Literary and Media Texts in Secondary English

New Approaches

Edited by Andrew Goodwyn

CASSELL
London and New York

Cassell

Wellington House	370 Lexington Avenue
125 Strand	New York
London WC2R 0BB	NY 10017-6550

www.cassell.co.uk

First published 1998

British Library Cataloguing-in-Publication Data
A catalogue record for this book is available from the British Library.

ISBN 0–304–70359–1 (paperback)

Typeset by Kenneth Burnley, Wirral, Cheshire.
Printed and bound in Great Britain by Redwood Books, Trowbridge, Wiltshire.

LITERARY AND MEDIA TEXTS IN SECONDARY ENGLISH

Also available from Cassell:

E. Bearne (ed.): *Greater Expectations: Children Reading Writing*
C. Fox: *At the Very Edge of the Forest: The Influence of Literature on Storytelling by Children*
M. Gilmour (ed.): *Shakespeare for All in Primary Schools*
M. Gilmour (ed.): *Shakespeare for All in Secondary Schools*
M. Styles, E. Bearne and V. Watson (eds): *The Prose and the Passion: Children and Their Reading*
M. Styles, E. Bearne and V. Watson (eds): *Voices Off: Texts, Contexts and Readers*

Contents

The Contributors   vi

Acknowledgements   vii

1 Introduction: Broadening the Literacy Horizon   1
   Andrew Goodwyn

2 Teaching the Classics   23
   Judith Baxter

3 Reading Plays   43
   Andy Kempe

4 Developing Poetry   62
   Michael Lockwood

5 Picture Books in Secondary English   81
   Vaughan Prain

6 Inside the Literature Curriculum   98
   Don Zancanella

7 Adolescent Girls' Responses to Female Literary Characters:
   Two Case Studies   110
   Holly A. Johnson and Dana L. Fox

8 Adapting to the Textual Landscape:
   Bringing Print and Visual Texts Together in the Classroom   129
   Andrew Goodwyn

Index   150

The Contributors

Judith Baxter is Lecturer in English in Education, University of Reading.

Dana L. Fox is Associate Professor, Department of Language, Reading and Culture, University of Arizona, Tucson, USA.

Andrew Goodwyn is Lecturer in English in Education and Director of the Centre for Languages, English and Media Education, University of Reading.

Holly A. Johnson is Assistant Professor, Department of Curriculum and Instruction, Texas Tech University, Lubbock, USA.

Andy Kempe is Lecturer in Drama Education, University of Reading.

Michael Lockwood is Lecturer in English and Education, University of Reading.

Vaughan Prain is Associate Professor, School of Arts and Education, La Trobe University, Bendigo, Australia.

Don Zancanella is Associate Professor, Division of Language, Literacy and Socio-cultural Studies, University of New Mexico.

Acknowledgements

I should like to thank Anne Goodwyn for her help with my chapters and for her love and support. Kate Findlay has generously helped with ideas for and revisions to both my chapters.

I should also like to acknowledge the support of the editorial team at Cassells.

I am grateful to the following for permission to reproduce extracts in this book:

Faber & Faber and Grove/Atlantic Inc. for *Rosencrantz and Guildenstern Are Dead* by Tom Stoppard;

Peters, Fraser & Dunlop for *An Inspector Calls* by J. B. Priestley;

Davis Higham Assoc. for *Under Milk Wood* by Dylan Thomas;

Phillip Pullman for *Sherlock Holmes and the Limehouse Horror*;

Chris Bond for *The Blood of Dracula*;

A Day in the Death of Joe Egg © 1967 Peter Nichols is published by permission of Faber & Faber and in the USA by permission of Alan Brodie Representation Ltd, 211 Piccadilly, London, W1V 9LD.

Part of Chapter 4 was first published in *Reading*, vol. 27, no. 3 (1993) as 'Getting into the Rhythm: Children Reading Poetry'.

To my dear sister, Pat Righelato,
who has devoted much of her life to literature and to teaching
and generously supporting its students
but who has always given even more of herself
to those very real characters who make up her family.

Chapter 1

Introduction:
Broadening the Literacy Horizon

Andrew Goodwyn

This opening chapter examines some of the major issues affecting the way teachers and adolescents encounter texts, both separately as individual readers and together in collective classroom encounters. A model of reading is put forward that argues for a broad definition of both reading itself and of what schools should include in their provision for adolescent readers; this consideration will involve some analysis of the shifting definitions of literacy. The main purpose of this collection is to offer an expanded vision of what 'English' should cover in school, the crucial phase of students' adolescent development. In the course of this discussion I shall draw, indirectly, on the work of the writers in the subsequent chapters but I shall also summarize these chapters at the end of the Introduction as a way in to the collection as a whole. I shall base some of my argument on Appleyard's (Appleyard, 1990) schema of reading development (see below) and offer the term of the 'sophisticated reader' as a potential model for our work.

QUINTESSENTIAL READING

This book is aimed at those readers for whom reading is quintessentially important but who retain an open mind about what is 'essential reading'. The last ten years in most English-speaking countries have seen a dramatic rise in the number of commentators desperate to tell everyone, and teachers in particular, what are the essential texts that will mark us out as truly well read. In the UK, for example, this is made plain in the increasingly prescriptive formulations of the National Curriculum for English (SCAA, 1995) and the enormous testing apparatus created around canonical texts, especially Shakespeare's plays. In the USA the debate has been more evident in the various polemics published claiming to define which books will mark someone out as truly civilized. These commentators are even more concerned that young people should be introduced to these texts by their teachers in order, as they see it, to civilize them before it is too late. In a paradoxical way then, books are seen as so powerful that the impressionable young must only encounter a few of them.

Educators working directly with young people, such as teachers, or indirectly, such as teacher educators and researchers, must deal constantly with the paradoxes of contemporary education. Some paradoxes have an essential truth. For example, in the 'information' age people seem to crave more and more fiction: as media technologies provide us with more and more realism audiences demand more, and more elaborate, fantasy. These are provocative paradoxes for those concerned with literature which itself is dominated by fictions and fantasies. False paradoxes also abound. More and more books are published each year and yet people are, so the media myth has it, apparently increasingly reading fewer books.

Readers of this book are likely to be those for whom paradoxes about reading abound but paradoxes that are productive of thinking and reflection. This collection explores many paradoxes about reading but it also attempts to provide some very direct help for people concerned about young people's reading. Its brief is explained in the title of this chapter, i.e. to broaden our literary horizon, and its argument is straightforward. How can we work more effectively with young people to make them more accomplished readers of the range of texts that they will encounter in their current and their adult lives? The writers of this collection share a conviction that schools are struggling with a profound difficulty about what to read with their students and how to make those reading experiences meaningful and purposeful. This is not because schools and teachers are 'failing' but because they are currently trapped by controlling forces locked in a nostalgia for the past, particularly a specific kind of literary past, and these forces are holding back educators from introducing the changes that they themselves are enthusiastic to make. There is enormous pressure to fit in with the culturally narrow views of cultural literacy gurus, such as Hirsch in the USA (Hirsch, 1996). All of these gurus have many political allies. Meanwhile the students themselves struggle to make sense of both the wide and the culturally and linguistically diverse multimedia world. The fact is that our diverse student readers have diverse reading experiences and needs. We are all advantaged but also limited by dominant identity-forming factors such as our culture, ethnicity and gender; given our differences, the act of reading cannot be neutral and there are no angelic texts, somehow free from contestable meanings, that float above the ground we ordinary mortals must all walk upon. This collection focuses on the challenges we all face in the diverse and pluralistic societies in which we live and work and on how we may get more from some of the domains of literature already familiar in school, such as poetry, dramatic and classic texts, as well as from the less familiar, such as picture books and media texts, particularly adaptations. It also focuses on the way our definition of what it means to be literate, to be 'well read', is expanding and evolving, and on the implications of this profound change.

LITERACY AND ADOLESCENCE

Readers of this book will tend to be knowledgeable about young people and, regardless of their location in the world, will probably share mixed feelings when someone, usually a person with opinions but not much knowledge, starts to criticize teenagers. Such critics usually begin 'Young people nowadays . . .' and unravel a long list of faults that their own generation, in their opinion, somehow avoided. Young people, of course, are unable to help being 'nowadays' as they have no choice in the matter. However, the question 'What does it mean to be young nowadays?' is of real significance for those of us trying to create a learning environment for young people which connects with the past and prepares for the future and which finally accepts that 'nowadays' keeps changing but was not created by the young people who experience it as the present. The serious point is that developed societies and their economic structures are undergoing so much rapid change that such regressive criticisms are worse than useless; what we need to do is to offer support to the young who face these changes without our cultural baggage.

One of the most frequent complaints about young people is that they read too little and watch too much, i.e. that they actually make use of the world that their parents have created, and here the majority of people working in education tend themselves to have very mixed feelings. Working with teenagers is both highly rewarding and extremely difficult and it is very hard to analyse whether they are getting harder to work with or whether other societal factors are making our job more complex and, at times, confusing. Some of my own recent research (Goodwyn, 1997a) suggests that many teachers feel that teenagers are not in any sense different beings to those of, say, twenty years ago but they are more knowing about the world and they are more critically aware of what is happening to that world. Most teachers attribute this to the omnipresence of the media, a subject about which they have even more mixed feelings, but they consider adolescents to be more aware of the world than students of the past and that this awareness is important and generally advantageous. As teachers we can recognize that students come to school with considerable knowledge and resources but also that these elements come from outside the conventional curriculum; teachers can struggle at times, hampered by that curriculum, to make active use of this student knowledge. In his important research, *Common Culture,* into young people's actual behaviour, Paul Willis suggests that they have a very active and creative role in relation to all the media and he argues, 'The young are the most sophisticated readers of images of any group in society' (Willis, 1990, p. 30). The question is: to what extent is that sophistication made use of in school?

To return to young people and their current relationship with reading, we do have a reasonable idea about some of their habits and can certainly base the way we organize our teaching on some reasonably clear evidence. Reviewing recent research and comparing it to work done twenty or thirty years ago does provide very useful evidence. Peter Benton's research (Benton, 1996) examined the reading and viewing habits of adolescents in England and compared it to the well-known study by Frank Whitehead (Whitehead, 1977) and his team. There is a host of detailed findings in the study but some simple points emerge that can help us here. The majority of adolescents appear to read less as they get older, and boys in particular turn away from written fiction. However, this is exactly the same pattern as twenty years ago. What makes this surprising, ironically, is that 'common sense' might have predicted that reading as a leisure activity might have disappeared altogether as adolescents have so much else now to select from for their leisure activities. They are surrounded by proliferating television channels, videos, radio stations and teenage magazines, and the computer now also provides a potentially vast range of sources of information and entertainment. However, as the Book Marketing Report, *The Children's Book Market: An Overview* (1995, p. 29), comments,

> There has been much concern over the threat that new leisure pursuits have posed towards reading . . . There is no evidence that this has yet happened . . . reading has probably maintained its position in the leisure hierarchy, whilst others such as outdoor games, cinema and even TV appear to have lost out.

The Benton study also shows that there is almost no discernible difference between the time spent watching television in 1971 and now; for example, about 50 per cent of teenagers watch 2–3 hours a day. Equally, the study by Nottingham University of children's reading choices, which also replicates the Whitehead study (Hall and Coles, 1995), finds no evidence of any significant decline in reading, except amongst 14-year-old boys. The study's findings state that 'Most children view reading positively and have positive views of themselves as readers' (p. 10), that 'over 70 per cent of children say they borrow books from the public library' (p. 13), and that 'over 90 per cent of children from all social groups report owning their own books' (p. 12). The comprehensive study *Young People's Reading at the End of the Century* (Children's Literature Research Centre, 1996) offers masses of data but no surprises and its findings support those cited above.

It appears that students choose slightly fewer 'classics' to read in their own time now but it is also quite likely that the original Whitehead report was not as accurate as Benton's or Hall and Coles, and the earlier research may have encouraged students to fit in with their teachers' preferred texts when reporting their chosen books. All the above studies do show that adolescents seem to read quite different magazines to those read by their parents who, when they were adolescents, read mostly comics; current teenagers read more directly about their perceived interests in music, fashion and sport.

Despite much societal angst there is no real evidence in the studies of declines in literacy. The key change is in the terms of the debate surrounding literacy, which has been joined by thoughtful commentators who are trying to analyse how the concept of literacy is expanding. In simple terms, people in the developed world are asked to make more sense from more sources of meaning and to do it faster and more effectively than ever before. Since there is this enormous pressure to educate for a much more demanding future, what kind of readers are we trying to develop?

In its conventional sense literacy is generally still defined as to do with letters, interpreting them and producing them, whether on a page of print or on a screen. This concept, that literacy is knowledge of print, remains very powerful. It is important to reflect on the fact that language itself, until quite recently, was studied and taught as if it was essentially writing. The terms 'oracy' and 'orality' (Wilkinson *et al.*, 1990) were created specifically to help us see the crucial differences between the spoken and the written. The relatively recent recognition that the spoken and the written are different forms of language is part of our developing understanding of how context-dependent language is. For example, the word 'visual' can now be inserted before literacy to help us focus specifically on images. This is, in fact, closer to the conventional definition of literacy than it seems because almost all visual texts rely on conventional literacy for part of their meaning; advertising especially demands a genuine visual literacy. The recent work of a number of researchers has begun to look more closely at the visual nature of writing and the influence of visual design on our perception (Kress, 1995; Walker, 1993). Again, then, we see literacy being expanded towards a truer reflection of what it is. And, as a more speculative example, what of a person listening to the radio: are they using aural literacy – especially perhaps if they are listening to a 'reading' of a book? I am not aware that this is a current term: certainly 'auracy' has no currency and yet 'listening skills' and being a good listener are common enough terms. So auracy might be quite a useful term to help us think about particular interpretative contexts, especially what makes them significantly different from other contexts.

The important point is that many researchers from quite different fields are now increasingly arguing for an extension of the term 'literacy' to areas such as media literacy, computer literacy and so on; in other words it is common to see writers arguing for literacies, multi-literacies, etc. This is a valuable attempt to move thinking on because it refuses to accept a simplistic definition of literacy and it recognizes the importance of context. The notion of a plurality of literacies or of multi-literacies is, therefore, productive but also problematic in its own way. Work in, for example, anthropology (Street, 1984) and linguistics (Gee, 1990) has revealed that the term 'literacy' is never neutral and that it is always a social and ideological construct; in other words literacies are controversial and even competitive and are in a hierarchical relationship, some being far more dominant and powerful than others. The fact that conventional literacy in itself does not actually create the sophisticated, rational mind in the way that has been claimed (Goody, 1977) does not diminish – indeed, it may increase – the social fact that those who have the literacy status are very protective of it and will judge others by its standards. In other words those people intuit that having the right kind of literacy does not make you a better person than someone without it but it does make you, and your children, more powerful. Those groups who have acquired this apparently omnipotent literacy also have a vested interest in preserving literacy's mythic status. Schools and universities are especially caught up and implicated in this myth and all teachers struggle in its invisible web.

Some terms from the multi-literacy approach have certainly entered ordinary conversation. People often define themselves in relation to degrees of computer literacy as in 'Oh yes, I am reasonably computer literate' and so on. Presumably this means that they have developed an understanding of how to get computers to do things for which they are designed, such as writing, manipulating figures and acting as communication devices. In a strict sense this is non-sense, i.e. they are just using their literacy and numeracy with a machine. They perhaps could say that they are a computerist in the same way that one is a cyclist or motorist, i.e. one who can use the particular machine for its purpose.

However, they are also including in their self-definition an award of status; in other words they are saying that computers are now a normal, essential part of a professional person's life, part of the current repertoire of what it means to be an educated citizen. This is an important change because until the 1990s many literary people, including many English teachers, would have rejected the inclusion of computer use within this definition and it helps us to see that definitions of literacy will always evolve to reflect societal change. In this sense computer literacy is becoming an extension of the universal assumption that to be educated is to be highly literate. Surely when people say they are computer-literate they do not mean that they are good at playing games on a computer? This helps to remind us that being literate is about much more than being able to read and write. It is about being able to read and write certain kinds of text.

Computer literacy is arguably now as acceptable as, say, knowledge of Latin and Greek once was, because it is a sign of belonging to the powerful and influential strata in society. Computer literacy is bound up with economic status and wealth generation but it is becoming just as important as a sign of belonging to a group. As computer literacy is becoming part of that literacy status so we see the definition of literacy being revised once more.

It is noticeable that teachers themselves are increasingly aware of this change (Goodwyn *et al.,* 1997) and that they worry (which they always do) that some children may be doubly disadvantaged because not only do they come from homes where there are few or no books, but their home also has no computer except perhaps a games console. This acknowledgement of the power of computers as an aspect of literacy by teachers is further evidence that the concept of computer literacy has the emphasis on literacy rather than knowledge about computers *per se* and also that teachers recognize that it confers not just a functional skill but status.

In this way we can see a simple, but crucial difference from 'media literacy'. People simply do not say, 'Oh yes, I am reasonably media-literate.' Knowledge about the media is, as yet, not associated with literacy in the sense of being well educated; indeed its general associations are in opposition to being well educated. However much the statistics show us that, for example, all 'levels' of society watch television, 'educated' people might not publicly admit to some of the things they watch. My own, qualitative research (Goodwyn, 1997) suggests that many teachers may fall into this category. This value association surrounding literacy is one reason why advocates of media education (Buckingham, 1993a, 1993b; Buckingham and Sefton-Green, 1994) want to annex the term 'literacy'. Once the term is associated with media study it may help to raise the dignity and status of media education, placing it within the frame of being well educated. Politically, this is a sensible, strategic move as it would make media education in the curriculum both safe and mainstream. However, for exactly the reason that it would become respectable, this move has met strong resistance from the guardians of literacy (including many literature teachers) in many English-speaking countries, England and Wales being prime examples; in contrast, New Zealand (Davies, 1996, pp. 54–8) seems to be rapidly incorporating media education into the mainstream curriculum. This issue will be discussed in much more depth in Chapter 8. The essential points are that the media remain associated with the popular and that literacy status is constructed around at least some knowledge of certain canonical, print texts; this is the whole basis, for example, of the current National Curriculum for English in England and Wales (SCAA, 1995).

This differential between the acceptability of computer and media literacy illustrates that what it means to be 'literate' continues to be hotly contested and that it is not really about simply being able to read and write. It also helps to demonstrate the general perception that literacy is a simple, stable term is untenable. It has a continually shifting meaning yet still operates as if it was a unified term that can neatly categorize people. Whether educators like it or not, that categorization is the way society expects school to work and to pass or fail students so that the world can treat them differently. We need, therefore, to acknowledge the power of literacy in this dogmatic sense but then to construct a curriculum that goes well beyond its limitations and that beats it at its own game. This acknowledgement also recognizes that commitments to media or computer literacy will not in themselves make the key difference. These 'new literacies' can easily be absorbed into the functional view of literacy that sees them as part of being an efficient citizen rather than an active and critical one.

We can work with the general idea of literacy and show our students where that definition tends to be narrow and inadequate and then stress certain emphases, such as the visual. This should help them to reflect on the 'given' definition and, eventually, to question it. Perhaps the term 'literacy', continuing to be one that is contentious and generally divisive, can open up students' thinking; perhaps its value for educators lies in the fact that we cannot pin it down and so we must constantly review our terms of reference.

At this stage I would sum up by arguing that the way the term 'literacy' is generally used (but not questioned) is as a multi-layered term which includes the following: the functional, i.e. the capability to read and write at a simple level; the literary, i.e. knowledge of certain predetermined texts; and the social, i.e. having an understanding of the social and economic status brought by the first two. This general use does not, for example, add the political layer which allows the individual to question the justice of that social and economic status; this is the critical literacy associated with the work of Freire (see for example Freire and Macede, 1987). To expect students to reach this stage is to have very high expectations of them and this is what we should all strive to achieve. However, this effort is in spite of, not because of, rhetoric about so-called high standards whose main intention seems usually be to make everyone, students and teachers alike, work on a treadmill of testing and summative assessment. This treadmill will allow us to prove that teachers can teach to tests and that many students can be taught how to pass them. It seems to me to be in direct opposition to promoting real critical literacy because critically literate students would be likely to refuse to take tests that they understood were largely empty exercises. Literature teachers are currently in a very difficult position, increasingly compromised by the systematic reduction of teacher independence, and this is why we need to beat the curriculum at its own game. We can get closest to critical literacy in school by extending and expanding the types of text that we work with and by adapting our classroom approaches to make this inclusiveness, this comprehensiveness, the main principle of our everyday practice.

STARTING WITH READING

The key term continues to be 'reading'. I accept that, for example, reading a film and reading a novel have differences but the act of reading seems to be the unifying principle (see Chapter 8). It can be argued that reading a poem and a novel or a biography and an autobiography provide different reading experiences and were written with differing intentions. In many ways our definition of reading has changed and expanded over the centuries but one strand remains constant. Whether as in Old English, where reading was often applied to making sense of dreams, to more modern variations such as the late eighteenth-century addition of a 'reading of' that is producing a specific interpretation of something, so the essence of reading has been the creating of a tenable (not permanent) meaning.

Making meaning, therefore, lies at the heart of all good English teaching; students can, and must, be challenged and puzzled by reading but they must become meaning-makers and encounter experiences that make them confident meaning-makers. Ultimately this implies that their reading in English will also need to be connected to their experiences of the world; it will need to be meaningful and, more profoundly perhaps, meaning full. We need a way then to engage students in the long process of becoming confident, sophisticated readers (see below).

I am, therefore, going to use our, i.e. literature teachers', textual knowledge as a basis and so will make use, as a starting point, of Appleyard's schema of reading development, set out in his valuable *Becoming a Reader* (Appleyard, 1990), to consider how teenagers in particular deal with visual and print texts. I am using his ideas as I feel his work represents an excellent synthesis of the ideas of many others from literary theory, developmental psychology, education, philosophy and linguistics. He makes no claim for the suitability of his schema for anything but printed fiction texts so any distortions are my own.

His view is that readers seem to learn in 'a fairly predictable sequence' (p. 14) and to adopt five roles in the following order:

1 *The Reader as Player*. In the pre-school years the child, not yet a reader but a listener to stories, becomes a confident player in a fantasy world that images realities, fears and desires in forms that the child slowly learns to sort out and control.
2 *The Reader as Hero and Heroine*. The school-age child is the central figure of a romance that is constantly being rewritten as the child's picture of the world and how people behave in it is filled and clarified. Stories seem to be an alternate, more organized and less ambiguous world than the world of pragmatic experience, one the reader easily escapes into and becomes involved with.
3 *The Reader as Thinker*. The adolescent reader looks to stories to discover insights into the meaning of life, values and beliefs worthy of commitment, ideal images and authentic role models for imitation. The *truth* of these ideas and ways of living is a severe criterion for judging them.
4 *The Reader as Interpreter*. The reader who studies literature systematically, typically the college English major or graduate student or teacher, approaches it as an organized body of knowledge with its own principles of inquiry and rules of evidence, learns to talk analytically about it, acquires a sense of its history and perhaps even a critical theory of how it works.
5 *The Pragmatic Reader*. The adult reader may read in several ways, which mimic, though with appropriate differences, the characteristic responses of each of the previous roles: to escape, to judge the truth of experience, to gratify a sense of beauty, to challenge oneself with new experiences, to comfort oneself with images of wisdom. What seems to be common to these responses is that adult readers now much more consciously and pragmatically choose the uses they make of reading.

Appleyard argues that these roles 'are no more than shorthand labels for a cluster of distinctive responses, a set of attitudes and intentions readers bring to reading and of uses they make of it, which appear to shift as readers mature' (p. 14). He is very clear that he is not offering a rigid, schematic sequence of the kind usually associated with Piaget. He draws more on Erikson's view of developmental stages as 'halting and uneven, and at later stages the work of earlier ones may need to be repaired – higher roles may be better – if they successfully integrate what is positive in the lower ones' (p. 17).

A further reason why I feel Appleyard's schema can help teachers of literature to think about literary and media texts is because he has considered the 'authority' of the text issue in careful detail. This, he argues, is the central area for the professional readers of literature, the professors and, to some extent, the teachers; they are engaged by theories of literature of all kinds, they daily struggle with finding an interpretation. In a sense, they stay in the fourth role, endlessly interpreting texts and never really acting like a typical adult reader who simply knows what he or she likes and likes what he or she knows. For most readers the issue of interpretation is important but it is much less central to their actual use of texts for much of the time. Appleyard argues that the great majority of readers choose to be involved with texts that are, for them, interpretively unproblematic:

> Thus for young children the authority of any interpretation of the text is simply a non-issue; indeed, at this stage texts are not interpreted, they are only enjoyed or rejected. Interpretation first becomes a matter of concern to older juveniles and adolescents, who are concerned with figuring out the truth about the world and their own lives and therefore with discovering what the writers of books have said about these subjects. But even here the possibility of interpretation is not in doubt; readers are convinced that a text has a meaning, put there by its author, that the reader is meant to discover. Older students start from this assumption and learn more and more skilful ways of dissecting texts and uncovering their meanings. But then a curious thing happens. As they become more sophisticated analysts of literature, they discover that meaning is unavoidably situated in historical contexts and within literary structures and cultural codes. They also discover the conflict of even authoritative interpretations and the conflict of theoretical positions about interpretation advanced by persuasive critics and by their own instructors.
>
> (p. 18)

Later Appleyard comments that this developmental view of reading 'permits us to picture the trajectory of our reading experience as a movement from unreflecting engagement to deliberate choice about the kind of readers we will be and the uses to which we will put our reading' (p. 19).

For many teachers of literature there is an immediate problem to do with the relationship between reading in a broad, functional sense and reading as in close, literary reading; they tend to concentrate on the latter, subsuming the former into that activity. I am sure this is the right approach in the sense that there is very little to be gained from restricting adolescents to the 'basics'. As they have reached the thinking and questioning stage in their development so they need an appropriate challenge. They have also understood that literacy is a status symbol and are insulted by attempts to treat them as if they have no status. However, the development of what might be called higher-order reading capability has no necessary connection with reading 'serious' and 'worthy' literature. Very sophisticated readers may have no interest in Literature with a capital L although they will be aware of the way knowledge about Literature carries status and value.

Appleyard argues that adults make deliberate choices and adopt a mostly pragmatic view of reading; that is, they know enough about texts and the effects of reading texts to select what they want. One could substitute the terms 'drinkers' and 'drinks' and the functionality of the whole process would be clear. To develop that analogy, most adult drinkers do not choose the finest wines and would not recognize one; equally, if they tasted a range of basic and fine wines they might find them merely wines. The teacher is rather like the connoisseur who loves only 'the best' and thinks: surely adults should recognize and choose the best? If we introduce young people to the best surely they will at least know what it tastes like? However, we have very little evidence of the general effects of literature teaching. One of the few examples is Tanja Janssen's (Janssen, 1997) examination of the attitudes of 24-year-olds towards literature; her findings suggest that nearly 50 per cent 'dislike reading literature'. If literature is so good why have they 'rejected' it? We must face up to the need to recognize our own limitations as well as our strengths since connoisseurs can be very prejudiced. My main point is that we need to stand back from our own obsessions and to have a perspective that allows us to see them for what they are.

So we know that a complex set of issues surrounds the concept of reading and purpose as in 'What is worth reading?' This tradition of values has a history that predates reading itself, and Plato had much to say about it. For teachers the issue can be limited to one of textual selection, the question usually being something like 'What is worth studying with a particular age group that will advance them as people and as literary readers?' The assumption here is that reading texts, at the right level of challenge, will make an intellectual difference to the readers. The students will be better readers first in the sense of being more accomplished, moving closer to the reader as interpreter role. The second sense in which they will be better is as moral beings living in a morally complex world. As a result of their affective involvement with a text, through, for example, feeling sympathy and revulsion for the characters in a story, they will come to reflect on human behaviours, including their own, in the real world. My own research (Goodwyn, 1992, 1997b), mostly in the UK but also in the USA, shows that English teachers consistently make great claims for the moral power and civilizing influence of literature. It is arguable then that literature teachers are generally looking for texts of increasing complexity both in a literary (i.e. cognitive) sense and in an affective and moral sense. This partly explains why in the 1970s in the UK, when television began to become a universal feature of industrial societies, a growth can be seen in the study of film in schools, that film could be art. Watching and discussing films was reasonable for literature teachers because they could select texts that were, in their terms, of sufficient difficulty and moral complexity; such films were of 'artistic' merit (and in the UK, rather ironically, were usually French). In that sense, film is unchanged: there are still easy ways to sort films into categories of difficulty. However, the media environment, part of the textual habitat (see Chapter 8) in the twenty-first century, will be markedly different to that of the 1970s. The point is that literature teachers tend to look for texts whose 'message' and values they can endorse. It is arguable that this is one, important aspect of our work. However, as sophisticated readers ourselves we know that texts actually carry many and mixed messages and that contemporary interpreters create new and exciting meanings. So we should be less worried about endorsing every text and more concerned about the contribution that a text may make to the exploration of meaning in the classroom. This does not imply that 'anything goes', but rather actually reinforces the opportunities for teachers to acknowledge and state their position; by reading texts we do not accept them. As all texts carry messages and exemplify values so we must bring into the classroom a wider range of texts broadening students' understanding of how variously values are conveyed. A useful irony to consider is that some English teachers, certainly in the UK, have always been ready to analyse advertisements for their message and for their attempts to persuade consumers whilst they have usually treated books as if they were entirely different. The point is that there are some differences but the similarities between books and advertisements are just as interesting.

It may be useful to be explicit about the fact this concern over textual selection immediately suggests that some texts have 'questionable' values. What such a term as 'questionable' illustrates perfectly for us is that its implication is that some texts have values that need not be questioned. What all literature teachers know through experience is that all texts, however canonical, must be questioned. This questioning is arguably the basis of good literature teachers' expertise and not the fact that they know, through their literary education, what the received opinions of various texts are supposed to be. I am arguing that there is a need to make more of this textual expertise by reflecting on a greater range of differing texts and by questioning the values of these texts and in this way literature teachers make the most of their textual knowledge and develop that of their students.

Literature teachers know a great deal about literature and how to 'teach' it but ironically they feel relatively ignorant about adult readers. What happens to readers once they leave the institutions in which they were encouraged, sometimes forced, to read is something of a mystery. As mentioned above, we have very few studies of adult readers as such. Of course, a few of those readers become professionals in education and perpetuate the cycle of interpretative readers. What we all know is that very few adults, at least in statistical terms based on sales and library loans, actually choose to read 'serious' literature although they read masses of fiction. One of the occasions when adults (and adolescents) do seem moved to look at a well-known serious text is when it has been filmed or serialized on television; at such times large numbers of the 'original' text are sold (I will return to this later in Chapter 8). Some teachers of literature themselves, however, certainly choose to read non-serious fiction. In fact, they make a very deliberate choice to read something 'light' as a relaxation and to escape from the pressures of their teacherly and personal lives. In that way teachers do know about adult, pragmatic readers. They know that reading a text can serve escapist and relaxing functions and so provides textual pleasure of a usefully predictable kind. However, they might find it difficult to 'admit' this in the classroom.

As Appleyard points out, one thing that truly distinguishes adult readers, at least in a democratic society, is that they can read what they like and many choose to read all kinds of texts. However, it is incontrovertible that many adults generally prefer to view texts rather than read them, although there is nothing mutually exclusive about the two habits; indeed the two activities may be going on at the same time, such is the ingenuity of human consciousness. Of course, a literature teacher might instantly say that such mixing of stimulations typifies the lack of genuine attention to texts that characterizes the superficiality of much modern living. If you are truly involved in the world of the book there is no escape from it – you must stay in it until you reach the end. However, this is just as true of a particular film or television programme and strikingly true of serials such as soap operas. The phenomenon of being completely absorbed in a text does seem to be a common experience but what makes it phenomenal is that it is more the exception than the rule. Whilst celebrating and encouraging such moments of textual intensity we must not lose sight of the ordinariness of most reading experiences. Finally, it is always salutary to reflect on the simple point that such experiences seem to happen when readers have chosen the text themselves and are reading at a time that suits them; schools simply do not allow for such opportunities. What would happen to the student who insisted on missing their biology class because they had to know what happened at the end of *Moby Dick*?

I have tried so far to build up a clear case for thinking more openly about what we mean by good reading. I now wish to consider the kind of reader that we want to develop.

ADOLESCENT READERS READING THE ADULT WORLD

A term that I consider useful is the 'sophisticated reader' and I will define it below. However, as a premise I will first distinguish sophistication from maturity and consider also the role that students adopt when responding to texts. I would argue that adolescents are capable of sophistication beyond their literal age, especially in the appropriately artificial and constructed conditions of the classroom. Adolescents cannot be mature readers, they cannot be the pragmatists that Appleyard describes – they are, despite appearances, immature even in the strict biological sense and certainly, psychologically, adolescence is a necessarily immature stage. Also the institutions of education clearly extend this stage because school students are never genuinely viewed as adults. However, it can be argued that their textual maturity is potentially greater. They certainly can respond to dense and difficult texts. Shakespeare is an obvious example since his treatment of profound themes does not in itself put teenagers off his work; it is that institutional and even political pressures can do the off-putting very efficiently but good teachers know how to overcome these institutional limitations.

The concept of maturity seems to have a particular and crucial meaning in English. In some of my previous research it became clear that for many English teachers what they meant by 'high ability' in English was equivalent to 'being mature' (Goodwyn, 1995). Very able boys in particular were frequently described as 'unusually mature'. Much research about girls' consistent success in English points to their emotional maturity compared to boys. English as a subject seems to demand a kind of ideal maturity that by definition is beyond the reach of most teenagers. However, this point helps us to see that our students, being immature in the adult sense, need help and support in their struggle for meaning, especially in English, but that they aspire to adulthood and will respond to pathways offered towards it. One must accept the need to construct a kind of artificial maturity, manageable in a well-run English classroom, where a teacher's presence can sustain a high level of discourse and critical thinking.

This approach is supported by Vygotsky's well-known theory (Vygotsky, 1962) of the 'zone of proximal development' and his concept of 'scaffolding', that is, supporting students who are building their own, independent understanding. A great deal of research in the last few years has taken Vygotsky's theories as a starting point. Here two points are vital. Vygotsky's zone of proximal development helps us to understand what literature teachers can achieve. Adolescents are endeavouring to be adults in their responses to texts but they need support and stimulation ('scaffolding') to move on and, in a sense, up towards such responses. Examining texts, with the teacher's help, for what they reveal about adulthood can be a means to this end.

Vygotsky's other point is that learning is not a discrete, individual process but a messy, social activity, and much recent research has also focused on the essentially social nature (Gee, 1990) of literacy. Reader response theory has also examined the essentially transactional nature of interpretations. Individuals attempt to make meanings but these meanings become much more meaningful through interaction with other students, usually working at a similar level of interpretative struggle. The teacher has to support but also hold back until the interpreter has enough meaning to make 'some sense' of a text. The temptation, on both sides, is for the teacher to provide the right answer but this would fix teacher and students at the immature level; perhaps a few in the group, already in the English sense 'mature', might secretly contest the teacher's authoritative interpretation. However, the students' interpretative struggle is vital and the teacher provides that zone of crucial development by sustaining the struggle until it begins to offer a number of potential meanings. One of the values and strengths of any group of students is its generation of a number of contestable meanings. To be able to recognize a range of meanings seems a sign of sophistication and a sign of the kind of maturity both manageable and desirable in the classroom.

Well-supported students can then speak and behave in the sophisticated way to which they generally and genuinely aspire. Texts, whether intentionally or not, offer a critique of adult life which adolescents can enjoy from the safety of their non-adult position. They can adopt a sophisticated critical stance. The creation of this stance has long been the goal of much of the rationale for English teaching and it fits well with the most influential model of English teaching, the personal growth model. This model is consistently the preferred model of English teachers. Without discussing its historical importance here, it is relevant to consider that it derives significantly from the way Harding (1962) and then Britton (1970) developed the concept of the spectator role in relation to reading literature specifically. To simplify their complex argument for use here, spectating allows us to look on at what is 'happening', to engage our feelings and contemplate the 'scene', but without the expectation of immediate action. I find the term 'spectator' valuable but I do not fully agree with Britton's argument.

Spectators are supposed to observe and enjoy and to stay in their seats. However, in the real world, when they get very involved, they get out of their seats and into the action. Here we have a necessary complexity. Texts can make us, for example, very angry and also very frustrated when we have our experience of the text and then can 'do' nothing. Adolescents are especially prone to emotional melodramas and outbursts; they feel very frustrated and want to 'do something'. However, it is equally the experience of many adult readers to 'love' or 'hate' a book. The spectating metaphor works well for many reading experiences. However, it essentially suggests that observing might be enough, sitting back so that literature itself presents to us what we, the onlookers, need. Spectating is very much a learned perspective, a sophisticated one at that. It requires maturity and the understanding that as one experiences the 'scene' of the text one cannot participate in its action; later, however, one may take action in the scenes of one's own life. Adolescents inevitably are also spectators of the adult world but they want to participate in it.

Britton proposes that the spectator role is liberating, allowing us to enjoy the textual scene whereas other uses of language are more participatory (see Britton, 1970, Chapter 3). Britton's distinction was immensely helpful in helping English teachers to gain a perspective on literature as an important part of language rather than as its supreme function. However, I feel adolescents are, and should be, much more participatory when engaging with texts. Appleyard defines the reader-as-thinker as follows, 'the adolescent reader looks to stories to discover insights into the meaning of life, values and beliefs worthy of commitment, ideal images, and authentic role models for imitation. The *truth* of these ideas and ways of living is a severe criterion for judging them' (Appleyard, 1990, p. 14). In this sense the adolescent both looks on and participates in the text, as they do in life, in that sense they lack maturity and distance. This is how the study of texts is developmental: adolescents, with teachers' help, are developing judgements, using all kinds of criteria, about texts and life.

Hence for adolescents at least the spectator and the participant role need to be applied to literature. If reading is to fulfil the expectations that adolescents bring to the activity, it must frequently make real connections with their lives and not be treated as somehow separate and special, remote from their everyday experience. This point does not simply equate realistic texts with everyday life: fantasy is equally present in everyday experience, especially for adolescents. However, the notions of simply contemplative reflection, even response, are often inadequate terms to describe this richly complex area in which the literature teacher has such great influence. All literature teachers know that this is true because their classrooms are always sites of struggle where adolescents particularly contest definitions of what is worth reading. It is arguable that this is not just adolescent questioning of adult authority; it is also that the definitions of literacy bound up with their own gender, their race, their parents' education (or lack of one) and many other factors generate a real and profound questioning of what is worth reading. The work of Graff (Graff, 1979) and others has shown that certain societal groups know from their collective experience that traditional, school literacy will not necessarily advance them economically; when they 'reject' this model of literacy it may be on quite sound evidence.

At times this struggle is wearisome for all of us but fundamentally it is a healthy sign of active thinking and critical engagement; no choice of text is neutral and the 'automatic' selection of texts is a contradiction in terms. I suspect that all teachers hate teenage indifference ('This is boring') much more than debate. It is also salutary for literature teachers to consider that anthropological research (Street, 1984) certainly suggests that we do not actually need literacy for higher-order thinking skills *per se*. However, discussing texts certainly draws on and develops higher-order thinking and reasoning.

Teenagers definitely engage with a vast range of 'adult' visual texts out of their own choice and often against the wishes of adults who might describe the subject matter as 'too adult'. I appreciate that 'adult' here may be a euphemism for the representation of the themes, i.e. the theme might be love but the representation is through explicit sexual content – the implication being that the adolescent is not 'mature' enough to handle such material and frequently the adults are right in this view. My point is that adolescents strive for a kind of maturity and that texts are a vital area for them to explore adult concepts and themes. Literature teachers constantly offer adolescents certain texts on that very basis. If we are honest we know that adolescents will experiment with 'adult' texts whether we help them or not; the question is whether we can make a valuable difference to the way they experiment.

THE SOPHISTICATED READER

I am arguing then for an approach to adolescent readers that treats them, quite deliberately, as more mature than they actually are, but that recognizes the vital support the teacher provides in scaffolding that 'maturity'. To help our students consciously engage in this process we can most usefully offer them the model of the sophisticated reader. The word 'sophisticated' first needs examining. It has a long and varied history but I would suggest its current meaning is principally positive, suggesting refinement, subtlety, considerable experience, some critical capacity and so on; in other words to be described as sophisticated is mostly a compliment. However, being sophisticated also suggests being rather cynical, no longer able to appreciate simple pleasures, rather demanding of the special and the unusual, and so on. Most people probably do not consider themselves very sophisticated although they may own objects or machines (the latest video recorder, for example) that they would be happy to describe as 'very sophisticated'.

One of its original meanings was to be adulterated, i.e. a pure substance was mixed with something else, and this led to a later meaning which was to make something natural into something artificial. In 1603 sophisticated could mean 'altered from, deprived of, primitive simplicity or naturalness; rendered artificial or worldly-wise' (*Shorter Oxford English Dictionary*). Being sophisticated is not therefore a claim to being morally superior but to being more worldly-wise. Whatever readers of this book consider to be their moral level compared to that of others, they will be sophisticated readers, i.e. they will have assimilated vast numbers of texts, many of which would lay no claim to being morally enlightening and many which would. All of these texts, to greatly varying degrees, have affected you, the reader. In that sense they have adulterated you, mixed with whatever is 'you', and created something artificial. There is nothing 'natural' about the act of reading a text; it is a complete human invention, although it draws very powerfully on our natural need to comprehend the signs in our habitat. You are also a sophisticated reader because you are critical and even cynical, you expect a great deal from some texts, and if they do not provide what you wanted you are likely to reject them; I suspect that you are, at least at times, a very suspicious reader. However, you are also capable – in that famous phrase – of the suspension of disbelief, you are prepared to trust a text for the immense rewards that such investment of faith can bring. This is another sign of your sophistication as a reader, not of your innocence or naivety. When you first learned to read, your reading was relatively innocent, you mainly trusted the texts; now you have learned to re-adopt this trusting stance when it suits you.

Some recent writers (Corcoran and Evans, 1987; Hayhoe and Parker, 1990; and Corcoran *et al.,* 1994) have argued for reading against texts, reading against the grain. This is an important idea and, as Chapter 7 shows, we need to recognize that, for example, the representation of our gender in fiction is only a representation and that adolescent girls can read in a properly feisty way! Reading against the grain may seem an enormously challenging task, which is beyond the scope of insecure adolescents, but we need to recognize that they will adopt this stance with the right support. If the text presents a version of the world which is at odds with their own experience and identity then they should feel a need to challenge the text. The greatest danger with current pressures to narrow the literature curriculum is that 'good' students will simply learn how to produce the 'right' and approved answers to pass the necessary tests; teachers will inevitably collude with this because they can only offer their students this version of success.

However, the 'reader as thinker' is not fully formed enough to resist all textual pressures. Whether we approve or not, a great deal of readers' reception of texts is to have the pleasure of recognizing and identifying with characters and situations; this is an essential textual pleasure. All the studies of children's preferred reading cited above show how children love to re-read certain texts in order to prolong this satisfaction. I would argue for a balance between reading against and reading with the grain, an honest acceptance that real readers, sophisticated ones like us, do this all the time.

We need to offer adolescents this model of sophisticated reading partly because it is far more honest and genuine than a more traditional literary model that implies, without ever stating it, that most readers, if left to their own devices, are bad in both senses, literal and moral – that is, they read poorly and they read unenlightening trash. The studies cited above confirm earlier studies that adolescents tend to read rather less than pre-adolescents. However, one factor in this is that they are more knowing readers and they tend to make informed choices, boys frequently turning to non-fiction for its efferent qualities. There seems to be plenty of evidence from the studies that some adolescent boys become very sophisticated readers of certain kinds of non-fiction text whilst remaining, in a sense, almost simplistic about print fiction. It is surely the case that the study of non-fiction as writing (as opposed to, say, a source of information as in history) would be an invaluable extension to the reading curriculum.

It is important to accept, then, that sophisticated readers are not pure readers. They are – in the way that sophisticated can mean adulterated, impure readers. Various models of literary reading have offered the illusion of purity in different forms. For example, the Leavis school offers the elitist position of reading as moral perfection; the New Critics proffer the hope of finding the perfect, self-referential text, a well-wrought urn without a crack; the structuralists posit a text so transparent that you could measure its dynamics, and Marxists offer to liberate us all from the prevailing ideology of which we are unconscious victims. These theoretical positions have all helped in their critiques of literature. Some sophisticated readers, depending on age and choice of courses in school, may become acquainted with these various theories, learning to inhabit them and to view them, eventually, from a distance.

However, many of our students will not choose to study literature or its theories, but they will continue to read in multifarious ways. We must not pretend to them that there is one, 'pure' way of reading. Instead we must discuss the way reading operates in the adult world. Part of this process will involve helping students to form views of their own about that contestable term 'literacy', i.e. we can help our students to see that literacy has different emphases in different contexts and that there are astonishing similarities and profound differences between texts across a spectrum of media. For example, we can show them the differing demands on a reader of a novel and a film of the same story whilst illustrating their textual similarities, so helping them to be and also feel literate, i.e. feel capable of making manageable sense from meanings that both converge and simultaneously diverge. The essential point is that we process and experience text in a sophisticated manner that allows us to decode specific meanings in a knowing way. For example, I am reading a horror novel and can expect certain things of novels and horror novels in particular. We are likely to draw most strongly on this particular aspect of our textual repertoire, i.e. horror novels. However, as active meaning-makers we do not close off our immense textual knowledge of all texts, we draw on it whenever the interpretative mind seeks for help in making sense. As agents of meaning we draw on our total literacy. I would argue then that we use our literacy in a broad way, a comprehensive way in order to assimilate and create meaning whilst drawing very specifically on the aspect of it that is most productive, e.g. we principally understand film through our previous experience of film.

Whether they like literature or not, most adolescents if asked 'Can you read?' are going to reply 'Yes'. However, if asked 'Are you literate?', I suspect they will be less sure and will want more information before answering. This seems reasonable given that we are still grappling with what being literate means at the end of the twentieth century and that we all know that it is a 'loaded' term. It is a term that adolescents would benefit from discussing in literature lessons.

To sum up at this stage, a sophisticated adolescent reader will be impure, imbibing all kinds of texts. Some will be purely, unselfconsciously for pleasure, some will be 'work', the kind of work that we do in school. However, it will be, in Paul Willis' sense (Willis, 1990), necessary symbolic work. That is work we need to do to make sense of a world full of bewildering texts and signs. We have to make sense of this world and adolescents do find it is worth working with teachers because they choose texts that help to make sense of that world; the reader has help from the teacher and classmates in being an interpreter. That act of interpretation, becoming increasingly sophisticated, means making more and more connections with the common and uncommon culture of our everyday experiences. We can only be sophisticated if we can make use of all our textual and cultural resources as we form our interpretations and, usually, revise and refine them.

THE SENSE OF A BEGINNING

I move to the end of this chapter with a sense of a promising beginning. I think we should face up to reality. If, as so many literature teachers propose, their main mission is to instil a love of literature into their students, then we are all failures. Very few students leave school in this worthy and rather emotional condition; one might fear for their lives as they crossed the road with their heads in books. Literature teachers are not failures but we might all bear in mind the words of Brian Johnston, whose book on assessment makes two points that we can learn from. He comments that

> overstrivers . . . have grown up with a sense that one's achievements define one's own worth. Consequently they work compulsively to avoid failure, and because of the amount of effort they expend, they are all the more easily threatened; for if they were to fail they could not attribute it to lack of effort. Consequently they regard failure . . . with a dread that is far out of proportion to its actual significance . . . the overstriver has fallen victim to a misunderstanding of the proper role of failure in the learning process.
>
> (Johnston, 1987, pp. 5–6)

I suspect many literature teachers will recognize themselves, certainly as strivers and definitely as individuals who work incredibly hard. If we set ourselves impossible goals then we will never reach them. What we can help students to do is to understand literature and why some of it has this special, capital L status. I think we can, more modestly, help them to really enjoy all kinds of texts and to develop judgements about them, properly informed by the judgements of others. We can also reveal just how much we love the stuff ourselves but we should not blame them, or ourselves, if they do not like it much. Because, as Johnston so succinctly puts it, 'Finally, the ability to make accurate assessments of ourselves, our products and our future goals, is a basic characteristic of a psychologically healthy person' (*ibid.*). We all like all kinds of texts, we dislike a lot too, we even love and hate a few of them, although all these feelings are subject to change.

I believe that the goal of making adolescents sophisticated readers is a difficult challenge but it is very possible. Our job might be much more satisfying and even more important than it already is if we adopt an inclusive approach to texts and work towards engaging our students across a wide range of texts using a broad spectrum of reading strategies. We will make more difference to our students' lives if we open up a broader reading horizon for them. The rest of this collection seeks to scan that wide horizon and to build on current good practice, recognizing the real constraints and contexts in which teachers presently work.

For example, Judith Baxter's chapter 'Teaching the Classics' takes a fresh and challenging look at a vexed area for literature teachers. Most of us received a literary education based on the canon of literature and, in whichever part of the English-speaking world, much of that literature was pre-twentieth-century British. However, teaching these classics to modern children is a difficult process and seems to place teachers in a dilemma: do you simplify these texts in some way so that students can 'appreciate' them or do you just dip into them so that students have an 'acquaintance' with these texts? Combining recent critical theory with reader response, Baxter offers teachers a way to approach such texts that shows that the above dilemma is a false one. Teachers can work closely with such texts without forcing their students into a false sense of homage or bewilderment and by helping them to see the connectedness and constructedness of all texts. This approach treats our students as sophisticated readers who can respond to 'classic' texts and generate meaningful interpretations that can be connected to contemporary fiction and media texts of all kinds.

If teaching 'classics' presents literature teachers with problems then dramatic texts seem even more challenging. For many teachers the simple answer has been to treat plays, Shakespeare's particularly, as a form of poetic novel. Andy Kempe's chapter outlines how to approach plays as plays and defines ways of reading dramatic text that keep the concept of drama in the foreground while offering teachers and students understandings of how such texts are constructed. For many students aspects of dramatic texts such as stage direction and even page layout have been an unexplained mystery. As Kempe shows, it is not just that these conventions need understanding; it is much more about reading plays in such a way as to make these parts of the text essential in themselves. Students have to engage with the staged nature of the performed text in order to make sense of dramatic structure and momentum. The chapter contains a wealth of practical approaches that illustrate for literature teachers how to make play reading into dramatic understanding.

Michael Lockwood also offers a great many practical approaches to the teaching of poetry. His motive is to help teachers to bring poetry into the realm of ordinary reading. He reviews the research that shows how frequently poetry tends to get left out or is treated in such a way as to be perceived by students as the ultimate reading chore. He investigates the views of many students themselves and brings their voices into his text to support the need for a more active and engaging approach to poetry in the classroom. As he argues, there is now a wealth of material for teaching poetry, and ideas from reader response theory have been developed to offer numerous ways of easing students into poetry reading so that they enjoy it before their usual objections are raised. Lockwood also looks at students producing poems and links in with the other authors in the collection who view literature as something that students participate in making as well as consuming. Essentially, poetry seems something that young children actively enjoy and play with; literature teachers gain everything by approaching it as a robust and flexible material, and not as some china ornament to blow the dust off occasionally. The difficult transition is to balance a playful approach with more thoughtful engagement with serious and emotionally demanding poetry. Lockwood shows that students are prepared to see poetry as providing a range of reading experiences but they want, and need, that range.

If poetry is appropriate play for young children then picture books are often viewed as not such appropriate 'play' for teenagers and even adults. For some, picture books represent all that is wrong with contemporary reading; for them, such material is simplistic, trashy and a distraction from all forms of serious reading. Such critics have a point, although this description might be applied to any type of literature. However, what they are ignoring is the rich, complex and extremely challenging nature of the inter-relationships between images and text. Vaughan Prain's chapter describes the enormous possibilities for the teacher prepared to extend his or her repertoire to include picture books. As well as discussing the powerful role that these texts can play in helping students reflect on the text–image relationship, he also indicates how essential such reflection is for contemporary literacy. Our students live in a world, a textual habitat (a phrase developed in my final chapter), which makes enormous demands on their visual understandings. Many texts that such students encounter may appear simplistic but even these texts will carry messages that are loaded with layers of meaning. The picture–text combination has an extraordinary and extensive history and it is only in relatively recent times that it has been seen, by some, as essentially trivial. Vaughan Prain offers a clear and coherent rationale for using picture books with our students and provides a range of approaches to developing their understandings as readers.

Picture books are at once more accessible than certain print-only texts and, simultaneously, more culturally bound by the visual style of the artist and the typographical traditions of a particular society. However, this complexity is not a problem, least of all for our students. In fact, it is an important and potentially illuminating perspective into a world enlightened by increasing global awareness at the same time as tribal strife and ethnic cleansing seem to dominate sections of our globe. In the midst of much rampant and often barbarous nationalism, literature is not neutral and can be used, in the wrong hands, as functionally and dogmatically as any political manifesto or religious tract. Much more insidious is the increasing tendency for governments in the English-speaking world to prescribe more and more texts that students must encounter on the grounds that this is all part of 'their' essential literary heritage. All our students have a number of legitimate heritages and the classroom should be a place where the concept of heritage is explored and understood, both its positive aspects and its negative tendencies.

In his chapter 'Inside the Literature Curriculum' Don Zancanella provides us with an inspiring example of a single teacher who resists the increasing narrowness of the literature curriculum and who has designed a culturally pluralistic course to help his students understand the cultures around them, to make aesthetic use of it for their own writing and to offer an alternative to the monolithic culture of the nation state. One of the fascinating aspects of the chapter is that Zancanella's patient research reveals the complex, subtle and continuous changes surrounding this course's original design and ongoing evolution. It also demonstrates the way various teachers, working in the same department, justify their teaching of literature in diverse ways and for differing outcomes, even fundamentally opposing each other's beliefs and yet always with the students' interests at heart. It is to be hoped that readers from around the English-speaking world will value this chapter as a source of optimism because it shows a teacher responsive to students, constantly reflecting on what literature can do for them, looking for ways of making literature matter. Here is a literature teacher for whom cultures are a means to understand one's identities and to enjoy and value the identities of others.

When it comes to identity there can be no question that gender often dominates our adult thinking and, for adolescents perhaps more than any factor, gender is a crucial and often confusing issue. Holly A. Johnson and Dana L. Fox offer us a chance to consider the power of gender in its relationship to the thinking and reading of adolescent girls. Their focus on two, individualistic yet also typical, teenage girls gives us an insight into the interaction between their school and home lives, their sense of identity and its complex relationship to the characters they encounter in fiction. Johnson and Fox offer both the richness of case studies of real readers and also a broad theoretical perspective on the kinds of literature classroom where genuine learning can take place. This kind of learning is not centred on literary knowledge. It is centred on real questions about the complexities of identity and, for example, gender, and on the necessary dissonance between the presentation of female characters in literature and the actual experience of being a young woman subject to powerful conformist pressures. In such a lively, questioning classroom, literature becomes both a source of knowledge and a subject worth investigating. All literature teachers know that 'English' is a peculiar subject. At one level it is apparently much dominated by the female, retaining its popularity among female students, in higher education in particular and taught mostly by women at the elementary and secondary levels. Yet literature, it can still be argued, is dominated by the male writer, especially within the canonical tradition. Hence literature teachers, as Johnson and Fox clearly demonstrate, must pay full attention to gender throughout their teaching.

My final chapter invites literature teachers to consider what I call our textual habitat. It seems that this habitat – once apparently dominated by books – is now threatened by the seductive proliferation of electronic and visual texts; the omnipotent screen seems destined to overwhelm the sacred book. However, as I try to show, this is an old story and the predictions of the demise of the book are mostly a tedious reminder of how certain commentators simply repeat the apocalyptic pronouncements of their forebears. Readers simply have more choice about where they get their facts and fictions from. My argument is that literature teachers should be less paranoid and more celebratory of the myriads of texts that are now available to all of us. Humanity remains in love with fiction in all its forms and consumes it insatiably. I focus on the burgeoning field of adaptations, not because literature teachers might treat them as 'almost as good as the real thing' but because they are real texts. In fact, I go further and suggest that we might now think of adaptation as a central element in the literature curriculum. Adaptations as individual texts, as forms and as a concept in a media-suffused world, are all rich material for us and even more for our students.

Finally, it remains for me to say that English teachers, of whom I am one, face a fascinating challenge. We have already had more advice about how to do our jobs than any other profession on the planet. It is my opinion that much of this advice has been ill-informed, negative and ultimately stifling. This collection offers a great deal of insight and a considerable range of ideas. It is various and varied. It covers a range of topics and comes from a range of countries. I hope it does not advise in that prescriptive and dogmatic way that has become all too familiar to teachers. Instead, it attempts to provide a source of stimulation for those teachers who, in their turn, want to make literature classrooms sources of challenge and stimulus for their students.

REFERENCES

Appleyard, J. A. (1990) *Becoming a Reader: The Experience of Fiction from Childhood to Adulthood*. Cambridge: Cambridge University Press.

Benton, P. (1995) Children's reading and viewing in the nineties. In C. Davies, *What is English Teaching?* Buckingham: Open University Press.

Book Marketing Ltd (1995) *The Children's Book Market: An Overview*. London: Book Marketing Ltd.

Britton, J. (1970) *Language and Learning*. London: Penguin Books.

Buckingham, D. (1993a) *Changing Literacies: Media Education and Modern Culture*. London: Tufnell Press.

Buckingham, D. (ed.) (1993b) *Reading Audiences: Young People and the Media*. Manchester: Manchester University Press.

Buckingham, D. and Sefton-Green, J. (1994) *Cultural Studies Goes to School: Reading and Teaching Popular Media*. London: Taylor & Francis.

Children's Literature Research Centre (1996) *Young People's Reading at the End of the Century*. London: Roehampton Institute.

Corcoran, B. and Evans, E. (eds) (1987) *Readers, Texts, Teachers*. Milton Keynes: Open University Press.

Corcoran, B., Hayhoe, M. and Pradl, G. (eds) (1994) *Knowledge in the Making: Challenging the Text in the Classroom*. Portsmouth, NH: Boynton/Cook.

Davies, C. (1996) *What is English Teaching?* Buckingham: Open University Press.

Freire, P. and Macedo, D. (1987) *Literacy: Reading the Word and the World*. London: Routledge & Kegan Paul.

Gee, J. (1990) *Social Linguistics and Literacies: Ideology in Discourses*. London: Falmer Press.

Goodwyn, A. (1992) English teachers and the Cox models. *English in Education* **26** (3).

Goodwyn, A. (ed.) (1995) *English and Ability*. London: David Fulton.

Goodwyn, A. (1997a) The secondary school and the media: how are schools preparing for the global mass media environment of the 21st century? Paper delivered at the European Conference of Educational Research, Seville.

Goodwyn, A. (1997b) English teachers' theories of good English teaching and their theories in action. Paper given at the International Association for the Improvement of Mother Tongue Education, University of Amsterdam.

Goodwyn, A., Adams, A. and Clarke, S. (1997) The great god of the future: views of current and future English teachers on the place of IT in English. *English in Education* **31** (2), 54–63.

Goody, J. (1977) *The Domestication of the Savage Mind.* Cambridge: Cambridge University Press.

Graff, H. J. (1979) *The Literacy Myth: Literacy and Social Structure in the 19th Century City.* New York: Academic Press.

Hall, C. and Coles, M. (1995) *The Children's Reading Choices Project.* Nottingham: University of Nottingham.

Harding, D. W. (1962) Psychological processes in the reading of fiction. *British Journal of Aesthetics* **II** (2), 135–47.

Hayhoe, M. and Parker, S. (eds) (1990) *Reading and Response.* Buckingham: Open University Press.

Hirsch, E. D. (1996) *The Schools We Need: And Why We Don't Have Them.* New York: Doubleday.

Janssen, T. (1997) What every literature teacher would like to know. Paper given at the International Association for the Improvement of Mother Tongue Education, University of Amsterdam.

Johnston, B. (1987) *Assessing English: Helping Students to Reflect on their Work* (rev. edn). Milton Keynes: Open University Press.

Kress, G. (1995) *Writing the Future: English and the Making of a Culture of Innovation.* Sheffield: National Association for the Teaching of English.

SCCA (Schools Curriculum and Assessment Authority) (1995) *English 5–16.* London: HMSO.

Street, B. (1984) *Literacy in Theory and Practice.* Cambridge: Cambridge University Press.

Vygotsky, L. (1962) *Thought and Language,* trans. E. Hanfmann and G. Vakar. Cambridge, MA: MIT Press.

Walker, S. (1993) *Desktop Publishing for Teachers.* Reading: Reading and Language Information Centre, University of Reading.

Whitehead, F. *et al.* (1977) *Children and Their Books.* London: Macmillan.

Wilkinson, A., Davies, A. and Berrill, D. (1990) *Spoken English Illuminated.* Buckingham: Open University Press.

Willis, P. (1990) *Common Culture.* Buckingham: Open University Press.

Chapter 2

Teaching the Classics
(with special reference to Kate Chopin's *The Awakening*)

Judith Baxter

> The past is a foreign country: they do things differently there.
>
> (L. P. Hartley, *The Go-Between,* 1953)

The 'classic' novel seems to have come of age, thanks to the world of mass media and marketing. We are in a cultural climate that is currently fostering a love affair between the media and a variety of fictional representations of our pre-twentieth-century past. Recently there has been a marked and unprecedented rise in the release of film and television adaptations of pre-twentieth-century 'classic' novels. Following the success of several Shakespearean plays, there have been big-screen versions of *Sense and Sensibility, Emma, Jane Eyre* and *Jude (the Obscure)*, and a thick-and-fast succession of British- and American-made television serializations of such novels as *Gulliver's Travels, Moll Flanders, The Tenant of Wildfell Hall* and *The Mill on the Floss* – not to mention another version of the ubiqitous *Emma*.

For many viewers, the classics have become fashionable and compulsive entertainment, and this has meant big business for the restless, profit-seeking world of film and television. For whatever motives, this commercial, media and audience fascination with classic fiction appears to signify a revival of public interest in our cultural and literary past. Certainly publishers and bookshops are benefiting massively from the 'tie-ins' industry by selling pre-twentieth-century fiction revamped in TV and film publicity jackets, and even from a spate of 'sequels' written by modern authors.

In the UK there is currently a marked parallel between this popular and media-led trend and the educational establishment's recent requirements for the study of pre-twentieth-century texts in the National Curriculum for secondary English. An overtly canonical perspective on the value of the classics states that 'Pupils should be introduced to major works of literature from the English literary heritage in previous centuries' (DFE, 1995, p. 20) and cites Austen, George Eliot, the Brontës, Hardy, Swift and Defoe among others as examples of major writers who have written fiction of 'high quality'. More recently, a pilot study conducted by a team of education inspectors[1] suggested that English literature examinations had become easier, causing a spurious improvement in standards. This was thought to be a result of 'a shift away from the study of challenging, pre-twentieth-century texts – such as Milton and Donne – in favour of more recent, more "accessible" and supposedly more relevant works'. The study consequently recommended an increase in the study of pre-twentieth-century texts at all UK public examination levels.

Despite the apparently happy convergence of popular taste and official policy on the desirability of reading pre-twentieth-century texts for both pleasure and learning, their use in the English classroom is by no means unproblematic. Indeed there is a history of critical, public and political debate around cultural heritage texts that has caused many teachers to be rightly suspicious of their educational value. At the very heart of this has always been the question of what counts as literature, what is meant by a 'classic' anyway, who gets to make the selection, and on whose behalf it is made. Such questions are fundamental, and in this chapter I shall revisit the case for teaching pre-twentieth-century fiction by reviewing the way it has been located both in popular and academic discourses, and institutional practices.

I shall argue that there is a convincing case to be made for teaching such texts at the turn of the twenty-first century, but that we have to be very clear why we want our pupils to encounter them. I shall draw on findings from my preparatory research as editor of a series for secondary schools entitled Cambridge Literature.[2] This research investigated the views and reading experiences of a sample of school students, student teachers and teachers in relation to pre-twentieth-century fiction, and matched the findings against the requirements of the National Curriculum English Orders and the UK examination syllabi. From this, I consider that it is not necessarily helpful or relevant to argue a case for teaching pre-twentieth-century fiction from one single theoretical position or ideological perspective. Following from Cox's definition of five models of teaching English, Goodwyn[3] has shown that teachers do not simply adhere to one universalizing model of teaching literary texts, but adopt a flexible, versatile and pragmatic stance according to the needs of their students, the nature of the subject matter, and the learning outcomes. At times they may adopt, or are constrained to adopt, a 'cultural heritage' model of teaching, particularly in preparing students to write critical essays on set texts for public examinations. At other times, they will draw upon the personal growth model for encouraging students to explore their reading of texts recreatively. Teachers are also beginning to make more use of the cultural analysis model in their teaching of both literary and media texts: this approach helps students to examine basic questions about how meaning is made, to inform the critical rereading of texts, and to appreciate the competing theoretical frames within which different critics work.

It is sometimes considered to be a deficiency in intellectual rigour – a lack of clear thinking – if teachers or students shift pragmatically between different theoretical standpoints or teaching methodologies. Traditionally, academic discourse tends to argue its case from the point of view of a single, totalizing, theoretical framework that feels compelled to refute alternative or competing frames of reference. However, recent postmodernist thinking has challenged this form of rationalism:

> The grand narratives that unified and structured Western science and thought and philosophy, grounding truth and meaning in the presumption of a universal subject and a pre-determined goal of emancipation, no longer appear convincing or plausible. Instead the anti-totalizing, post-modern perspective reveals the generation of

knowledge as singular, localized and perspectival. Knowledge is constructed, not discovered; it is contextual, not foundational.

(Elliott, 1996, p. 19)

I shall argue that it is this pluralist and contextualized approach to learning which accommodates different and competing voices, values and perspectives, and which allows for differing methods and approaches to be used according to the needs of a particular purpose, situation and audience, that is supported by the teachers surveyed in my own research study. Such an approach does not obviate the value of critique, nor does it mean that 'anything goes'. Indeed, a postmodernist perspective on learning requires that all models and systems of thinking should be continuously reviewed and criticized so that, in the spirit of change, revision and renewal, new ideas and approaches can emerge, subverting, replacing or co-existing with the old. It is therefore vital that we question the relevance and value of a particular approach to teaching a literary text: is it one that is meaningful for that cohort of students at that stage of their personal and reading development, or for that course of English literature? What would an approach to teaching pre-twentieth-century fiction look like that actually serves the interests and needs of our own students?

THREE CASES FOR TEACHING PRE-TWENTIETH-CENTURY FICTION

Currently there are three cases for teaching pre-twentieth-century fiction that have dominated pedagogical discourse in English: the first two are consistent with, and flow from, two established models of teaching English literature; the third is more of a response to a popular, commercial trend. There is good reason to scrutinize all three.

Case 1: Pre-twentieth-century fiction is part of a 'great tradition' of literature that all pupils are entitled to study

The heritage version of English literature is in many ways still the most powerful voice to be heard, both in its definition of what is meant by a 'classic' and in its influence on English teaching policies and practices. At the root of this discourse are essential issues to do with the nature of Englishness as an index of linguistic identity and monocultural power. Based on Leavisite and New Critical models of literary criticism, it initiated the construct of a tradition of texts that qualify for 'great' or 'classic' status (and hence become 'Literature') according to a set of literary critical qualifications generally agreed by appropriately qualified critcs. In his hierarchial selection of a 'great tradition' of fiction, F. R. Leavis (1948) was making judgements both on formal stylistic features and upon the link between a text's aesthetic properties and its moral messages, presumed by him to be universally relevant. In short, he proposed that great literature was good for the soul, and contained the educational power to teach children 'to discriminate and resist' the crude blandishments of pulp fiction and popular culture. This is directly reflected in recent UK National Curriculum documentation which urges that 'as many pupils as possible should have contact with some of the great writing which has been influential in shaping our language and culture' (DES, 1989, 7.15).

Linked to this canonical version of English literature are three further strands, all based on liberal-humanist notions of personal, political and educational progression, and ultimately, enlightenment. The first is that of access and entitlement: that is, the democratic right of all pupils, whatever their linguistic capability or level of interest, to be put in touch with their heritage, through the medium of subjects like English literature or history. According to this, pupils are entitled to connect with their own national identity and understand better the contribution of great literature to political progress and a more 'civilized' society. But entitlement is inevitably a tricky concept and raises more questions than it answers. Does, for example, entitlement guarantee access only, or does this also include egress – the right to opt out of knowledge, out of a course, or out of assessment on that knowledge?

The second strand might be termed 'literary enlightenment': according to the heritage view, learning to understand and appreciate great literature is a long and arduous journey, full of challenges and pitfalls. The modernist presumption here is that a hard slog through the classics will help the student reader to grow inexorably towards a more refined appreciation of literature. Popular and modern fiction, on the other hand, are far less likely to make a literary critic out of you – it may be more 'accessible' and 'relevant', but it is often perceived to be less demanding, and by a puritanical twist of logic, less good for you. On this basis, one wonders how many pre-twentieth-century texts have acquired their 'classic' status as much for their linguistic difficulty, hidden meanings and impenetrability as for their ability to enchant readers with their poetic ambience or to inspire them with great truths.

The third strand of the heritage argument suggests that students will better understand and appreciate recent fiction by gaining a sense of its place within the tradition of literature. This is the issue of 'influence': each great work of fiction is connected chronologically by its influence upon the next, as if attached by an invisible string. However, this presumes in the modernist spirit that 'great literature' is on its own journey which culminated in the work of experimental writers like T. S. Eliot and James Joyce. Did the invisible string break after the work of Joyce? What can we make of the chaotically diverse range of often excellent contemporary and multi-ethnic writing in the light of the unbroken string theory? Where was the beginning of this tradition, and where is the end? Such questions remain largely unanswered by the heritage theorists.

The counter discourse to the 'heritage' case has posed fundamental questions about the relevance and accessibility of such monocultural versions of English. Whose canon is it, and whose interests does it serve? Which criteria were used to select it? Can there be just one canon in a multi-ethnic and multilingual society? According to this opposing view, an English curriculum based on such a 'selection from culture' (Williams, 1965) appears to be privileging the interests, language and literacy tastes of the dominant social class – in this case, a group of white, Anglo-Saxon, Protestant, educated and largely male novelists who prefer the classic realist genre of the *Bildungsroman* above other fictional forms. Cultural materialists such as West (1994) have attacked the hegemonic tendencies of the heritage version of English for its concern with 'the task of nation building, the literary heritage being the vehicle whereby the standard form of the language is established in its dominant role' (p. 127).

This supports Eagleton's (1983) contentions that 'English Literature' is no neutral medium capable of transcending ideological debate, but a site for contesting and negotiating issues of national identity, language and power.

Literary theory has also problematized heritage notions of literature, by questioning the authority upon which judgements about 'greatness' are based. Deconstructionists like Barthes (1977, p. 146) have claimed that no text is original or unique, but rather texts act as 'multi-dimensional spaces' in which 'a variety of writings . . . blend and clash'.

> All literary texts are woven out of other literary texts, not in the conventional sense that they bear the traces of 'influence', but in the more radical sense that every word, phrase or segment is a reworking of other writings which precede or surround the individual work. There is no such thing as 'originality', no such thing as the 'first' literary work: all literature is intertextual.
>
> (Eagleton, 1983, p. 138)

So, according to the deconstructionists, literature is an ideologically constructed field of discourse, and is therefore in itself a cultural construct. Rather than studying individual 'great works', students and teachers should be studying the nature of this construct – what is counted as literature, what defines and characterizes the canon, what reading practices we use, and which values these practices affirm or deny. But this field of theory, for all its radicalizing intentions, is often perceived by the school students and beginner teachers I have worked with as alienating, mystifying, jargon-bound, and above all, difficult. Where is the place, they ask, for empathy, pleasure and their own response to a treasured book, in this cold world of constructed subjectivity and undifferentiated texts? Where is there room for a work of fiction that has a transforming effect on a reader's emotions and thoughts? And what about the process of reading – the business of picturing and imagining, of reminiscing and anticipating, of reflecting and making judgements upon a good story?

To sum up, then, the 'heritage' case for teaching canonical texts causes problems for English teachers today because of its lack of critical awareness of its ideological and aesthetic constructedness. This 'critical awareness' has been supplied by the deconstructionists who rightly place an emphasis upon the culturally determined nature of texts at the expense of inherent greatness. But those teachers and students in my study who had experienced teaching methods grounded in literary theory found little space there for exploring and developing their own, at first tentative readings of pre-twentieth-century fiction.

Case 2: There is a collective teacher guilt about having ignored pre-twentieth-century fiction during the last twenty-five years

This 'lurking neurosis', as Barton (1994) terms it, originated from a generation of schooling in the UK since the 1960s influenced by the personal growth model of English that consciously chose not to teach the classics. There was a complex mix of reasons for this: the inception of comprehensive schooling and mixed ability grouping; the rise of the personal growth model of teaching literature, and later, the growing popularity of reader response theories which put the emphasis on a pupil's personal response to a text at the expense of its literary status. Accordingly, English teachers considered 'classic' fiction to be inappropriate for children's language development, interests, abilities and home culture. Instead they turned towards texts that were modern, linguistically accessible, and perceived to be enjoyable and relevant to students' own experiences. Many of the texts featured teenage protagonists and were set in familiar environments – school, home, or the local community. Ironically, what has since emerged is an alternative canon, now over twenty-five years old, that is still alive and flourishing in British schools. Instead of Jane Austen, George Eliot, Henry James, Joseph Conrad and D. H. Lawrence, we have John Steinbeck, William Golding, Barry Hines, Laurie Lee and Harper Lee: still Wasps and largely male, but nonetheless still perceived to be 'accessible'.

British teachers have felt vulnerable to the charge from various camps that there is a lost generation of pupils who never received their entitlement to pre-twentieth-century literature (and, linking with West's argument above, also failed to pick up a knowledge of formal English grammar and Standard English). My experience as a teacher educator of young beginner teachers (who perceive themselves to be a part of that 'lost generation') suggests that there is a sense of having 'missed out' on the experience of learning about pre-twentieth-century literature as it was rarely taught before advanced level. Encountering Jane Austen or Shakespeare at this stage was considered 'a struggle' and 'too late'. Not only do they feel inadequate about teaching it themselves, but it has also made them quite evangelical about the need to introduce pupils to pre-twentieth-century literature from the very start of secondary school.

There is a danger, however, that teachers will seek 'quick-fix' solutions in their search for strategies and materials that will overcome their insecurities and help them to deliver the demands of a curriculum or examination syllabi:

> Suddenly it seems that classic literature is the equivalent of the one-minute dash around the supermarket, with publishers and anthologists toppling all the most attractive items into their trolleys leaving behind unappealing tins of corned beef and chunky chicken.
>
> (Barton, 1994, p. 135)

At least one UK examination group has already used the bait of an anthology of snippets of texts from novels and plays, as well as a selection of short stories and poetry that purports to cover all the pre-twentieth-century requirements of its examination English syllabus. Why – the argument runs – invest in expensive sets of books when a single, all-purpose anthology will do? But the risk is that students will encounter classic fiction in a superficial and piecemeal way, rarely experiencing a novel as whole, and (unless there is tender, loving care from the teacher) failing to appreciate the full social context, generic links and histories of such texts.

Case 3: Classic fiction is a media fashion – in film, television, radio and book publishing – so let's make the most of it

Returning briefly to the opening of this chapter, the revival of media interest in the 'classics' is certainly having its effect on the world of English teaching. Its advantages are clear: any concerns English teachers may have about the remoteness and irrelevance of pre-twentieth-century texts are likely to evaporate as cheap, readily available videos provide the possibility of powerful and stimulating classroom resources. Several of the adaptations have made serious efforts to connect with young people's experiences today, and have quite consciously aimed to strip away the clutter of period cultural and linguistic barriers. The film *Jude* is one such example:

> So we say, okay, free yourself from what's said in the novel and try and imagine how people might have spoken and then try to make it sayable by actors to seem real and natural and fresh as possible . . . We tried to clean out any linguistic complication that comes between the audience and the story; maybe at times we pushed it too far, but hopefully not that often. [4]
>
> (Andrew Eaton, director, 1996)

However, this comment also problematizes the issue of using film resources of this type, in two particular ways. The first is to be found in that group of films, including *Jude,* which has primarily aimed to connect the film with the experiences of a modern audience by more or less transposing the story of the original text, complete with period detail, to the cultural and linguistic idiom of the present day, as if the difference between then and now were merely one of houses, costume and furnishings. Not all film critics have agreed with Eaton's view that we should 'try to imagine Sue and Jude as if they were living now', and that historical conditions make no difference:

> [*Jude*] is set in the late 19th century; the tension between sombre Victorian values – such as the pressures of a couple living out of wedlock – and the first hopeful glimmers of the dawning century is a key element; it's misleading, even mendacious to claim it is a contemporary story.
>
> (Johnstone, *Daily Telegraph,* 4 October 1996)

The second problem area lies in the 'heritage' tendencies of certain other adaptations, such as the film version of *Emma.* For marketing reasons these tend to romanticize the socio-economic conditions of the past, offering up rather nostalgic, folksy notions of how people lived, dressed and spoke in pre-industrial Britain, while omitting conditions or marginalizing characters that might expose social inequalities and injustices. Film companies have understandably capitalized on the entertainment value of picturesque classic fiction; they have played to the audience's desire to escape, to be transported to a different historical period that appears on the surface to suffer less from modern 'ailments' such as the effects of urbanization, pollution, racism and unemployment, 'for a peek at a vanished world rather than one that merely mirrors their own' (Johnstone, *op. cit.*).

So there are critical questions to be asked about the use of film and TV adaptations in the classroom alongside literary texts. If we are to take Andrew Eaton's argument that 'the most accurate way of dealing with a historical situation . . . is to try and imagine Sue and Jude as if they were living now', then we might ask: is a film's main function to be a way of bypassing the difficulties of the text by presenting students with a palatable and comprehensible alternative to reading it? In her insightful work on teaching Shakespeare, Leach (1992), has challenged such an approach:

> I feel that using video is in many ways an opting out, seen by teachers as a panacea for the difficulties of having to deal with long texts with students who may not be very receptive to them. An inability to use those televisual texts in radical ways, along with a failure to understand the particular codes by which they are working results in the whole unsatisfactory nature of the undertaking . . .
>
> (p. 71)

Leach suggests that if videos are to be used at all, they should be used in a 'cultural analysis' spirit – as a particular interpretation or re-reading of the original literary text. Teachers must be prepared to use them 'in stages, to rewind and reinspect scenes or small parts to see what is happening'; and to make time and effort. Indeed this argument might be taken one stage further: perhaps the film or TV adaptation shouldn't be regarded as a tool for comprehending the novel at all, but as a media text in its own right, with its own sets of semiotic codes, discourses and audience positions.

In summary, it may well be that film and TV adaptations provide teachers with an incentive for teaching pre-twentieth-century novels, and a handy set of resources for making these texts accessible and entertaining to students of ranging abilities. But this might in the end be more harmful than good if the teaching approach does not accommodate a sophisticated handling of the media text itself.

TEACHING PRE-TWENTIETH-CENTURY FICTION

Connection and distance

Each of the three cases for teaching pre-twentieth-century fiction given above presents teachers with problems if it is to be adopted as an overarching pedagogical rationale. I suggest that if we want our students to enjoy reading and studying classic novels, we must be prepared to be much more eclectic, versatile and critically mobile in our teaching approaches. Andrew Goodwyn's research (1992) on English teachers' views of Cox's five models drew the conclusion that 'the personal growth model, developed in the 1960s and 1970s, remains dominant' and furthermore, that while some English teachers subscribe to the cultural analysis model, 'as an approach and seem to be adopting it increasingly, it is not sweeping away personal growth' (p. 9).

Pre-twentieth-century fiction is best encountered by drawing upon an interplay of principles and approaches from the personal growth and cultural analysis models. As we have seen, the personal growth philosophy was accompanied by reader response methodologies that have highlighted the value of personal engagement, or connection, with a text through a range of active and exploratory teaching methods, while the cultural analysis model has emphasized the value of critical distance by asking students to deconstruct the cultural fabric of texts. Within this section I shall explore both principles, and the value of developing an interplay between them in our teaching of pre-twentieth-century fiction.

Connecting with the text
It is no accident that most canonical fiction tends to be works of classic realism, aiming to reconstruct the illusion of a realistic and believable story about the lives of

'ordinary' men and women. They are 'readerly' rather than 'writerly' texts, rarely deliberately experimental or playful with their fictional form, nor consciously self-referential. The implied reader postion is usually one that requires a connection with, and simultaneously, a critical distance from the narrative stance. Typically the protagonists featured behave in ways that threaten to, or actually do, transgress the norms of their culture; these characters momentarily appear to 'step out of' the cultural framework of the novel and may review their predicament ahistorically; their actions may threaten to subvert their place in society, and as a consequence, they are variously punished or rewarded, learn a lesson or are reabsorbed into their social context. As classic realist fiction thrives on closure, solutions are usually cyclical and conservative, and dominant readings tend to elicit fairy tale-type messages and morals about the struggle between free will and fate.

It is these generic features which contain the key to understanding the continuing popularity of classic fiction. A 'Waspish' selection it may be, but these novels sell today precisely because male and female readers from all classes as well as all ethnic, regional and educational backgrounds have discovered them to be significant texts which have a transformative effect on our lives and development as readers. For example, students I interviewed found powerful points of connection with the transgressive role of certain protagonists, such as Tess of the d'Urbevilles, Maggie Tulliver, Heathcliff or Oliver Twist, in mirroring their own feelings of frustration, entrapment, need for independence or desire for escape. For me, Jane Eyre's famous 'freedom' speech, as culturally referenced and nuanced as it is, spoke down the ages to my teenage self, and nudged my reading interests towards the field of women's fiction writing:

> Women are supposed to be very calm, generally; but women feel just as men feel; they need exercise for their faculties; and a field for their efforts as much as their brothers do; they suffer from far too rigid a restraint, too absolute a stagnation, precisely as men would suffer; and it is narrow-minded in their more privileged fellow-creatures to say that they ought to confine themselves to making puddings and knitting stockings, to playing on their pianos and embroidering bags.
>
> (Brontë, 1996, p. 123)

This is paradoxically both a culturally situated statement and a robustly timeless one – and I would suggest that there is room in our responses for the co-existence of both readings. It also exemplifies how particular features of pre-twentieth-century fiction can lead readers outwards, enabling us to make links and parallels with our personal and social experience, teaching us to reassess and reshape our perceptions in the light of reading a powerful text. Our prior reading experience also plays an intricate role in this process. This is partly the subconscious Barthian business of our making sense of the text in hand in the light of all other texts we have encountered; but it is also the more explicit, personalized pleasure of making reading connections between one text and another. For example, I recall being made keenly aware of the echoes of Jane Eyre's story on first reading Kate Chopin's *The Awakening*: an influence and a parallel that, as I learned later, Chopin recognized and probably intended herself.

Classic fiction can therefore lead the reader outwards to explore lived and fictional experiences, but it also carries us inwards, into the imaginative, other-world of the text, where the story acts as the medium for making a journey of exploration through what is initially a culturally and historically remote landscape. By the end of that journey the world of the text has been assimilated into our own: the sense of strangeness has mostly been dissolved by our powers of imagination and empathy, by the way we bring our own personal experiences and memories to the text, and by our abilities as readers to fill in the gaps and omissions in the work.

Establishing a critical distance from the text
While empathy and connecting processes help students to cross the pre-twentieth-century barrier, it would be wrong to belittle the challenges of such texts both culturally and linguistically. From a modern young reader's perspective, what happens in the cultural world of a pre-twentieth-century novel can at times seem mystifying, irrelevant, trivial or pointless. It is not hard to see, for example, why students of Jane Austen's Emma often feel an initial lack of sympathy for the affluent and complacent heroine, in a novel seemingly full of small-minded social snobbery, interminable gossip, afternoon teas, calling cards and stage-managed courtship. When a novel does appear initially to be more culturally accessible in its story and themes, this may be misleading if read 'at face value'. For example, in *The Awakening*, a text I shall use as an example of pre-twentieth-century fiction, Kate Chopin's heroine, Edna Pontellier, appears to be expressing a modern perspective when we are told that she is no 'mother-woman', and that 'she would never sacrifice herself for her children or anyone'. But, to understand this with any real sense, we must reframe it within the context of a hierarchial New Orleans society with a leisure class of affluent, white married couples who paid demeaningly low wages to 'quadroon' women to look after their children. In short, Chopin's heroine could afford to look for freedom and personal fulfilment on the basis of her wealth, race and class. From this we see the inherent problems in 'reading' the subject of a pre-twentieth-century novel from a present-day perspective without taking account of the cultural conditions that shaped it.

On the lingusitic level, modern expectations of reading and styles of reading practice have changed considerably since the late nineteenth century. For example, Thomas Hardy's novels presume an educated reader with ample leisure time to engage with his long, complex sentence structures, his figurative vocabulary, his verbosity, his detailed descriptions of landscape, and dense allusions to myth, religion and other literature. Today the kind of fiction favoured by young people presumes a reader in a hurry who is easily tempted away by the visual pleasures of TV, film or interactional computer games. The Point Horror and Romance series, for example are characterized by a range of attention-grabbing techniques: pacy, action-packed plots, bold but sketchy characterization, and only as much setting detail as is instrumental to the action.

Language and culture may therefore be a barrier for our students, and it would be wrong to suggest to our students that Thomas Hardy or Jane Austen will ever be easy reading. But I would like to argue that it is this very cultural and linguistic 'otherness' that offers our students a foothold on the more critical study of such texts. What pre-twentieth-century fiction does is to draw active attention to our culturally situated roles as readers. We are made explicitly aware through the medium of the language that a nineteenth-century text is about a milieu that is socially and historically strange and removed from our own, and that characters' experiences and psychological insights are constructed in rather different terms from our own. This 'strangeness' in itself draws attention to the fictionalized world of the novel; it can never be a direct representation of our own, however 'universal' certain elements of it may feel. Rather it presents a selective version of reality, situated in a specific historical moment and cultural space.

I suggest therefore that as teachers we can use pre-twentieth-century fiction to draw our students' attention to the constructedness of fiction in general, precisely through the difficulty they may experience in making sense of it. This does not preclude students from suspending their belief as readers, from entering that version of reality offered by a novel, and from allowing the characters to 'speak to them', for this would take away one of the great joys of reading. Indeed we must find ways actively to encourage this kind of empathy. But this must be an empathy with a critically distancing edge: one that seeks to ask questions about what version of reality the novel is constructing both overtly and subtextually, whose version it is and where this ideological framework comes from. Our students are in the business of critical readership, of learning to recognize the historical and cultural elements that are shaping their own readings and responses. The study of pre-twentieth-century fiction can make this kind of meta-textual reflection particularly explicit and focused, and may give a new meaning to the traditional distancing analysis of 'lit-crit'.

PUTTING THEORY INTO PRACTICE

So far I have argued for a teaching approach that brings together best practice from two theoretical perspectives: the value of empathy and personal engagement with a text as put forward by personal growth and reader response theorists; and the value of reading with a critical awareness of cultural history, as advocated by cultural analysis theorists. More particularly from a practical standpoint, I believe that our students will find the study of pre-twentieth-century fiction both accessible and stimulating if these two qualities – empathy and critical readership – can be brought into some kind of reciprocity, interplay or co-existence in the classroom. To illustrate what I mean by this, I outline below the study approach of the Cambridge Literature series as the outcome of my research into the teaching of 'classic' fiction, and follow this by suggesting some general, longer-term principles and strategies for achieving this aim in the classroom.

The Cambridge Literature approach

The study approach aims to help readers think about what happens when they read a pre-twentieth-century novel – that they are not passively responding to words on the page that has only one agreed interpretation – but that they are actively exploring and making new sense of what they read. They are encouraged to reflect on their own position as readers: that the way they read and interpret a text is both a consequence of their individual experiences and point of view, as well as their belonging to a culture and a community rooted in a particular time and place. They are also asked to consider the parallel between the way they read a text and the way that this text has been written: that is, the process that begins with the author's first, tentative ideas and sources of inspiration moves through the stages of production and publication, and ends with the text's reception by the reading public, critics and students.

The study approach centres on a common framework of five questions to open up demanding texts and encourage students to explore their responses in an engaged and critical fashion:

- Who wrote the novel and why?
- How was the novel produced?
- What type of text is it?
- How does the novel present its subject?
- Who reads the novel, and how do they interpret it?

Teachers and students might use this framework of questions in the order they appear (and as such would mirror the communication process of 'production–mediation–reception' instrumental to all texts, whether literary, non-literary or media). However, as each question is free standing, it is just as likely that it might be used selectively and flexibly to support a teacher's individual scheme of work as required. In order to illustrate the practical study value of each of the questions below, I have referred to two works of classic fiction used internationally in secondary schools: *The Awakening* by Kate Chopin and *Great Expectations* by Charles Dickens. The significance of each of the following questions is explored below, because they each serve as a way of stimulating the student to explore the text through methods of connection and critical distance.

Who wrote the novel and why?

Given the challenge of recent literary theory to the concept of the authorship-function, it is no longer possible to pose this question to our students in any simplistic way. Foucault (1977) and Barthes (1977) have demonstrated that the concept of the author is a constructed one, and a fairly recent and modern notion. Whereas in medieval times literature was more likely to be seen as part of a collective enterprise, and not associated with an individual author or point of view, in recent times the author has been linked with notions of 'individuality', 'originality' and 'intentionality':

> The image of literature to be found in ordinary culture is tyrannically centred on the author, his [*sic*] person, his life, his tastes, his passions . . . the explanation of a work is always sought in the man or woman who produced it, as if it were always in the end, through the more or less transparent allegory of fiction, the voice of a single person, the author 'confiding' in us.
>
> (Barthes, 1977, p. 143)

Certainly it important to problematize the concept of authorship to our students: to ask them to consider why it is that certain discourses in society are characterized by the name and identity of their author, whereas others, such as much non-fiction writing, are not. This can be linked to the many examples today of the extraordinary power of the 'personality cult' in mass media discourses: for example, the opening of any new film is always heralded in newspapers and magazines by an interview with the starring actor probing personal life, family background and, where it exists, personal philosophy. Political debates are invariably reported less according to the quality and range of ideas, and more according to the failings and foibles of politicians' personalities. On a different level, it is useful to question the assumption of authorial intentionality that still persists in the expression of so many examination questions on most UK English literature syllabi.

By questioning the role of the author and the spurious notion that understanding the intentions of that author is a route towards a definitive interpretation of the work, our students can move towards a greater appreciation of the work as a text. With less attention placed on the author, no single voice in the text is privileged; and a reading can becomes an active opening out of the range of meanings possible, rather than a passive closing in to a single, intended or expert reading.

But should the role of the author cease to be of any interest at all, when studying a text such as a pre-twentieth-century novel? As I suggest in my editorial notes to *The Awakening* (Chopin, 1996), we need know nothing at all about the life of an author like Kate Chopin in order to interpret and appreciate her writing. But, and it is a very big 'But', reading Chopin's stories does awaken a very powerful curiosity about the author herself. Why was she constantly writing about freedom in her stories: whether freedom through notions of an 'open' marriage; through love affairs with charming and passionate men; through separation and divorce; or through the escape of art, music or writing? After reading a number of her stories, I was intrigued to find out the answers to these questions and fascinated by what I discovered. Chopin's life was colourful, vibrant and highly unconventional. It led me on a reading quest to find out more from her autobiographical writings, her pieces of journalism, letters and the biographies written about her; and the experience of reading these non-fiction writings in parallel with her fiction spurred me on to a greater appreciation of how a writer can be both situated in and standing on the margins of their own culture.

I would suggest therefore that we can enhance the pleasure students may derive from reading pre-twentieth-century fiction by giving them opportunities to read 'narrative parallels': that is, 'stories' about the writer's biographical and cultural circumstances that run parallel to, or indeed in contradistinction to, the focal novel. These are not intended as devices to 'explain' the novel. Rather they can be read primarily for curiosity as narratives in their own right, but they may also incidentally reveal intriguing parallels, points of contrast, links and influences upon the novel itself.

How was the novel produced?
Recent literary theory has done much to demystify the business of how writing a novel 'gets done'. Traditional romantic notions of the author, usually male, in his garret suddenly being seized by a moment of inspiration, or on his travels, undergoing a mind-transforming experience later to become the raw material of a brilliant novel, have given way to a rather more prosaic construct – the novel as artefact:

> Like cars, computers, clothing and other consumer goods, written texts are products of culture. As cultural artifacts, these things are made to fit into people's lives and to support certain ways of thinking and acting. Also like manufactured goods, texts are created as part of a process: raw materials are gathered; designs are consulted; guidelines are followed; the final product is distributed and consumers buy and make use of the article.
>
> (Moon, 1990, p. 30)

The kind of cultural materialist imagery used here – that of the market place and consumerism – allows little place for the humanist perspective on creativity with its notions of original thinking, ingenuity and the individual imagination. It has been the argument of this chapter to suggest that there should be enough intellectual space in a postmodernist environment to accept the co-existence of both individual human creativity and the powerful socializing influences of a given set of historical and cultural conditions upon that writer's creativity.

Whenever I have invited a professional writer to give a reading at a school, I have noticed that the first question students always ask is a variant on 'Where did you get your ideas from?' The writer's answers are never guessable – always unusual, complex and highly personal – and it is hard to equate their imaginative ingenuity and playfulness with the analogy of writing as an assembly of textual parts on a cultural production line. For this reason, I think it is fascinating for students to know that, for example, Mary Shelley's *Frankenstein* originated from a ghost story-telling competition also involving her husband, Percy Bysshe Shelley, and Lord Byron, while they were on holiday in the Swiss mountains; or that Chopin's *The Awakening* was partly based on a true and tragic story she heard from a friend. It is also useful for students to know that a novel's content and form are often intricately related. The evolution and serialized form of *Great Expectations* (Dickens, 1995), written for the periodical *All the Year Round*, was partly influenced by the author's own enjoyment of travelling.

Described by him as a 'pilgrimage of being', it is organized into three stages like a stagecoach journey. But its 'staged' and episodic structure was just as much determined by the pressure he was under to meet the periodical's regular deadlines. Similarly, the novel's thematic preoccupation with Pip's past suited the periodical's series form very well: readers of weekly instalments needed to be reminded constantly of what had gone before. Idiosyncratic and cultural details such as these can only enhance a student's understanding of a novel's structure, and why that structure is significant.

From a wider cultural perspective, students should understand that the process by which a novel, or any text, gets written and then eventually published is neither simple nor automatic; that novels written by talented people throughout history never got published; and that those selected for academic study are the survivors of an elaborate system that begins when a publisher accepts a manuscript, and ends with the official approval of the literary and educational establishment. This kind of cultural contextualizing of the means by which a text gets selected and approved for study in schools is a useful antidote to the view that texts 'make it' on the basis of inherent 'greatness'. It allows for the development of 'critical literacy' (West, 1994), in helping our students to speculate why, for example, there are so few canonical texts by working-class writers, or by men and women from a range of ethnic and cultural backgrounds.

What type of text is it?
This question allows students to consider the complex generic nature of a given novel, and to read for evidence of the text's connections with other texts. It invites students to consider issues of intertextuality, and the Barthian view that every text is to some extent a reworking of other texts. Eagleton has pointed out (1983) that this is not a

question of direct influence in the Leavisite sense, but much more a subconscious process of each new text being inevitably constructed from the texts that 'precede and surround' it. For this reason, the resource notes in *The Awakening* (1996) ask students to compare the novel's generic form with those of a variety of other genres in popular use in nineteenth-century American literature such as the *Bildungsroman*, the 'domestic' novel and the 'local colour' novel. This should never be a simple 'spot the genre' exercise: it is intended to help students explore the extent to which a novel may borrow from its antecedents, and the extent to which it may imitate, revise, manipulate, exploit and subvert these forms, or move beyond a genre's more formulaic constraints to develop a unique character of its own. Students should also be making intertextual comparisons between the generic make-up of the novel and other fiction they have read for pleasure. This could extend to film and media adaptations. For example, they might be asked: 'What are the links and parallels; what are the contrasts and differences?'

Beyond this, it is useful for more senior students to know that certain novels also bear very conscious 'traces' of individual texts that their authors have been consciously and profoundly affected by. It is no accident therefore, that students of *The Awakening* routinely describe how they are reminded of Charlotte Brontë's *Jane Eyre*, Leo Tolstoy's *Anna Karenina* or George Sand's *Lelia*. Moreover, as I have already suggested above, novels that have an enduring appeal do much more than, in a manufacturing sense, 'rework' other texts or genres. They are experimental and adventurous with conventional forms, playfully refashioning them into potentially new modes of literary expression. They have a potentially revolutionary power, able both to challenge traditions of established writing and to construct new generic frames of reference. Elaine Showalter (1988) suggests that *The Awakening* was banned from American libraries and bookshops for almost fifty years for precisely this reason:

> A writer may work in solitude but literature depends on a tradition, on shared forms and representations of experience: and literary genres, like biological species, evolve because of significant innovations by individuals that survive through repetition and revision. Thus it can be a very serious blow to a developing genre when a revolutionary work is taken out of circulation . . . *The Awakening* was just such a revolutionary book.
>
> (p. 170)

How does the novel present its subject?
The question may be read in a Leavisite spirit ('How does the novel present its subject through characterization, plot, setting, themes and style?'), or from a deconstructionist's viewpoint ('How do the textual strategies of the novel, as well as its gaps, silences and ambiguities, position the reader to respond?'). But it is likely that a teacher's initial aim is to help his or her students to engage with a new novel, find some pleasure in reading it, and begin to understand its language and cultural context. When a student asks 'Why do we have to read this book? What has this novel to say to me?', the design of the study activities should encourage students to find their own answer.

The way to achieve this kind of personal investment is through active methods that open up a text's imaginative, dramatic and creative possibilities. Active methods are learner-centred, acknowledging the active part every reader plays in making meaning, and creating their own 'readings' of a text. Such methods allow students to enter into the world of the text, visualize it through artwork, experience it through role-play and drama, and take the writer's part by inventing new episodes, or rewriting existing ones. According to those who advocate 'active' methods (Benton and Fox, 1985; Gibson, 1994), the text is something to be 'made', not 'taken'. Indeed students will only learn to demystify texts with 'classic' status by treating them with a certain amount of disrespect that demands intervention, challenges to the authority of the text, and creative reworking.

This requires social methods: pupils working together with others, sharing ideas and possibilities in collaborative work. It involves creative methods that allow students to 'visualize' or 'physicalize' episodes and scenes, for example, by inventing and dramatizing 'absent' chapters; hot-seating a character who has made a controversial decision; or staging a court trial or inquest. It asks for methods that rely on visual, graphic or tabular means of presenting ideas – drawing a family tree, designing a class map of a character's journey, or storyboarding the plot of an episodic novel as a large mural in order to envisage it as a feature film. There is a range of imaginative writing possibilities such as creating a chapter from the point of view of a 'silent' or peripheral character; rewriting the novel's ending; or turning a scene into the script for a play. Such active methods aim to release students from the difficulties of fighting with the language of the text, and help to get to the 'heart' or 'essence' of a key chapter or turning point in the plot. They are designed to liberate students from the traditional role of literary critic and begin to enjoy the possibilities of collective class study of a more difficult text.

However successful these active methods can be, they must also be backed up by more explicitly critical methods that allow students the opportunity to reflect on what they have learnt about the novel from each activity. Well-directed active methods should lead towards more formal evaluation of aspects such as plot, characterization, setting and language. Reflection will also help them to articulate both the 'connectiveness' and 'otherness' of the pre-twentieth-century novel: both what is familiar, relevant, accessible and appealing about the version of reality offered by the novel, and what seems strange, different, unappealing or removed from their own experience.

More senior students can be encouraged to build on this understanding of the 'connectiveness' and 'otherness' of pre-twentieth-century novels in various ways. One approach is to consider the strategies that classic realist novels use to convey an illusion of 'truth' and reality. What version of reality and truth is it? And whose version is it? Which textual strategies work to produce this illusion, and which undermine it? Within this critical framework, students can consider the novel's use of more formal aspects such as characterization, plot or social setting. But they can also learn to interrogate a novel's ideological terrain by exploring both what is foregrounded and highlighted and what is marginalized, omitted, ambiguous or contradictory. For example, in *The Awakening*, Edna Pontellier's struggle for liberation is sometimes perceived by students as a victory for feminism. But when a more critical perspective is taken on the cultural frames of the novel, Edna's attempts at 'liberation' must be reconceptualized in the light of the underclass of silent and marginalized, female servant characters on whom her new-found lifestyle depends. By seeking to reflect on such ambiguities, students are learning to appreciate the constructedness of the pre-twentieth novel, and to reflect on the often contradictory social and moral values it supports.

Who reads the novel and how do they interpret it?

Drawing from reader response theory, this area of study asks students to consider the nature of the reading relationship between reader and text. If we want a novel to matter to the students we teach, it is clearly vital that they develop a personal response to literature – a response that they should learn is shaped by their personality, experience of life, prior reading experience, views and attitudes to issues, events and relationships. My experience of interviewing postgraduate English students for Initial Teacher Training courses has repeatedly shown how disillusioned some of them are by the lack of emphasis in their degree courses on developing their own responses to literature at the expense of the readings of critical theorists.

Clearly it is a priority to give space to personal response with students of all ages, particularly by means of the range of 'active' methods described above. However, as students become more experienced readers, this 'personal response' should become more subject to critical scrutiny as they learn to interrogate their own cultural situatedness in reading practices. By asking questions such as:

- What is my response to this novel?
- Where does this response come from?
- How similar or different is it from my peers?
- What do our collective responses have in common?

students will be able to consider that factors such as age, gender, language, the area in which they live, upbringing, background and so on have a marked effect upon the nature of their responses, and may account for the differences between theirs and those of readers from other backgrounds, times and places.

The value of the pre-twentieth-century novel in this learning process is to draw explicit attention to the cultural factors that have shaped the changing nature of reading practices. When *The Awakening* was first published, there was a public outcry throughout the USA as newspaper and magazine critics called it 'trite and sordid', 'morbid', 'essentially vulgar' and 'sad, mad, and bad'. It is sometimes difficult for students today to imagine firstly, how this particular novel's themes could have provoked such an uproar in comparison with the subject matter of published novels today, and secondly, how attitudes could have changed over seventy years to such an extent that a nationally banned book is now part of the literary canon in American high schools.

Certain canonical texts like *The Awakening* have attracted volumes of modern literary criticism, encompassing many schools of theory, which can have quite an inhibiting effect on young student readers struggling to formulate their own responses. It is my view that we must provide our students with a learning 'space' initially, to articulate their own responses, both individually and with their peers, before they encounter the readings of the 'experts'. When they have had this 'air time' they will be more confidently placed to make their own evaluations of a classic novel, and probably more capable of assessing the readings of critics. Such readings might also be perceived as 'parallel narratives' (see p. 40): discrete texts that are not being read simply in order to seek explanations or interpretations of the novel, but rather as readings that offer insights into a personal stance or a culturally situated theoretical perspective, such as feminism, cultural materialism or psychoanalysis. Because this understanding of critics' readings can be an academically challenging business, even at degree level, I feel that critics' readings should be used selectively and with some discretion at school level.

IMPLICATIONS FOR TEACHING PRE-TWENTIETH-CENTURY FICTION

There are two further points about teaching pre-twentieth-century fiction to add. The first is that English departments will need to plan their students' encounters with pre-twentieth-century fiction with their longer-term reading development in mind. If possible, this plan should span the whole school career so that students meet such literature in a gradual, varied, accumulative and recursive way. This would allow for early experiences with demanding texts to be selected and structured appropriately according to age, aptitude and interest, and for later encounters to reinforce what they have learnt, as their study becomes gradually more challenging.

I believe that it is important to get away from the notion that a pre-twentieth-century novel must be taught religiously from beginning to end. There are many possibilities that allow for a valuable experience of the text by encountering it selectively, particularly at the primary and lower secondary stages. For example, a primary class might hear the whole story of a novel in a simplified or modernized version, or even better, hear an abridged audiobook reading. They might read, or hear a reading of, a single chapter, exciting episode or sequence of episodes from a novel like *Great Expectations*, and then experience the whole novel a couple of years later. Or, students might look at pivotal moments in one Thomas Hardy novel, and later in their school career they might read another Hardy novel as a complete work. Alternatively students might be introduced to shorter texts such as poetry or short stories in the lower secondary years, which would provide a preparation for longer texts by the same author later at the senior secondary stage. With younger classes, teachers should focus on the pleasure of the story, the dramatic potential and imaginative possibilities of such texts drawing on active methods. With more senior classes, there should be more emphasis on moving from exploratory, active methods towards critical and reflective work.

The second additional point about teaching pre-twentieth-century fiction is this. In order to demystify classic novels and to challenge their monolithic status, they should be taught where possible in conjunction with other texts that are linked in some way, say by theme, author, historical period or genre. Rather than according the novel a 'stand alone' authority, it should become one of a cluster of texts, being studied comparatively for the intertextual links, parallels and contrasts between them. The aim would be to gather together a mix of 'classic', modern and popular texts that provide varying and appropriate reading opportunities for students in your class. So, for example, you might choose to teach Mary Shelley's *Frankenstein* in conjunction with a cluster of 'satellite' texts on the theme of mystery and horror. You could link it, for example, with a selection of older texts such as Edgar Allan Poe short stories, Henry James' *Turn of the Screw,* or Bram Stoker's *Dracula,* as well as with more recent texts such as extracts from Stephen King and Point Horror. The value of this exercise would not be to get students to appreciate 'classic' fiction and 'discriminate and resist' the effects of popular fiction. Rather it should be to encourage an understanding of the evolution, diversity, playfulness and attractiveness to readers of a popular genre like horror.

So, if students are to enjoy the experience of studying pre-twentieth-century fiction, they must, above all, have opportunities to make their own meanings from texts. They need to discover the 'connective' qualities of a novel through active, collaborative methods that promote personal engagement. Thus they will be able to feel some empathy with the text, but not entirely lose that sense of distance that will give them the critical edge to make sense of the more 'foreign' and difficult elements, to reflect on how classic realist novels fictionalize reality, and to make links and comparisons with alternative versions of reality from their own reading or lived experience.

The essence of my argument is therefore that English teachers should not be hidebound by limiting beliefs which advocate the transcendence of one teaching model over others. Recent postmodernist thinking has argued for the parity and co-existence of diverse and sometimes competing theoretical insights, frames of reference and methodologies. Translated to the teaching context, this would imply that teachers have at their disposal a repertoire of theoretical models and teaching methods that may be deployed in varying ways according to purpose, context and student group. While it is an approach that actively sustains paradoxes in learning, it is not a recipe for anarchy, for 'anything goes'. It allows greater scope for making informed decisions about the use of a particular model, a teaching methodology or a given text. But it also accepts that any given framework for study must inevitably face competition and challenge, and – if the reasons are strong enough – be prepared to review its practices and make changes.

If the postmodernist view is applied to fiction, a 'classic' novel can also be perceived paradoxically, both as a finely honed novel full of rich moments of drama, insight or satire that may speak directly to us about our lives, and, just as legitimately, as a cultural artefact, a product of its time, constructing a version of reality quite removed from our own. Like expatriates learning to enjoy life in a new country, our students may feel a strong sense of creative engagement with a pre-twentieth-century novel, but simultaneously be aware that it is 'a foreign country: they do things differently there'. Let's help them to enjoy that paradox.

NOTES

1 This joint report by the School Curriculum and Assessment Authority (SCAA) and the Office for Standards in Education (OFSTED) was reported in a feature article in *The Times Educational Supplement* on 12 June 1996. The name of the report was not given.
2 Cambridge Literature is a series of study texts which presents writing in the English-speaking world from the sixteenth century to the present day. The series includes novels, drama, short stories, poetry, essays and other types of non-fiction.
3 See Goodwyn 1992. This article was based on research carried out in the USA and the UK to assess English teachers' views of the Cox Report (1989) describing five models of English teaching.
4 This quotation is taken from 'Jude the Renewed', an article by Jenny Grahame that appeared in *The English and Media Magazine*, **35** (Autumn) 1996, 24–8.

REFERENCES

Barthes, R. (1977) *Image, Music, Text*. London: Fontana.

Barton, G. (1994) Explorers and sightseers: approaches to pre-twentieth-century literature. *The Use of English* **45** (2), 134–45.

Benton, M. and Fox, G. (1985) *Teaching Literature: Nine to Fourteen*. Oxford: Oxford University Press.

Brontë, C. (1996) *Jane Eyre*, ed. S. Cockroft, Cambridge Literature series. Cambridge: Cambridge University Press.

Chopin, K. (1996) *The Awakening*, ed. J. Baxter, Cambridge Literature series. Cambridge: Cambridge University Press.

DES (1989) *English for Ages 5 to 16* (The Cox Report). London: HMSO.

DFE (1995) *English in the National Curriculum*. London: HMSO.

Dickens, C. (1995) *Great Expectations*, ed. T. Seward, Cambridge Literature series. Cambridge: Cambridge University Press.

Eagleton, T. (1983) *Literary Theory: An Introduction*. Oxford: Blackwell.

Elliott, A. (1996) *Subject to Ourselves: Social Theory, Psychoanalysis and Postmodernity*. Cambridge: Polity Press.

Foucault, M. (1977) *Language, Counter-memory, Practice: Selected Essays and Interviews*. Oxford: Blackwell.

Gibson, R. (1994) Teaching Shakespeare in schools. In S. Brindley (ed.) *Teaching English*. London: Routledge.

Goodwyn, A. (1992) English teachers and the Cox models. *English in Education* **26** (3), 4–10.

Leach, S. (1992) *Shakespeare in the Classroom*. Milton Keynes: Open University Press.

Leavis, F. R. (1948) *The Great Tradition*. Harmondsworth: Penguin.

Moon, B. (1990) *Studying Literature*. London: English and Media Centre.

Showalter, E. (1988) Tradition and the female talent. In *Kate Chopin, The Awakening; Cases in Contemporary Criticism*, N. Walker (ed.). Basingstoke: Macmillan.

Williams, R. (1965) *The Long Revolution*. Harmondsworth: Penguin.

West, A. (1994) The centrality of literature. In S. Brindley (ed.) *Teaching English*. London: Routledge.

Chapter 3

Reading Plays

Andy Kempe

Peter Nichols' play, *A Day in the Death of Joe Egg* (Nichols, 1967) explores how a young couple cope with their severely disabled daughter. Nichols' key technique is to use comedy in a way which effectively throws the sensitive and tragic content of the narrative into sharp relief. This juxtaposition of form and content can be particularly challenging for the audience, who are not allowed to settle into one emotional state. This is how Nichols opens his play:

> BRI *comes on without warning. Shouts at audience.*

BRI   That's enough! *(Pause. Almost at once, louder.)* I said enough! *(Pause. Stares at audience. He is thirty-three but looks younger. Hardly ever at rest, acts being maladroit but the act is skilful. Clowning may give way to ineffectual hectoring and then self-piteous gloom.)*

       Another word and you'll all be here till five o'clock. Nothing to me, is it? I've got all the time in the world. *(Moves across without taking his eyes off them.)* I didn't even get to the end of the corridor before there was such a din all the other teachers started opening their doors as much as to say what the hell's going on there's SOMEBODY'S TALKING NOW! *(Pause, stares again, like someone facing a mad dog.)* Who was it? You? You, Mister Man . . . I did not *accuse* you, I *asked* you. Someone in the back row? *(Stares dumbly for some seconds. Relaxes, moves a few steps. Shrugs.)* You're the losers, not me. Who's that? *(Turns on them again.)* Right – hands on heads! Come on, that includes you, put the comb away. Eyes front and sit up. All of you, sit up!

So where are we? Well, as you read this you might be in any number of places. As a class reads this they would most likely be in a classroom. As an audience watches this they would be in a theatre. But where is Bri? At first glance he also seems to be in a classroom. Or does he? The class he is speaking to are the theatre audience who will doubtless recognize much of what Bri is saying to them as they are transported back to their own days in school. But their reactions in the auditorium, safe in their numbers and the knowledge that this is theatre, will be very different from the reactions of a real class being berated by a real teacher in a real classroom. How can they 'all be here till five o'clock' when it's probably already 7.30 p.m.? What corridor did Bri fail to get to the end of? Apart from the auditorium the audience have only seen a foyer. Bri is clearly in a fictional world up there on the stage, yet the audience delight in the novelty of the way that world is being spread beyond the fringe of the stage to include them. Indeed, within his speech Bri reminds them that they both are and are not in the fiction: 'You, Mister Man? . . . Someone in the back row?' But what will the reaction be when Bri tells them to put their hands on their heads? Nichols is here employing a trick originated by J. M. Barrie in his play *Peter Pan* when the audience were invited to cheer if they believed in fairies in order to bring Tinkerbell back to life. Imagine yourself in the auditorium: would you put your hands on your head? Perhaps you wouldn't want to but felt you ought. At that moment you'd be experiencing the delicious fear of drama – of being in the fiction, yet not being in it.

I once had a student who started a drama lesson by yelling at a class for their appalling behaviour the previous week when she was absent. They protested their innocence; some became aggressively defensive while others looked genuinely upset. Snapping out of what she had considered a 'role' she asked them how they felt and claimed that was how drama worked – she was using fiction to make them feel something. The trouble was that they weren't in a fiction; for them the experience was real. But Nichols' audience know they are in a fiction and that Bri is a fictitious person not just because of the context in which a performance takes place but because his writing of the speech makes it clear. And for the reading audience too I would suggest that, with due care in the reading, the theatrical trick is similarly clear.

In England, teachers are required to study plays in ways that specify that plays studied should 'extend pupils' understanding of drama in performance' (DFE, 1995). This chapter is about the problems involved in helping young people read plays 'with due care' in order to facilitate this.

THE PROBLEMS IN CONTEXT

There is a conundrum in the teaching of plays, and in order to move forward it is pertinent to recognize how it has arisen. The fact is that while it may be appropriate to emphasize the importance of helping pupils understand plays in performance, many teachers of literature feel they lack the knowledge and skill required to do this. Their backgrounds are often in the traditional 'lit crit' approach to the text. Even those who have come to terms with more recent theories such as reader response have not been given much help as to how to apply these essentially literary theories to the study of plays. As has been pointed out, 'The outstanding failure of the new criticism (and the old) has been to perceive drama as some kind of aberration from poetry or the novel' (Styan, 1983, p. 4). Teachers will find that while there are now several books explaining and expounding how semiotics or feminist theory, for example, may be applied to the critical study of plays, little is available by way of practical guidance on how to apply these alternative lenses to the classroom.

And an alternative is now needed when one considers what the 'traditional' way of teaching plays looks like in reality. The stereotype of the approach has involved reading through the whole work as a class, with different pupils taking on the nominated parts. Given their stumbling and droning delivery and frequent interruptions by the teacher to explain what's happening, this could take several weeks – by which time the pupils hate the teacher, the teacher hates the pupils, and everybody has gone off the playwright. If older students could remember anything about the play they might set about 'lit criting' it come that magical word 'Curtain'; while younger initiates may set about comprehension-style questions which largely ignore the fact that the work studied was a play and not a story. The ultimate aim of both types of task has frequently been to delve into the assumed intentions of the writer in order to understand, not what the play might mean to a member of the audience and how it achieves resonance and effect in the theatre, but what mental aberration the playwright might have been suffering when he or she wrote it.

An exaggerated analysis? Maybe. Certainly the study of plays is dogged by practical problems. Should the teacher 'cast' the roles? How will those not cast in a role maintain their interest? How does the teacher avoid those cast in minor roles from shutting their ears to the reading while they skate through the text looking for their bit? How can the class acquire even the rudimentary story when the dialogue is so often just the tip of the narrative iceberg?

There is an axiom which says that the best way of coming to know and understand a play is to perform it. But as Kelsall points out, 'the imperfect nature of the untrained technique is a handicap, and the very mechanics of performance can interfere with a deeper understanding of the playwright's craft' (Kelsall, 1985, p. 2). Rehearsals designed to improve performance skills might serve only to draw the students' attention to their existing ability or inability rather than help them appreciate what the play in performance is saying to them personally or how it might elicit response from an audience. Any performance also begs the question of whose vision of the play text is being performed and for whose benefit. Without being given the opportunity to 'play' with the script and experiment with different ways of realizing elements of it in performance, pupils will have only a limited chance of understanding how their perception of its potential meaning is being formed (Kempe, 1994). And of course, on a purely practical level, producing a whole play is enormously time-consuming and unlikely to engage an entire class with every aspect of the script.

Given the continuing rise in popularity of drama as a discrete subject on the curriculum, readers may be forgiven for asking why the practical skills involved in studying plays are not being tackled in the drama studio. I'm sure that many, if not most, people who had no immediate experience or knowledge of drama in education would assume that the subject was principally concerned with how plays are made, performed and received. In some schools this is clearly the case, but the recent history of drama education indicates that the systematic study of playwriting and production has been rejected by many drama specialists. Arguments against a 'theatre skills' approach to drama have arisen partly from a recognition that formal performance can either over-inflate or thoroughly deflate self-esteem. There has been a resistance to treating pupils as puppets to serve other interests, such as the money-spinning public relations exercise of the school play or preparation for externally set examinations, in favour of promoting pupils' own creativity and providing a forum to explore issues which are deemed to have more immediate import for them.

David Hornbrook (1991) has sharply criticized the way in which an 'orthodoxy' in drama in education in the 1970s and 1980s turned actors, theatre and plays into 'conceptual outcasts' from a drama curriculum which emphasized drama as a learning medium rather than an art form in its own right with its own specific corpus of knowledge and skills. Playwright Noel Greig looks further back to the 1960s where the emphasis on individualism and self-expression resulted in 'a couple of generations of would-be chair-makers' producing 'a vast array of bean-bag seats' (Greig, 1994a, p. 117).

The current situation in many schools is that teachers of literature tend to want to study plays with their classes but are not sure of the best way to do it. All too often, the choice of reading a play is made either because it is a syllabus requirement or because it is perceived as a little light-relief from the more taxing business of grappling with novels, poetry and grammar. The former choice, particularly in the lower years of secondary school, tends to result in simply preparing the pupils to answer the obligatory question on Shakespeare in the examination (in England pupils aged 14 years are required to do this as part of the Standard Attainment Target tests). The latter choice tends to do a disservice to the text by focusing more on the fun pupils can have by reading aloud and interacting with each other rather than revelling in the creative possibilities of interpreting the text in terms of performance.

Drama teachers, for their part, do have many proactive and effective techniques which focus on making, performing and responding to drama but their work all too often focuses on drama generated by the pupils themselves rather than on models provided by professional playscripts. In one survey in England (Kempe, 1994), 47 per cent of drama teachers saw plays as an important ingredient of their teaching against 65 per cent of their colleagues in the English department. These rather desultory figures are further tempered by the findings of another survey of students at Reading University and Homerton College, Cambridge, which revealed that, on average, by the age of 16, they had each studied just three plays and, out of the total, over half were by Shakespeare. Of the 99 respondents to a questionnaire just 9 could name a play they had studied in drama as opposed to English before the age of 16.

With the study of plays being largely removed from the drama studio and seen as the business of the English department, English teachers might have turned hopefully to books such as Ken Byron's *Drama in the English Classroom*. But of the 167 pages only three are devoted to 'Working on a Playtext' (Byron, 1986). This short chapter espouses using a variety of strategies familiar to drama teachers in the exploration of issues and stories. The main thrust of many such exercises is to avoid the 'threat' of naturalistic enactment. While this may appear to be sound, it is interesting to note that the first exercise involves stage-fighting in a 'controlled game-like physical activity' designed to hook the class (or does he mean the boys?). The next activity involves reading Act 1 Scene 1 then watching Franco Zeffirelli's film version, though there is no indication of any discussion regarding the differences between the film and the script. A later activity asks groups to prune Act 3 Scene 4 to a 'barebones version – nothing essential omitted'. While not arguing for the sanctity of the text, this kind of editing surely warrants an exploration of why current editions of Shakespeare include any text which isn't 'essential'. Such an exploration would, I submit, usefully guide pupils towards an understanding of the importance of context and audience and be one step towards a reconsideration of the nature of the playscript.

THE NATURE OF THE PLAYSCRIPT

While it is commonly recognized that seeing a good production of a play may be an invaluable tool in helping pupils understand the written text, the problem is that this simply isn't always possible and, even if it was, matching the performance seen to the script still isn't the easiest task in the world. Drama educator Cecily O'Neill (O'Neill, 1989, p. 16) states that 'Without the presence of an audience the theatre event is not complete' – a sentiment which echoes those of the Player in Tom Stoppard's *Rosencrantz and Guildenstern are Dead* (Stoppard, 1966, p. 45) when he says:

> You don't understand the humiliation of it – to be tricked out of the single assumption which makes our existence viable – that somebody is watching . . . There we were – demented children mincing about in clothes that no one ever wore, speaking as no man ever spoke, swearing love in wigs and rhymed couplets, killing each other with wooden swords, hollow protestations of faith hurled after empty promises of vengeance – and every gesture, every pose, vanishing into the thin unpopulated air. We ransomed our dignity to the clouds, and the uncomprehending birds listened. Don't you see? We're actors – we're the opposite of people!

Ken Robinson (Robinson, 1980, p. 149), similarly recognizes the complexity of theatre by proposing that 'Theatre does not refer to what the actors do, or to the presence of the audience. It refers to the encounter between them.' To study a play effectively in the classroom means discovering how the playwright has set about predicting and shaping that encounter. Peter Nichols cannot know precisely what the reaction will be when Bri demands the audience put their hands on their head. Some will, some won't. But he has recognized the presence of the audience and doubtless had a good idea about how the demand would make them feel and the embarrassed laughter the moment will induce.

The extract from *Joe Egg* is useful because it exemplifies so many facets of the actual craft of writing plays. Roman Ingarden (Ingarden, 1973) distinguished between the *Haupttext* (what the actors actually say) and the *Nebentext* (those other instructions that are needed to realize the play in performance). Nichols supplies the reader with a number of different types of this latter category. The first ('BRI comes on without warning') is a stage direction, that is, an instruction as to what must be seen to happen in the performance space. The second ('Shouts at the audience') is directed at the actor in terms of how he is to deliver the line. But later we are given: 'He is thirty-three but looks younger. Hardly ever at rest, acts being maladroit but the act is skilful.' This instruction is clearly going to be used for the actor in performing the rest of the play but is also a vital piece of information to be used in casting it. As J. L. Styan (Styan, 1983, p. 7) rightly points out, in the theatre 'the primary signals to the eye do not consist of characters, but bodies; male and female, young or old, tall or short, fat or thin'.

But within what Bri actually says, there are other implicit instructions regarding action. A little further on from the extract given above, he says: 'Who was that? Whoever did – that – can open the window before we all get gassed . . .' Although no explicit stage direction is given to the effect that the actor playing Bri should precede this line with sniffing and pulling a disgusting face, the content of the line suggests that this is the obvious thing to do. Shakespeare's plays are, of course, full of these kinds of 'intra-dialogic' instructions, that is, directions locked within the dialogue which give the actor an indication of what needs to be physically shown to support the words spoken (Veltrusky, 1991).

It is these kinds of instructions which make plays what may be called 'procedural texts'. 'Reading a procedural text does not depend so much on reading to discover what occurs next, but rather how it occurs' (Michaels, 1993, p. 25). Reading a play thus requires a very different mode of operating to reading a novel. The reader is constantly being invited to stand outside the fictive world in order to visualize what is happening on the stage rather than being drawn into the story in a way which may happen in performance, but that only happens because the actors, directors and designers have gone through the process of extricating all the information they need to realize what has been described elsewhere as 'the design brief of the text' (Kempe, 1997).

Recognizing the nature of the procedural text may well be the first step towards an effective study of plays in the classroom. It involves changing the questions 'What is happening in the story?' to 'What is happening on stage?', or 'What is this character thinking?' to 'What might the actor be doing at this point?' What becomes apparent through engaging with such questions is that there is never one simple correct answer. Even the subtlest changes of tone or gesture will alter the perameters of an audience's interpretation. No matter how precise a playwright's instructions regarding what is to be said and shown on stage, designers, directors, actors and technicians will always offer different interpretations of the brief in the process of realizing the text. The role of the teacher is thus to guide students towards making conscious decisions in this process.

In his useful book *Studying Drama*, Kelsall (1985) draws a comparison between the playwright and the wheelwright. Plays, like wheels, are made to be used rather than looked at and admired. If either falls to pieces in the process of being used then they are no good. And this process involves many people, not least amongst them the audience: 'it is clearly as important to know what is being returned by the spectator to the actor, and by the actor to the script, as to know the intentions of the script in the first place. Arguably, intentions are of no consequence whatsoever' (Styan, 1960, p. 7). This shift of emphasis away from the words written to the response they provoke needs a little more consideration. While the playwright's intentions regarding the *meaning* an audience will perceive may be of little consequence to the student of drama, as I suggested above with reference to Nichols' play, we can inspect the writer's intentions regarding an audience's *reaction*. As Jean E. Howard (Howard, 1990, p. 15) explains: 'I assume that in writing plays for performance Shakespeare was partly writing with an eye to the potential responses of the audience; that is, as he orchestrated the play, he was indirectly orchestrating the theatrical experience of the viewer.'

Plays employ complex and diverse structures and linguistic forms. Without appropriate guidance, pupils find these difficult to embrace. In the case of Shakespeare in particular, this difficulty is often expressed through the pupils' focusing on the use of obsolete words and phrases. 'But this is not the real source of the difficulty – rather, it lies in the unusual discourse structures of the procedural text', says Wendy Michaels (Michaels, 1993, p. 32). This suggests that careful choices need to be made regarding the plays read with younger students. Teachers might, for example, usefully select texts or just short extracts; these give clear and simple stage directions which help pupils envisage the scene and make a distinction between the fictive scene and the artifice of its stage representation. Here is the opening of Philip Pullman's play *Sherlock Holmes and the Limehouse Horror* (Pullman, 1992)

> *A winter evening in Holmes's sitting room in Baker Street.*
>
> *It's a comfortable Victorian room, with a coal fire burning in the grate, two armchairs, a table set for supper, a desk with a chair, and a sofa which is partly concealed from the audience by a folding screen. The walls are lines with bookshelves, and every surface seems to be cluttered with papers, chemical apparatus, racks of tobacco pipes, soda-syphons, Holmes's violin . . . a Persian slipper is hanging next to the fire, and a jack-knife is stuck through a pile of letters on the mantelpiece.*
>
> *There are two doors: one to the landing and the rest of the house, the other to Holmes's bedroom.*
>
> *When we first see it, the room is lit only by the dim light coming through the half-drawn curtains.*

There is conscious reference here to what the audience sees set against a vivid description of the atmospheric room. Asking pupils to spend a few minutes annotating a copy of this in order to consider *how* the effects might be achieved will help them to keep the artifice of the whole thing clear in their mind. The next stage is to consider the resonance of such effects (as an example see Figure 3.1).

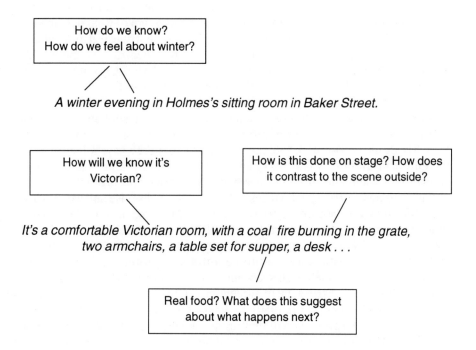

Figure 3.1 *Interrogating stage directions*

Contrasting the winter scene outside Holmes' room with the cosy scene inside may be discussed in terms of both how it will be achieved practically, how it positions the audience as the lights go up, and how it will determine the way in which characters will make their entrance.

The world of the play is not the real world. In a world dominated by televisual naturalism, it is all too easy to interpret plays as showing on stage what happens in real life. Selecting playscripts which lay bare their artifice helps pupils see that this is not so. At the end of Pullman's play, for example, we are given the direction:

> *Moriarty has made a dash for the door. Mrs Hudson brings down the saucepan on his head. He falls stunned.*

and just a page later:

> *He [Watson] points to Moriarty with horror.*
> HOLMES: Is he dead?
> *He kneels to look more closely – then jumps in stupefaction.*
> I don't believe it!
> *Watson picks up Moriarty with one hand. It is a dummy!*
> WATSON: A dummy Moriarty! How on earth –

Before our very eyes, the real Moriarty has disappeared and been replaced by a dummy! Is this possible? No, of course not, but this is a comic thriller and the rules of real life do not apply here. Pupils who read such a play just for the story might well react by dismissing this impossibility and seeing it as a sign of weakness in the writing. Those who have considered the play as something to be witnessed by an audience will have no trouble speculating on their reaction to this theatrical moment and may be enthralled by asking not what has happened to the real Moriarty but how the trick was achieved technically. (Pullman himself admitted to me that when he wrote the instruction he had no idea how the director would achieve the effect!)

Laying bare the *artificial world* of the play is essential if students are to understand how an audience can be drawn into its *apparent reality*. In 'The anatomy of drama' Marjorie Boulton (Boulton, 1985, p. 9) attempts to offer a psychological justification for Olivia in *Twelfth Night* marrying a man she hardly knows and then seeming undisturbed when she finds she has actually married the brother of the man she thought she was marrying, who turns out to be a girl in disguise anyway. Such attempts at justification are, according to Kelsall, fruitless: 'The fact is that characters in romantic comedies do not perform like characters in real life . . . Characters in comedies do not behave like characters in tragedies' (Kelsall, 1985, p. 10). From this, one might see how students need to be introduced to the implicit rules governing different genres. Stanley Fish's account of how readers belong to 'interpretive communities' who share a tacit agreement of the different conventions used in literature is helpful here (Fish, 1980). In the study of drama, recognition must be made of two distinct interpretive communities: those who take the script to performance, and those who constitute the theatre audience. To understand how an audience interprets a performance, students need to acquire a knowledge of the conventions used by those who perform.

CHOOSING PLAYS

In the upper years of secondary school it is reasonable to expect students to be able to read and work with texts drawn from mainstream professional theatre in the same way they are expected to engage with other works from a broad literary canon. The problem is that these plays, most obviously those by writers such as Shakespeare, require considerable skill to read if they are to be understood as the brief for a performance rather than a finished piece of literature. My contention is that success in this enterprise is dependent on a suitable induction into this particular form of writing. This might be achieved through choosing plays which are written specifically for young audiences, but may also be achieved by employing practical methods focused on revealing the dynamics of the playtext and which are flexible enough to apply to any play.

The first option is clearly dependent on the existence of suitable material. While there is a plethora of good children's and teenage fiction around which initiates young people into the world of the novel and similarly there are many fine poets who write for children, there is a constant cry from teachers regarding the dearth of good playscripts aimed specifically at young and inexperienced readers. Certainly, in comparison, the options are small, but it is helpful to consider the expectations that teachers, and by proxy their pupils, have of a playscript. One such expectation, reported by publishers of playscripts, is that 'there are enough parts to go round'. Why? Teachers do not pick out novels for use in the class because they have lots of characters, and only a tiny minority of the plays looked at in schools are ever taken on to production where the corporate enterprise can be thrilling no matter how small the acting part. By comparison, being in a class reading of the play is often an insignificant, not to say demeaning, experience.

Secondly, interviews with teachers have shown that they tend to look for plays that focus on young people. Certainly the majority of children's and teenage novels do likewise, but by their own choice many young people are avid readers of a broader and often more adult range of fiction and the television they watch would seem to indicate that they are as enthralled by the adult world as by the dramatic imitation of their own. Why then shouldn't plays concerning the world of adults also be admissible?

Part of the answer here is a question of accessibility. Given the difficulties of reading playtexts discussed above, one can see why the plays chosen for study in the classroom often tend to be ones which offer a strong storyline over and above interesting theatrical possibilities. I would speculate that this factor is largely responsible for the success of dramatized novels in the classroom. The problem here is that while the play version might offer a slightly quicker and more communal way through the story than a novel, such versions are not necessarily a good preparation for the subsequent study of 'real plays' (there are of course exceptions: Mary Morris's stage version of Morris Gleitzman's novel *Two Weeks with the Queen*, which is quoted below, being one of them). In a similar vein, published versions of film and TV scripts are popular. Their immediacy may be appealing but the corollory is that exposure to this type of script still doesn't prepare students for the complex functions of intra-dialogic and extra-dialogic instructions (i.e. stage directions) in *theatre* texts and nor can it encourage pupils' own writing in this form. Having said that, using TV scripts in which the technical information on the camera shots is included can certainly contribute towards building an understanding of how what the viewing audience ultimately sees on the screen is carefully predetermined (see for example Kempe and Warner, 1997). The point is that the media of theatre and TV are different, and an understanding of how one works is not immediately and unquestionably transferable to the other.

Through a survey of 600 schools in the UK it was discovered that the most commonly studied play other than one by Shakespeare was J. B. Priestley's super-natural thriller, *An Inspector Calls* (Priestley, 1947). This was followed by Willy Russell's *Our Day Out* (originally a television play) and then *Gregory's Girl* (originally a film) (Kempe, 1994).

The case of *An Inspector Calls* is a revealing one. It does not have a large cast and it does not focus on children or teenagers. Written in 1945 but set in 1912, its character can hardly be said to relate to young people today in an explicit way. It does, however, have a strong storyline which can be construed from the dialogue alone, and the concerns of the younger characters about the attitudes of their elders may resonate to contemporary readers. But the play is not one which relies on depicting 'real life' in the way that popular TV soaps do. In fact, it is very similar to Pullman's *Sherlock Holmes and the Limehouse Horror*, a play written especially for a young audience. Compare this opening stage direction to the one printed above:

> *The dining room of a fairly large suburban house, belonging to a prosperous manu-facturer. It has good solid furniture of the period. The general effect is substantial and heavily comfortable, but not cosy and homelike. (If a realistic set is used, then it should be swung back, as it was in the production at the New Theatre. By doing this, you can have the dining-table downstage centre during Act One, when it is needed there, and then, swinging back, can reveal the fireplace for Act Two . . .)*

and on it goes addressing would-be producers of the play. How many teachers, I wonder, actually draw the pupils' attention to these directions?

At the end of the play, we are invited to believe that Inspector Goole – no coincidence in the name, obviously! – is not a real character but some kind of premonition. Is it possible? Probably not. Do we care? Certainly not. What we care about is that delicious effect of that moment when the father of this apparently respectable though actually somewhat morally bankrupt household says:

> . . . a police inspector is on his way here – to ask some questions –
> *As they stare guiltily and dumbfounded, the curtain falls.*

Notice just in this ending the intra-dialogic instructions implicit in the punctuation of the father's line followed by two different types of extra-dialogic instructions, one addressing the actors and one the stage manager.

However, *An Inspector Calls* is a rarity – one of the reasons, presumably, for its disproportionate popularity. It has all the narrative ingredients necessary to hold an audience not yet sophisticated in their reading of playtexts without losing its integrity as a play.

David Booth, a Canadian drama educator, has said that 'there are almost no plays written for children of this age [grades 7 and 8] and perhaps there shouldn't be. They need so much to experience at understanding themselves and their own lives that role-playing should have been the answer all along' (Booth, 1995, p. 5). I firmly believe the contrary is true. Through what I have called elsewhere 'the convex glass' of plays (Kempe, 1995) people come to see reflections of themselves in different contexts and so increase their understanding of both their personal identity and the cultural framework within which it is shaped. Rather than adopting roles in improvisations which too frequently demand the pupils draw on their own experiences or caricatures of others, reading, acting in and watching plays give people the chance to study a wider range of characters in specific situations. The suggestion that role-play helps us to understand ourselves relies on accepting the possibility of an immutable inner self. More recent theories of 'multiple selves' (Nicholson, 1995) suggest that, far from being an identifiable kernal, the 'self' is more like a primordial mud which is constantly being reshaped into a range of character traits through social interactions. This process is revealed by creating and observing the characters in plays and considering the different ways in which they may be realized in performance. In simplistic terms, but clearly recognizable when we watch how young children adopt the behaviour of characters they have seen on screen or have encountered in literature, we can see how we'd like or not like to act – not for ever, but just in certain situations. Given this rationale, we need to adopt methods which will lay bare the artifice of drama in explicit ways for pupils if we want them to go on to enjoy and have mastery over the full range of drama in both its literary and its enacted forms. Thus, in choosing plays to study, we might consider two simple criteria:

- Do they work as plays?
- Is it clear how they work as plays?

While the plays of Shakespeare, which teachers in England at least are now obliged to teach, may well fulfil the first criteria, for the uninitiated reader they clearly present more problems in terms of the second criteria. However, my own work on Shakespeare with pupils in primary schools has shown me that the practical approaches described below offer a flexible and viable alternative to more traditional 'literary' studies.

PRACTICAL APPROACHES

Reading the play

It will be clear to readers that the practice of casting parts in the classroom is not one in which I have a great deal of faith. Some teachers have found that asking pupils to read a line each around the class is a way of giving everyone a chance to read aloud but this makes the play sound disjointed. Both methods can be time-consuming, as can recasting parts in each lesson in order to give everyone a chance. Andrew Goodwyn (1995, p. 21) relates that 'A great many pupils stressed how dull they found it to "plod through books"'. Given that most plays only run from two to two and a half hours in performance, spending weeks reading through a play obviously mitigates against experiencing the immediacy of the form.

Another method is to allow the class to work in small groups where they can cast a play for themselves and read it at their own speed. Teachers may feel that this doesn't give them the chance to monitor the pupils' understanding and that the pupils would be unlikely to consider the importance of the stage directions. In the first instance it is helpful to simply get to grips with what actually happens in the play as quickly as possible. One way of doing this is to divide the text into sections and ask different groups to just read that section. The groups may then report back in as simple a way as possible who was in their bit and what the main actions of the narrative seemed to be. This can then be mapped, in the original sequence, on the whiteboard.

A slightly more sophisticated, but certainly more enlightening method is to give each group a supply of small slips of paper. On these, they write simple, descriptive sentences of the key events of their section. These are then physically laid out on a large sheet of card while the group retell the story as they have understood it. The teacher can intervene to suggest where new narrative lines seem to be appearing. Incidents which seem to relate to each other can then be linked by lines drawn onto the sheet. In this way, even though each pupil will have read only a segment of the play, they will all come to see its overall storyline and have a visual representation of its structure in a short space of time. An example of the start of such a map of Mary Morris's *Two Weeks with the Queen* (1994) is shown in Figure 3.2.

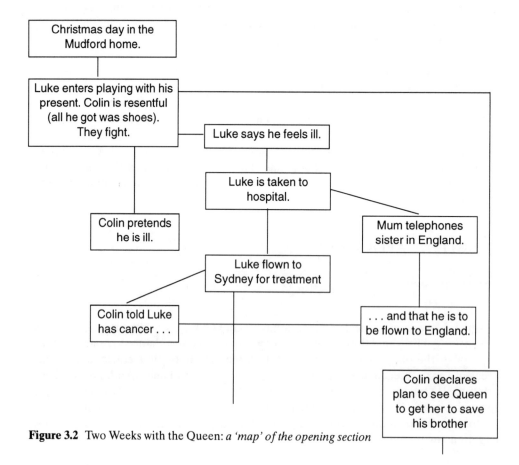

Figure 3.2 Two Weeks with the Queen: *a 'map' of the opening section*

Mapping just the opening section of a play in this way can be used to instigate predictions about how both the narrative and its structure are likely to develop. In the simple representation in the figure we can already see that although Colin and Luke fight at the start, Colin has ideas about using his trip to England to resolve the crisis. Will he be successful? What will the final shape of the play look like? Which character is most likely to develop from the information and structure employed here?

Playing the lines

An effective way of distinguishing between characters is to ask each group to select a line from their given section of the play which seems to be a key to that character – something that only that character would say. Having chosen these, the whole class mingle together, speaking aloud their lines in a way they think is appropriate to everyone else. Their task is to listen out for other lines that their characters might say in other parts of the play. After a few minutes of this, the pupils are asked to link up with anyone they think has chosen the same character as them. This leads to fruitful discussion not only about the register of the characters' language, but the way the playwright has used intra-dialogic and extra-dialogic instructions to inform the delivery of the lines. Pupils can again describe to each other in more detail what happens to their chosen character at different moments in the play.

The question of what is an 'appropriate' delivery may be addressed by experimenting with some obviously inappropriate ones. Here is a section from the beginning of Dylan Thomas' play 'for voices' *Under Milk Wood* (Thomas, 1954):

FIRST VOICE:	Captain Cat, the retired blind sea-captain, asleep in his bunk in the seashelled, ship-in bottled, shipshape best cabin of Schooner House dreams of
SECOND VOICE:	never such seas as any that swamped the decks of his S.S. *Kidwelly* bellying over the bedclothes and jellyfish-slippery sucking him down salt deep into the Davy dark where the fish come biting out and nibble him down to his wishbone, and the long drowned nuzzle up to him.
FIRST DROWNED:	Remember me, Captain?
CAPTAIN CAT:	You're Dancing Williams!
FIRST DROWNED:	I lost my step in Nantucket.
SECOND DROWNED:	Do you see me, Captain? the white bone talking? I'm Tom-Fred the donkeyman . . . we shared the same girl once . . . her name was Mrs Probert . . .
WOMAN'S VOICE:	Rosie Probert, thirty three Duck Lane. Come on up, boys, I'm dead.
THIRD DROWNED:	Hold me, Captain, I'm Jonah Jarvis, come to a bad end, very enjoyable.
FOURTH DROWNED:	Alfred Pomeroy Jones, sea-lawyer, born in Mumbles, sung like a linnet, crowned you with a flagon, tattooed with mermaids, thirst like a dredger, died of blisters.
FIRST DROWNED:	This skull at your earhole is
FIFTH DROWNED:	Curly Bevan. Tell my auntie it was me that pawned the ormulu clock.
CAPTAIN CAT:	Aye, aye, Curly.
SECOND DROWNED:	Tell my missus no I never.

THIRD DROWNED: I never done what she said I never.
FOURTH DROWNED: Yes they did.

Standing the class in a circle and giving each pupil just one line to say aloud, the passage is read through firstly with as little intonation as possible. The teacher might then suggest each line is read as if it is a piece of juicy gossip. What happens if the whole thing is delivered as a rap or a Sunday sermon? The exercise makes the pupils listen to rhythm and the sounds of the words and gets them playing with their own voices. Finally, the teacher suggests they use tone, volume and pace in a way they think is more appropriate. They do it and are asked why. The answers range from comments on the choice of words and the way they are set out on the page to a regard for the opening lines – it simply doesn't fit to do it as rap if you are a long-drowned sailor visiting an old friend's disturbed dreams!

Playing with voices in this way is an effective introduction to Shakespeare's language. Asking students to voice these lines from the 'Seven Ages of Man' speech in Act 2 Scene 7 of *As You Like It*, and to comment on the contrasting sounds they make and what the act of speaking them does to the speaker's face, quickly reveals how the choice of vocabulary helps determine the rhythm and tone and so reflects the meaning in a way that a purely literary reading may deny the inexperienced reader:

'At first the infant, Mewling and puking in the nurse's arms.'
'The lover, Sighing like furnace, with a woeful ballad.'
'The justice, In fair round belly, with good capon lin'd, With eyes severe and beard of formal cut.'
'Sans teeth, sans eyes, sans taste, sans everything.'

Attention may be drawn to the literary imagery by a similarly irreverent approach. In *Romeo and Juliet* (Act 3 Scene 5) for example, pupils may be divided into two groups. One is asked to underline all the words that suggest daylight and leaving, the other picks out words suggesting night and staying. Two volunteers are asked to read the lovers' speeches while the rest of the class echo the words they have underlined. Will they see the way Shakespeare is using imagery here to suggest action? The volunteers are asked to read through the parts again slowly while a few of the other pupils take hold of them and either gently pull them apart or push them together every time they come to one of the underlined words.

Changing perceptions

If one of the obstacles to teaching plays is the pupils' perception that they are difficult, a primary job for the teacher is to change that perception. Before even beginning to read the play they can be shown the whole text in its entirety. I personally have no aversion to cannibalizing two copies of a Shakespeare, or indeed any other play, and mounting each page onto card which can then be pinned on the classroom wall. The whole text should fit onto four or five sheets of cards. The immediate response from most people seeing this is that the play isn't very long! Somehow, this 'flat book' looks a lot more manageable than the bound edition with all its introductory and textual notes. The device can be used to chart themes in the play. Again, working in small groups on different sections of the text, students can be asked to select lines or actions which suggest key themes. These are plotted on the flat book using different coloured pins for different themes. The different coloured pins are joined by coloured wool; students can inspect how the themes are touched on in parts of the play they haven't yet personally read.

In a similar vein, different scenes may be pasted onto card and read by groups who then place different coloured counters onto them like casino chips. Each colour represents a character in the scene and the number placed onto the card reflects how much is at stake for each character in that scene. Simply making the exercise physical in this way engages the pupils as a precursor to explaining to the rest of the group what they feel to be the tensions for the different characters in the scene. Following the groups sharing their ideas, a simple line graph may be drawn showing the way characters, and thus the audience, experience rises and falls in tension through the course of the whole play.

Many teachers feel, particularly with Shakespeare, that showing classes film or television productions of the work is a helpful way of overcoming initial resistance to the text. However, this strategy is not without drawbacks. To mention just one: what motivation would many pupils have to read the play if they can say they have already seen it on video? Much more helpful in terms of raising questions about the play and inducing a sense of enquiry is to show a number of contrasting clips from different productions and relating these back to the text in order to appreciate the different possible meanings which can be created. Susan Leach (1992) offers a fuller account to the pitfalls of teaching Shakespeare through the use of video. (As a matter of interest, Film Education in the UK offer a number of videos and accompanying notes which compile contrasting scenes of various Shakespearean plays.)

Secondly, as has already been mentioned, film and television drama works very differently from theatre. In the film of *A Day in the Death of Joe Egg*, for example, viewers see Bri in the school setting berating a class of adolescents – a production decision that negates the way in which Nichols positions the theatre audience. Some might argue that the predominantly naturalistic forms of plays such as *An Inspector Calls* is too close to televisual naturalism to be of great value in helping pupils move on to less naturalist plays such as those by Shakespeare. I would argue, however, that a conscious investigation into the way Priestley writes his extra-dialogic instructions does serve as a clear introduction into stage craft. And there are of course other plays which are not so naturalistic but nevertheless accessible. Recently published plays such as *Final Cargo* (Greig, 1994b) and the already mentioned *Sherlock Holmes and the Limehouse Horror* fit this bill; as do, for example, Victorian melodramas which tend to be short, dynamic and great fun to play with.

Using extracts

In the same way that comparing different video clips can draw attention to the importance of production and highlight the manner in which audience response is constrained, so the use of contrasting extracts leads pupils to an understanding of how different theatrical genres work in practice. How do we know, for example, that one of these plays about a vampire is a melodrama which is presented (if not received!) in all seriousness, while the other is a blatant comedy?

A.

RUTHVEN: I'll hear no more! she is my bridebetrothed: this mad-man would deprive me of her.

RONALD: *(Loud thunder: Another gust of wind blows open the casement).* See! See! the moon already rests upon the wave! – One moment! – but one moment! –

RUTHVEN: Nay, then thus I seal my lips, and seize my bride.
(Ruthven draws his poignard: rushes on Ronald – Robert throws himself between Ruthven and Ronald, and wrenches the dagger from his grasp.)

LADY M.:   Hold! hold! – I am thine; the moon has set.

RUTHVEN: And I am lost!
(A terrific peal of thunder is heard; Unda and Ariel appear; a thunder bolt strikes Ruthven to the ground, who immediately vanishes. General picture.)
The curtain falls.

B.

Music. Thunder. Dracula appears on the stairs blocking their exit.

DRACULA: Too late Doctor. But I believe I have an appointment to view that brooch on your throat.

VAN HELSING: Keep off!
She raises crucifix in front of him. He snarls and hisses.

HARKER: No, Johnny wants it, keep Johnny safe, Johnny have it!
Grabs crucifix. He and Van Helsing struggle over it. It breaks in two pieces. Dracula laughs.

HARKER: You broke Johnny's crucifix . . .

DRACULA: Now, Doctor . . .

VAN HELSING: The garlic, Sir Robert!
Seward pulls on Mrs Crebbs' necklace of garlic. She moans and holds onto it. The string breaks and it rolls all over the floor.

SEWARD: It's brock! She's brock the bloody thing!

DRACULA: You see, Doctor, it is useless. Come!

VAN HELSING: No . . . please . . .
But she moves towards him against her will.

SEWARD: What art th'doing, Doctor?

DRACULA: Come!

VAN HELSING: I can't help it . . .
She is close to Dracula now.

DRACULA: Now Doctor . . . *(Exhales)* Your brooch . . .
Van Helsing takes choker off. Dracula caresses her neck. He howls like a wolf and is just about to sink his fangs into her when there is music, and a shaft of sunlight lights his face. He screams and leaps into the audience, snarling and fanging at them until he reaches the back row.

These two brief extracts, one from J. R. Planche (Planche, 1995, pp. 66–7) and the other from Chris Bond (Bond, 1995), illustrate how while reading plays aloud might be better than reading them silently, the full dramatic effect can be achieved only by using a whole gamut of factors not readily available in the classroom (including an unsuspecting audience!). By introducing pupils to dramatic literature through using such extracts, how much more able will they be to translate the following into a visual picture in their mind's eye?

ROMEO:	Wilt thou provoke me? Then have at thee, boy!
PAGE:	O Lord, they fight! I will go call the watch.
PARIS:	O, I am slain. If thou be merciful,
	Open the tomb, lay me with Juliet.
ROMEO:	In faith, I will. Let me peruse this face
	Mercutio's kinsman, noble County Paris

Acting out this short passage from Act 5 Scene 3 of *Romeo and Juliet* would certainly have a value in pointing out what action must take place even though Shakespeare doesn't specify it with any kind of extra-dialogic instruction. Another advantage of actually staging certain scenes in even the crudest way is that it reminds pupils that other characters are on stage even though they may not be speaking. The most obvious example is Hamlet's soliloquy 'To be or not to be'. Strictly speaking a soliloquy is spoken by a character alone on the stage. Indeed, in Laurence Olivier's film version the camera literally takes us on a journey through Hamlet's skull, yet according to the playtext he is being watched from behind the arras and Ophelia has not yet left the stage. What are these characters doing? What happens if the audience's attention is drawn to them? What radically different meaning would the speech convey if the actor playing Hamlet gave the audience the slightest suspicion that he was aware of Claudius and Polonius?

CONCLUSIONS

1 Young people need to be actively taught how to read a play as a play. Simply reading plays in class as if they are novels is an inadequate preparation for a higher level of study and does not even fulfil the demands of the National Curriculum in England.

2 Choosing plays which work as plays in their own right, and making it clear how they would work on stage, are preferable to choosing adaptations from other media.

3 Changing the pupils' initial perception of the play in order to show them its manageability, and selecting strategies which make them physically assault the tyrant of the text, gives them a feeling of mastery over it.

4 Help them paint the scene of the play in their mind's eye not as a real scene but as something constructed for an audience.

5 Find a way of getting the class through the whole play as quickly as possible in the first instance even if this means that not everyone reads everything.

6   There is clearly a value in speaking lines aloud but no necessity for any one pupil to feel they own a particular part. Be irreverent. Try to make the words do things they don't want to do and in this way find what they do want to do.

7   Reading the play aloud and moving through scenes can give a better insight into what is happening and how, but explicit attention needs to be paid to the effect sound and lighting, etc. might have. Similarly, the physicality of the part must not be ignored; a Year 10 girl might well be able to read the part of Sir John Falstaff fluently and with character, but can she possibly have the same effect on an audience as a large, middle-aged actor?

8   Pupils need to be taught how to read a play. Highly focused and carefully structured exercises, often using extracts of texts rather than the whole work, are used to introduce the novel. So it should be with dramatic literature.

REFERENCES

Bond, C. (1995) *The Blood of Dracula*. Walton-on-Thames: Nelson.

Booth, D. (1995) *Pre-Text and Storydrama*. Brisbane: NADIE.

Boulton, M. (1985) Action. In M. Kelsall *Studying Drama*. London: Arnold.

Byron, K. (1986) *Drama in the English Classroom*. London: Methuen.

DFEE (1995) *English in the National Curriculum*. London: HMSO.

Fish, S. (1980) *Is There a Text in This Class?* Cambridge, MA: Harvard University Press.

Goodwyn, A. (ed.) (1995) *English and Ability*. London: David Fulton.

Greig, N. (1994a) Educational drama as cultural dispossession. In P. Abbs (ed.) *The Educational Imperativer*. London: Falmer Press.

Greig, N. (1994b) *Final Cargo*. Walton-on-Thames: Nelson.

Hornbrook, D. (ed.) (1991) *Education and Dramatic Art*. London: Falmer Press.

Howard, J. E. (1990) Contemporary concerns. In S. Bennett (ed.) *Theatre Audiences*. London: Routledge.

Ingarden, R. (1973) *The Literary Work of Art*. Evanston, IL: Northwestern University Press.

Kelsall, M. (1985) *Studying Drama*. London: Arnold.

Kempe, A. (1994) Dramatic literature in the classroom. *Drama* **3** (1), 9–15.

Kempe, A. (1995) Intruders in the convex glass. In P. Taylor and C. Hoeppner (eds) *Selected Readings*. Brisbane: IDEA.

Kempe, A. (1997) Reading plays for performance. In D. Hornbrook (ed.) *On the Subject of Drama*. London: Routlege.

Kempe, A. and Warner, L. (1997) *Starting with Scripts*. Cheltenham: Thornes.

Leach, S. (1992) *Shakespeare in the Classroom*. Milton Keynes: Open University Press.

Michaels, W. (1993) Plots have I laid . . . Shakespeare in the classroom. *NADIE Journal* **17** (2), 23–9.

Morris, M. (1994) *Two Weeks with the Queen*. London: Pan Macmillan.

Nichols, P. (1967) *A Day in the Death of Joe Egg*. London: Faber.

Nicholson, H. (1995) Genre, gender and play. *NADIE Journal* **19** (2), 15–24.

O'Neill, C. (1988) Ways of Seeing. *2D Magazine* **8** (2), 10–29.

Planche, J. R. (1995) In C. Bond *The Blood of Dracula*. Walton-on-Thames: Nelson.

Priestley, J. B. (1947) *An Inspector Calls*. Oxford: Heinemann.

Pullman, P. (1992) *Sherlock Holmes and the Limehouse Horror*. Walton-on-Thames: Nelson.

Robinson, K. (1980) *Exploring Theatre and Education*. Oxford: Heinemann.

Stoppard, T. (1966) *Rosencrantz and Guildenstern Are Dead*. London: Faber.

Styan, J. L. (1960) *Elements of Drama*. Cambridge: Cambridge University Press.

Styan, J. L. (1983) *The State of Drama Study*. Sydney: University of Sydney.

Thomas, D. (1954) *Under Milk Wood*. London: Dent.

Veltrusky, J. (1991) Stage directions 1. In E. Aston and G. Savona (eds)*Theatre as a Sign System*. London: Routledge.

Chapter 4

Developing Poetry

Michael Lockwood

When the role of literature in reading development is under discussion, attention most often focuses on fiction: novels, short stories or traditional tales. Within media studies there is a similar emphasis on narrative texts, often derived from literary fiction or from plays. All these types of fiction, of course, represent important elements in any 'balanced diet' of reading and viewing which children and young people should experience. However, the list leaves out an important area of literary experience for pupils: poetry. Often poetry is treated as if it were the icing on the cake of reading experience (if not the decoration on the top) rather than the essential ingredient it can be. In this chapter I intend to use the views of pupils themselves in order to suggest what poetry can offer to readers at different stages of development and how teachers can use poetry to broaden and deepen the range of pupils' responses to texts.

READING POETRY AT 11 AND 15

The evidence to date suggests that the primary years (ages 5–11) are a more fertile ground for poetry reading than the secondary school (11–16). The surveys of pupils' attitudes to reading carried out between 1979 and 1983 by the Assessment of Performance Unit (APU) in schools in England, Wales and Northern Ireland consistently show a more positive response to poetry from pupils at age 11 than at age 15. The APU surveys, though covering only a limited period, are invaluable as sources of reliable and valid data and form a useful baseline against which to measure changes in pupils' attitudes. In the 1979 Primary and Secondary Surveys, for example, the most detailed of the APU reports, the responses to the statement 'I like reading poems' were as shown in Table 4.1 (APU, 1981, 1982).

Table 4.1

	Totals			Boys			Girls	
	% Yes	% No		% Yes	% No		% Yes	% No
Age 11	59.5	36.9		50.0	46.0		68.8	27.9
Age 15	32.4	67.0		23.6	75.4		41.5	58.3

The percentage of 11-year-olds professing to like reading poetry seems to have remained stable or risen slightly across the years of the survey from the (incomplete) figures available (APU, 1988) as shown in Table 4.2.

Table 4.2

	Total	% Yes		Boys	% Yes		Girls	% Yes
	1979	1983		1979	1983		1979	1983
Age 11	62 [*sic*]	65		53	57		71	72

Predictably, girls were consistently more positive than boys in their attitudes to poetry reading throughout the surveys.

The picture of poetry reading in the primary school presented in the APU surveys is not all positive. To put the figures quoted in context, 80.5 per cent of the 1979 primary school sample said they 'would rather read stories than poems' given the choice, and 82 per cent of the same sample agreed that they 'prefer funny poems to serious ones' when they do read poetry, with no significant differences between the sexes in either of these (APU, 1981). Humour and rhyme were the features of poems mentioned most often by children who said they liked reading poetry. In the 1982 Primary Survey, where pupils were asked about the kinds of poems and poets they liked, 'Spike Milligan [author of comic and nonsense poems] was the versifier referred to most frequently by pupils in the sample', to use the loaded words of the report (APU, 1984, p. 157).

From the evidence, the picture seems to be one of a more receptive audience for poetry at age 11, without the resistance which seems to have set in by the early years of secondary school, but also of a limited range of experience of poems and poets and an overwhelming preference for reading prose narrative.

One other, more unexpected finding of the APU reports is worth picking up also at this point. Taking an overview of 'reading as a source of pleasure and enjoyment' for 11-year-olds over the years of the surveys, APU concludes:

> There were clear indications that some pupils whose reading performance was lower than the average nevertheless enjoyed reading poetry and preferred it in some cases to other kinds of reading.

> (APU, 1988, p. 171)

If we reflect on this, it is less surprising. Research by Bryant and Bradley (1985) and Goswami and Bryant (1990), summarized most recently in Roger Beard's collection *Rhyme, Reading and Writing* (1995), has shown the importance of rhyming poems in the initial learning of reading. It should come as no surprise then that less fluent older readers sometimes prefer the experience of reading poetry to that of reading prose.

The APU overview confirms the picture of a decline in popularity of poetry at 15:

> The general trend was for there to be a significant decrease in the proportion of responses indicating an enjoyment of poetry reading from both boys and girls at secondary level.
>
> (APU, 1988, p. 173)

The 1979 Secondary Survey gives more detail as to why 15-year-olds responded negatively. Three-quarters of those questioned read little or no poetry outside school:

> Many comments implied that pupils perceived poetry as something highly complex in expression and meaning and so they either felt inadequate, without a teacher to mediate and explain, or were reluctant to embark independently on reading which required so much effort . . . novels were praised for their clarity of structure and expression in comparison with the convoluted complexity that seemed to characterize poetry for these pupils.
>
> (APU, 1982, pp. 54–5)

Interestingly, 'a few pupils remarked on the change in their own reading habits with regard to poetry, in that they remembered liking and reading poetry when they were younger' (p. 55).

As far as poetry within school was concerned, the 1979 survey found evidence to suggest a significant neglect in some secondary schools, with possibly as many as one-fifth of the 15-year-olds questioned reading 'very few or no poems at school' (p. 57). Of those four-fifths who did encounter poems, 36 per cent were 'completely negative in attitude', describing the poems read as: 'boring', 'long', 'monotonous' or 'difficult to understand'. The report comments:

> The impression given by these responses was that poetry was generally perceived in terms of 'set poets', studied because of their presence in an anthology, or in terms of a theme in which the work of individuals was subsumed. A sense of relevant choice and of meaningful purpose in this poetry reading was thus predominantly absent.
>
> (p. 58)

It is some fifteen years now since the APU's monitoring of language performance ended, a period which has seen the introduction and revision of a National Curriculum in England and Wales, with its attendant assessment procedures. In the same period there has also been an explosion in the number of poetry books being published for children and young people. So what is the position now as far as the reading of poetry is concerned at the ages of 11 and 15?

A report by Her Majesty's Inspectors (HMI) on the second year of implementation of English in the National Curriculum suggests an increase in the amount of poetry reading in primary and lower secondary classrooms ('poetry received more attention in the classroom than has been customary recently', HMI, 1992), but gives tantalizingly brief glimpses of its findings. However, large-scale surveys of poetry provision in primary schools in Wales and England in 1992–3, directed by Dennis Carter for the Clwyd Poetry Project, suggest that 'the 1988 act had only marginal effects on the status of poetry in primary schools', which continues to be 'rather low'. Carter concludes, for his part, that the surveys 'point to a patchy and declining role for poetry in primary schools' under a revised National Curriculum which defines literacy in a narrow and functional way (Carter, 1997, p. 5). I therefore interviewed groups of pupils (and their teachers) in different types of primary and secondary schools to try to get some idea of attitudes to poetry in English classrooms now, and of how these differ at the ages of 11 and 15. I was also interested in finding out just how pupils approach poems as a reading experience. I had in mind a remark by Michael Benton that 'Reading a poem is different from reading a story or any other text . . . [It is] a reading process that is more varied and unpredictable than any other' (Benton, 1992, p. 79).

POETRY AT 11

I started by talking to small groups of 10- and 11-year-olds in the context of a middle (9–13), a primary (5–11) and a junior school (7–11).

The middle school

My group of six middle-school pupils were a teacher-selected cross-section of readers. Moira enjoyed writing poems but said she only read them if they were exciting; Sarah loved reading poems but couldn't write them, although her mum did; Eleanor used to like poems, but didn't now; Max didn't find poems at all interesting to read or write; Tom liked books but didn't choose to read or write poems much; and finally Russell found poems OK, but wasn't particularly interested, preferring stories ('You get more involved in it in a book . . . character and things . . . than in a poem').

I would like to concentrate on the comments of Sarah, as the only reader in the group who sometimes preferred a poetry book to stories. For Sarah, how she read a poem was important:

> I think it's much better if you read the poem aloud . . . I find it difficult to read poems in my head because it's much nicer if you read them aloud and listen to your own voice.

This led Sarah to choose other kinds of poetry than the 'comicky sort of poems' which were the only ones Max and Eleanor liked reading (though Eleanor didn't really think they were 'proper poems'):

> I like poems that you have to use a lot of voice expression for . . . like if it's a dark poem then you have to lower your voice down.

Sarah's reading practice with poems was different from the other members of the group. Her response to the question 'Do you read poems differently from stories?' was: 'I actually read poems slower . . . because I like trying to listen to the sound and the rhythm.' Some members of the group said they read poems faster than stories. Max, who didn't generally read poems, read them more slowly if he had to, but for reasons of comprehension, 'so I can actually make most out of it and hear what it's saying'. In contrast to Sarah's savouring of the poem's music, Max and Russell said they would never read a poem twice except 'if it was really complicated and you rushed through it'. Max made a comparison with films, which he said he *did* often watch twice: 'You have to put effort into reading but a film you just stick it in the video and watch.' Poetry reading was equated for them with having to work hard at understanding something difficult.

Sarah's response to the question 'What is a poem?', following the reading of a shape poem, revealed a relaxed and tolerant attitude. Whereas Tom and other members of the group were anxious to define formally what was and wasn't a poem, trying out formulations such as:

This is a poem.
Do you think it is?

Sarah's feeling was that: 'There is no actual definition. Lots of people think lots of different things about poems, so it's your definition for your personal liking.' The personal nature of poetic enjoyment posed problems for the classroom, according to Sarah:

Some teachers make you read poems but you can't be forced to read a poem . . . it's just something you like or don't like . . . you can't be forced to write or read a poem because you won't enjoy it.

As an enthusiastic reader of poetry, Sarah reminds us of the importance of letting children read poetry aloud, of allowing children the time to choose what poems they would like to read and of giving them the time to read them effectively.

The primary school

Bearing in mind the comments made by this keen poetry reader, when I talked to another group of six 10- to 11-year-olds in the top year of a primary school I tried to find similarities of approach in those who enjoyed reading poems. The second group I talked to were again teacher-selected, but this time they were *all* children who were enthusiastic about poetry. Thomas expressed the group's feelings about the kinds of poems they liked when he commented:

I don't really like poems that are long and well they just go on a bit . . . and they don't rhyme . . . I think I like the shorter poems better really.

Discussing the difference between reading stories and reading this kind of poem, Emily expressed her experience of the two in this way:

> A story has a start, a middle and an end – well most stories do – and . . . a poem . . . can be a start of a story or a middle or an end or just, you know, whatever you want . . . and also a poem is sort of a way of expressing your feelings sometimes.

Thomas mentioned this expressive quality of poetry too when he commented: 'Poems are sort of a better way of expressing things than a story really.'

As far as actually reading poems was concerned the group as a whole did feel they read them in a different way from narrative. Emily felt it depended on the type of poem as to how slowly or quickly she read it, but Christine gave this very clear description of her own practice which the entire group greeted with a 'Yeah!' of approval:

> In a poem you stop for a while afterwards, longer than you do when it's just a full stop . . . you stop and then go on to the next line and you stop, go on to the next line . . . and you read it slowly . . . you need more time to think with a poem . . . 'cos stories you just read it through and get it all into your head but a poem you need to be reading it quite slowly to take it all in.

Here Christine seems to echo the kind of approach to reading poems Sarah described.

The junior school

My third group of 10- to 11-year-olds was drawn from a mixed ability class in a junior school. Of the group of eight picked for me by their class teacher, six were positive towards the reading of poetry, one was 'so-so' about it, and one, Jeremy, was emphatically hostile ('If it was the last book on Earth I might read some poems'). In general the group preferred stories to poetry ('Stories take me into a place', said Matthew), as with the children in the APU sample, and there was again a dislike of 'really long poems' and of 'descriptive poems', as with the children in the previous school. Roald Dahl was as popular for his poetry as for his fiction, a view echoed by all the groups I talked to, and other poets mentioned by this group were Brian Patten and Edward Lear.

With this group, when I asked them how they read poems they stressed to me the importance of rhythm. 'It depends what the rhythm is, how fast or slow you read it', said Jeremy, the non-reader of poetry, and Cheryl felt also that the crucial thing was 'if you can get into the rhythm'.

We read together Brian Patten's poem 'The Newcomer' (which Jeremy liked!) (Patten, 1985) and had a vigorous discussion about what or who this newcomer was ('It's about us', said Matthew; 'a mythological creature', said Jeremy). Keeping in mind the comments made earlier to me about reading poems more slowly than stories, when I read the poem aloud to the group, after their own initial silent readings, I consciously slowed down my reading and tried to bring out the poem's rhythm and metre. The group's reactions were mixed:

'You read it much more slowly . . .'
'It sounded a bit more interesting . . . I couldn't get into it.'
'It sounded very, very different when you read. I read it much faster.'
'I preferred my reading to myself.'

At this point I asked the group whether they had ever been given any guidelines for reading poems, and the reply was that they hadn't but had 'just picked up' how to do it. I then asked whether they felt the following sample guidelines would have been useful to them as poetry readers:

Reading poems
1   Choose any poem in the book. You don't have to start on the first page and you don't have to read the poems in any order.
2   Read the poem quickly to yourself. It doesn't matter if you don't understand it all.
3   Read it again more slowly to yourself.
4   Read it aloud, so you can hear what it sounds like.
5   Share it with someone else. Read it together and talk about it.
6   If you really like it, remember where to find the poem so you can read it again to yourself or someone else later.

The reactions to these guidelines were again mixed ('All poems are different', Cheryl rightly pointed out), so I asked the children to produce their own advice to give to beginner poetry readers. Their main recommendation for younger readers was to try to hear the rhythm of a poem:

'I'd say read it slowly a few times. Try to make it sound more exciting.'
'It's important to get the rhythm of a poem.'
'Read it carefully and slowly to yourself. If you don't understand it, get someone to help you.'

Conclusions from the primary sample

Talking to these children at the primary/secondary divide in a number of different schools confirmed my belief in poetry as an essential reading experience for the less fluent and also the independent older reader. I felt there were lessons to be learnt from those readers such as Sarah, Christine and Cheryl (all girls!) who were committed poetry readers and likely to continue to be so into secondary school and beyond.

As well as promoting and supporting poetry as a reading experience and widening children's awareness beyond humorous poetry (but not excluding it), it seemed helpful to talk about the actual process of reading poems. This might mean keen readers sharing their practice with others, or groups of children suggesting advice for younger readers on 'how to read poems', as distinct from prose stories or information books.

Almost certainly it would mean children discovering or rediscovering the music of poetry through reading aloud themselves as well as hearing poems read. As my third group reminded me, the single most important thing for children reading poetry was 'getting into the rhythm of it', rhythm being the 'litmus-test' of a poem, as Richard Andrews has suggested (Andrews, 1991, p. 17).

POETRY AT 15

I followed up my interviews with 10- and 11-year-olds, and the tentative conclusions reached, by talking to small groups of 15-year-olds in a number of different types of secondary school: two mixed comprehensives, a boys' comprehensive and a girls' grammar school. The groups were selected by their teachers to reflect a range of ability and attitude. Since the number of pupils involved was greater, I shall present my findings differently here, organized under the questions asked rather than by school.

The overall impressions I took away from my conversations with these groups of 15-year-olds contradicted some of the APU findings reported earlier. Nowhere in these mixed ability groups of young people did I encounter the positive hostility to poetry I had expected from some. To illustrate this through a rather crude statistic, the responses to the APU prompt statement 'I like reading poems . . .', which I repeated to the secondary groups, were as shown in Table 4.3.

Table 4.3

	Totals		Boys		Girls	
	% Yes	% No	% Yes	% No	% Yes	% No
Age 15	77	23	64	36	88	12

Even when allowance is made for the smallness of the sample (31 pupils, 14 boys and 17 girls, interviewed in five small groups) and the possibly unrepresentative nature of it, this still emerges as a much more positive attitude to poetry at 15 than previous research suggests (compare the figures at the beginning of this chapter). As in the primary school, fiction was of course more popular; 70 per cent of pupils said 'Yes' to the APU prompt 'I would rather read stories than poems . . .', an almost identical figure for girls and boys. At worst I found an indifference to poetry or a neglect because of the wider study demands of secondary school (finding a slot in the timetable to interview pupils proved much more difficult!). Overall I was impressed by the seriousness and the willingness with which all the groups talked about their experiences and views about poetry, and particularly so with the single-sex boys' group and the lower ability pupils interviewed. More than once I came across a complaint that *not enough* poetry was being experienced in the secondary school (and this in schools where the teachers devoted a lot of time to poetry activities!). There was also a suggestion that low expectations of secondary school boys in particular in relation to poetry might be a self-fulfilling prophecy, as one pupil suggested:

> I think the books we get given aren't the best pieces of poetry because they tend to be a bit silly, trying to get our attention . . .

When I repeated another prompt from the APU surveys 'I prefer funny to serious poems . . .', it was interesting that only 46 per cent of the pupils said 'Yes', with a figure of 50 per cent for the boys, again a good deal lower than I had been led to expect, given the figure of 82 per cent from the 1979 Primary Survey.

I would now like to review the secondary pupils' responses to the questions I asked them in more detail.

Poetry outside school

The APU surveys all included questions on experience of poetry outside the school: in the 1979 Secondary Survey, for instance, 73 per cent of those asked did not read poetry to any extent in their own time (APU, 1982, p. 54). So I began all my discussions by asking pupils whether they read or wrote poetry in their own time. Only 22 per cent of the pupils said they read poems outside school and in all but one of the cases it was emphasized that this was 'very occasionally' and 'funny poetry, not heavy stuff'. The exception was Jo, a pupil in a mixed comprehensive and another committed female poetry enthusiast ('I really like it!'). She was the only pupil interviewed who actively sought out poetry books in her own leisure time, though this was proving difficult ('There's only three teenage poetry books in the [local] library and I've read them!'). Jo's background as a poetry-lover was interesting:

> I used to do drama lessons and I used to have to read poetry as a matter of doing my grades.

Here was another example of interest in poetry being stimulated by reading aloud, as with the 11-year-olds. Jo also wrote 'songs and poems' outside school, and here again the context, as she explained it, was the pursuit of another practical arts activity:

> . . . it helps me with my music GCSE [General Certificate of Secondary Education] if I write poetry then I can change it into songs.

Jo's out-of-school activities suggest a cross-curricular potential for poetry even in the secondary school, particularly where other expressive arts subjects such as drama and music are concerned, which may not be exploited as much as it could in a packed and subject-dominated timetable. Poetry, after all, has been defined as 'a song with no music' and 'a dance in words' (Andrews, 1991, p. 11).

Another 22 per cent of the pupils in the sample said they wrote in their own time, though none of them read poetry significantly ('I don't read much but I write an awful lot', was a comment which could have applied to all). Again song lyrics were mentioned by a number of these pupils, including Ian in the all-boys school who felt that 'they could be considered poetry', a view endorsed by Matt for whom poetry was

> . . . a way of expressing your feelings. Poetry doesn't just consist of a few sentences which rhyme. It's saying what you want to say. Not saying it in a nice way, but in the most effective way.

Sadly, two higher ability boys said they had 'given up' writing poetry after primary school, except once again for song lyrics in one case.

The interest these 15-year-olds, mostly higher and middle ability pupils, had in writing poetry outside school suggested a potential which might be tapped further before premature 'retirement' from poetry writing could set in in the secondary years. Many pupils wanted more opportunities for writing their own poems beyond the first couple of years of secondary education, as will emerge in the next section.

Poetry in school

I began by inviting the pupils to mention any poetry activities they had enjoyed or not enjoyed in school. There was a familiar complaint here about a perceived over-emphasis on analysing poems. From the girls in the grammar school to the boys' comprehensive, a majority of pupils expressed a dislike for 'dissecting' poetry and 'writing ten-page essays' on it, as Yasmina put it. (In a minority of one was Katriona, who enjoyed analysis, since she found it 'quite easy to do'.) A clear preference was expressed for 'more just reading', as Kevin put it: 'Dissecting – it's all right for a while, but if you're dissecting more and dissecting more I don't think it would be quite as interesting.' Ross in the same school agreed: 'It depends what we do with the poetry. You can just read it and it's fine, but when you have to start writing, answering questions about it, then that's not so much fun.' Alicia summed up this view:

> You're made to read them and you go into them in so much depth and detail . . . when I read one I like to skim over it. I don't like to go into what everything means . . . it gets boring after a while.

Both the discussion of and the reading of poems were mentioned as enjoyable. 'I don't mind interpreting it . . . discussing what it means' and 'It's good to find out other people's views . . . but it gets a bit heated' were two comments from the same school, where the practice of group and whole-class discussion of poems was clearly well established, as it was in others too.

Choice of texts was an important factor in pupils' enjoyment or otherwise of poetry in school. Lower ability pupils in particular had found the transition from the 'simpler', 'fun' poetry for children of primary school to the 'more adult' secondary school texts hard: 'Ones that don't make sense is what puts me off, because I don't understand it', said one girl. 'Poetry is more serious now, it's not like it was', agreed two lower ability pupils, 'it was a lot more fun.' Another from the same school reflected:

> As you get older it gets more complicated and you don't enjoy it as much, I don't think, because it's harder to understand . . . when you were younger you could understand it quite easily.

The sort of poem which was enjoyed by the lower ability group was 'something that you read that you think that, oh, you can understand that'. There was little awareness by pupils of poets who have specifically written for a teenage audience in recent years. This seemed to be an under-used resource with all the groups interviewed, though teenage *fiction* was well established in the reading repertoire. They described a transition typically from Allan Ahlberg, the most frequently mentioned poet encountered at primary school (*Please, Mrs Butler*, 1983, is by far the most popular volume with primary teachers, according to research cited in Beard, 1995, p. 11), to 'more adult' poetry and expressed a need for 'something in between', with content they could relate to.

Pupils remembered enjoying practical activities with poems, such as performance work in groups; a dance based on W. H. Auden's 'Song IX', made popular by the film *Four Weddings and a Funeral*; cutting up newspaper headlines to make poems; writing a poem in the form of a recipe; and writing from the stimulus of a photograph. As mentioned, pupils in all but one of the groups wanted such opportunities to write poems: 'something different from reading all the time', as one of the lower ability pupils put it. The rationale was supplied by another pupil: 'If you write your own poems, it helps you get a better understanding' of other people's.

Transition from primary to secondary school

I asked the groups to recall poetry activities at primary school and to reflect on the transition to secondary school (as some already had done spontaneously). Most of those interviewed remembered 'a lot more' opportunities for poetry and particularly for writing poems in the primary school. Peter recalled:

> We had a poetry folder and once a week we had to write our own poem, so we ended up with quite a collection.

However, memories of the poems written were not always positive:

> 'We were pressured into doing it, so it wasn't quite as good as writing for your own pleasure.'
> 'There wasn't any meaning in it [rhyming poetry] or anything.'
> 'It's autumn, write an autumn poem!'

For a significant minority of pupils as well, there had been little poetry in primary school. 'In our primary school there wasn't a lot of poetry', said Jonathan, 'more the infants did poetry.' He enjoyed poetry more now in secondary school. Activities which were remembered as enjoyable from primary school were again practical ones. Jo, the poetry-lover, recalled acting out 'funny poems, like Michael Rosen's' (this had been with a student teacher). Owen, in the same higher ability group as Jo, remembered painting a picture about a poem; Sally recited Ogden Nash's 'Winter Morning', which she'd learnt by heart. A lower ability pupil reflected fondly:

> We used to have Poetry Days . . . a chap would come in and we'd work with him in the day and read out our own poetry to the rest of the school the next day.

The 'chap' was later recalled as the ubiquitous Allan Ahlberg! Other pupils remembered similar visits by writers and Peter summed up a general wish for visits by 'more poets and poetesses, as in primary school'.

When asked what advice they would give to teachers introducing poetry to younger children (I mentioned my earlier suggested guidelines here), pupils responded in similar ways, as follows:

- keep it simple;
- make it enjoyable, fun;
- more comedy poems;
- keep it going, keep their attention;
- work with images;
- singing;
- rhyming;
- read about something you understand;
- write about something you know about and like.

Rob, in the all-boys group, warned:

> I think at that age you shouldn't really have poetry hammered into you. You should just get familiar with it and then later on you should start looking at it more closely, because I think you're too young to appreciate it academically . . . strict guidelines aren't really the best idea.

Asked whether their attitude to poetry had become more negative between the ages of 11 and 15, as the APU surveys suggest, the pupils' responses were mixed. Eleanor in the girls' grammar school group felt her interest and enjoyment *had* decreased because poetry was more 'difficult', 'harder' now, though she still liked reading poems. Another able girl, Annabel, in one of the comprehensive school groups, agreed: 'I just don't read as much.' Less able pupils in the same group also felt they were not as interested now that poetry was 'more serious'. However, the majority view of these 15-year-olds was that their enthusiasm for poetry had not diminished, but that there was simply less time and opportunity available now to enjoy it.

Styles of reading poetry

I ended the group interviews by inviting the pupils to think about how they read a poem and again used 'The Newcomer' by Brian Patten as a text to read and discuss beforehand. The poem was seen by the secondary pupils as one which was suitable for both children and adults. The comments of the primary children about 'getting into the rhythm' were closely echoed. 'I try and get some rhythm into it', said David, though it depended on the type of poem; 'I automatically put it into a pattern, always trying to find a pattern for the words', said another boy. Tina described her practice like this:

> When you read it you always think a poem has a beat to it and it rhymes, so you try and say it like in a beat . . . trying to make it more interesting.

Clear differences with fiction reading styles were articulated:

'Poems I read more slowly and in stages. Stories I just read in one big go.'
'With a novel you don't read every word, just get the gist of it.'
'You have to understand most of the words.'
'In a story you try to take the role of the person in the story, but in a poem it's totally different, you just go with the flow.'
'It goes straight down to the point of what it's trying to say . . . within a poem it's got a message . . . so you try and find that by reading it and breaking it down and finding out what it means.'

Poems were almost always read more slowly than prose fiction, but not automatically re-read by all pupils interviewed. Peter, for example, said he would only read a poem again if he enjoyed it, not if he didn't understand it. There was the conviction though that there was a single 'message' or possibly two 'meanings' in poems which the reader needed to get at, sometimes through repeated readings:

'I always try to find a meaning, because there is one somewhere.'
'A lot of poems have two meanings to it, or different sides of it every time you read it, so if you read it again and again you understand more about it.'
'If I read them every day I'd find the meanings quicker.'

I asked the last group I interviewed to suggest ways in which poetry could be made more interesting for them in secondary school. Their suggestions, readily and speedily supplied, were as follows:

- more writing;
- more choice;
- more involvement;
- 'basically more of it' [poetry]!

DEVELOPING POETRY

It's interesting to discover from Linda Thompson's edited volume, *The Teaching of Poetry: European Perpectives* (1996), that the relative neglect of poetry in the language and literature curriculum and its perception as 'difficult' by teachers as well as pupils is not simply a feature of British education. Contributors from Germany and Denmark in this volume describe a similar situation. 'It is a common prejudice among Danish secondary school teachers that poetry is difficult, and they are therefore reluctant to teach it', observes Thorkild Borup Jensen in the book (p. 30). After outlining the important role of elements of poetic language such as rhythm and later rhyme in the experience of even the youngest children, Gundel Mattenklott describes a depressingly familiar development:

in Germany there is a perplexing phenomenon: young people, adolescents and students at universities, even those who study literature, tend to reject poetry. They find that they cannot relate to poetic form and language, and even at times find them tiresome. Given the original pleasure experienced through poetry, how did this rejection develop? If asked, young people point to school as the guilty party. In particular they identify the overwhelmingly analytical and interpretative nature of literature teaching.

(p. 13)

Of the situation in the UK, Linda Hall in the same book claims:

I do not think I am misrepresenting current school practice if I say that poetry does not enjoy a prominent place in the curriculum of our primary and secondary schools ... when it does make an all-too-fleeting appearance, it is unfortunately subjected to methods and approaches which distort and damage its very special qualities and seem to make it without exception the most detested subject that children meet during their schooldays ... There is no doubt that poetry is perceived by most people, including many teachers, as something highbrow, difficult and obscure ... It is no exaggeration to say that poetry seems to generate more antipathy in secondary pupils, particularly among boys, than does the supposedly dreaded maths.

(p. 22)

Hall goes on to quote the statistics mentioned previously from the 1979 APU survey and some even earlier ones. My own more recent but admittedly limited snapshots of pupils' attitudes suggest that there may be some exaggeration here and that the situation now in British secondary schools may not be as gloomy as is painted – or at the very least that some more substantial up-to-date research needs to be done. The pupils I spoke to demonstrated a good deal of real and potential interest in poetry well into secondary education. Many secondary schools *have* modified their approach to poetry and sought to give it a higher profile over the past decade, partly in response to National Curriculum requirements for English (a partial resurgence which matches the 'poetry boom' in British culture reported by, among others, *The Daily Telegraph* of 28 June and 3 July 1996). The challenge now for teachers is how to build on the mainly positive attitudes of pupils at the end of primary school in order to develop further and extend the potential interest in poetry in the secondary years, as public examination and assessment demands exert their growing influence.

I would like to consider in the final part of this chapter what can be learnt from the responses of British pupils in both primary and secondary schools to my survey of attitudes to poetry and how as teachers we might develop approaches to poetry teaching, drawing also on the experiences of colleagues facing similar challenges both in European and in other English-speaking countries.

WRITING POEMS

Poetry writing is a normal part of language development in the primary school, although the range of poetic forms and content experienced there might sometimes be limited. It tends to continue as part of English lessons in the first few years of secondary school but often then disappears and becomes an extra-curricular activity for a few, under pressure of public exam syllabi at 16 and 18. Clearly change here will always partly depend on how far those syllabi can be adapted to include elements of pupils' poetry writing as well as reading and analysis. However, the potential of poetry writing in Modern Foreign Language teaching in the secondary school has been convincingly demonstrated (by Carol Morgan, for example, in Thompson, 1996) and the argument for more writing in English is a strong one, not least because it enables pupils to build on their achievements at primary school. What are clearly required are challenges which extend the range of poetry writing rather than repeat familiar exercises ('We still do acrostics!' one secondary boy complained during interview). Opportunities to investigate the craft of poetry writing are valid in their own right as language development activities (to say nothing of personal development), but should also yield insights which easily transfer to poetry reading and indeed speaking. There is clear potential too for links with other arts subjects.

Writing is an activity which demands pupil participation and creativity, the kind of involvement my interviewees wanted more of. It also offers teachers the chance to be involved as writers and editors of poetry, an opportunity which the Arvon Foundation, for example, an established provider of residential writing courses in the UK, sees as crucial to raising standards in poetry teaching, as demonstrated by the subsidized writing workshops it now offers for teachers and trainees. Contact with published poets through workshops and residences, as the Arvon Foundation recognizes, can be a vital spark for a writing programme. Many pupils I spoke to remembered enthusiastically visits by poets to their primary schools, but this seems a stimulus that secondary schools could provide more and for more pupils, rather than only higher ability ones. Increasingly, writers in education are becoming involved in extended visits or 'mini-residencies' in schools or groups of schools, as well as the more familiar one-off performances or workshops (Harries, 1984). This kind of regular contact with poets, often leading to the publication of school anthologies, can not only demystify the art-form for pupils, but also establish the essential seriousness of the artistic activity (Calouste Gulbenkian Foundation, 1982). A series of visits to a school allows teachers as well to work in partnership with writers, both before, during and after the visits and during staff development sessions.

Contexts for poem-writing which build on pupil experience and provide for cross-curricular links might include:

- creating film/poems in the genre created by contemporary poets like Tony Harrison (e.g. *The Shadow of Hiroshima and Other Film/Poems,* 1995);
- writing poems to accompany paintings or photographs, possibly ones by pupils themselves (see Michael and Peter Benton's anthologies *Painting with Words* (1995) and *Double Vision* (1990) for examples by published poets);
- writing poems to music, either composed by themselves or by others (see Mick Gowar's poems for *Carnival of the Animals* (1992) for examples);
- writing poems for reading aloud, for dramatic performance or for dance, including rap poems;
- writing poems for dissemination on the Internet or via e-mail to a linked school, possibly in another English-speaking country;
- writing poems for public places in the school, on the lines of Benson, Chernaik and Herbert's *Poems on the Underground* (1993) project (e.g. poems in the dining hall, computer room, science lab, etc.);
- writing translations of poems from modern foreign languages.

All the above provide public contexts for poetry, without losing sight of personal creativity.

A range of poetic forms can be introduced or revisited in greater complexity: free verse techniques, imagism, poetic monologues and dialogues, syllabic forms (perhaps haiku chains or pupils' own syllable patterns), rhyming and metrical forms (such as the villanelle and the various sonnet forms). Pupils can build up a portfolio or collection of their own poems over time, including audio- and video-taped versions, perhaps organized into relevant themes which have an overall coherence. Some useful thematic headings are suggested by David M. Johnson in *Word Weaving* (1990), his valuable account of poetry writing activities with college and high school students in New Mexico:

- Origins.
- Home and family.
- Love and friendship.
- Work and holidays.
- Ageing and death.

The aim, in the end, must be to encourage the individuality of each writer, but through encountering models from other writers, including contemporary and classic poets, and also draft work and work from other students (such as Johnson helpfully includes in his book).

READING POEMS

More choice and diversity in their poetry reading was requested by secondary pupils I spoke to. There was also a need felt for 'something in-between' those poems written specifically for children and those for an adult audience. This suggests that as well as experiencing contemporary and classic adult poems, and continuing to have access to the sort of poems they enjoyed at primary school, including humourous ones, secondary pupils could be introduced more often to 'real' collections and anthologies written specifically for teenage readers, in addition to school anthologies, which inevitably tend to perpetuate a particular canon and a particular poetic (Andrews, 1991). Andy Kempe, in Chapter 3 of this book, comments on the lack of plays written specially for young audiences, which he feels can be a valuable resource. However, some excellent poetry anthologies *are* available, such as:

- Wendy Cope, *Is That The New Moon?* (1989).
- Anne Harvey, *The Language of Love* (1989).
- Carol Ann Duffy, *Stopping for Death* (1996).
- Judith Nicholls, *Sing Freedom* (1991).
- Naomi Lewis, *Messages* (1985).

There are also plenty of single-poet collections aimed at a teenage audience and dealing with experiences and issues important to this age-group, such as:

- Philip Gross, *Scratch City* (1995).
- Norman Silver, *The Walkmen Have Landed* (1994).
- Mick Gowar, *So Far So Good* (1986).
- Roger McGough, *Nailing the Shadow* (1987).
- Helen Dunmore, *Secrets* (1994).
- Benjamin Zephaniah, *Talking Turkeys* (1994).

Allowing secondary pupils to *choose* poems for performance and discussion from a selection of texts like these, in addition to and not instead of teacher-selected poems from other kinds of poetry texts, should increase pupils' involvement in and sense of ownership of poetry. Increased diversity and choice in the outcomes expected of poetry reading will also help. Thorkild Borup Jensen talks of ways Danish pupils can 'experience' poetry in the classroom, as well as ways they can 'acquire poetic knowledge' (Thompson, 1996). Group discussion of poems, allowing pupils to develop their own responses as readers in their own terms, before encountering critical interpretations, is well established (Benton *et al.*, 1988). However, this is often just a brief prelude to teacher 'dissection' of poems and written pupil analyses, such as my interviewees complained of. Despite the influence of reader response and other postmodernist literary theory, with its validation of plurality and diversity in interpretations of poetry, there was still a deeply held belief among pupils that poems do hold single definable meanings, which their teachers can reveal to them. The hold of New Critical approaches on teaching methodologies and pupils' attitudes, with their 'devaluation of the role of the reader', is more tenacious than we imagine and still an important part of 'the problem with poetry' (Andrews, 1991).

Practical activities can allow pupils both to 'experience' poems and to 'acquire poetic knowledge'. For example:

- reassembling cut-up poems;
- comparing translations of poems;
- comparing poems and prose texts in the same mode (realist, fantasy, horror, etc.);
- comparing contemporary and classic poems on the same themes;
- comparing the language of poems with popular media forms, such as advertising, journalism and song lyrics;
- compiling anthologies for younger readers, including notes;
- presenting poems to younger readers through performances;
- designing and creating video sequences to accompany poems;
- designing and creating multimedia presentations of poems, using IT.

These active methods of learning which encourage students to investigate the constructed nature of poetic texts, without diminishing the value and integrity of those texts, and also seek to show poetry's relationship to new media technologies, are consistent with those advocated in other chapters of this book, whether in relation to classic fiction, plays, picture books or media adaptations.

CONCLUSIONS

James Squire (in Hayhoe and Parker, 1990) has distinguished the role of the literature teacher in the following way:

> The task of teaching literary history is a task for the literary historian; the task of teaching about the lives of authors, a task for the literary biographer; the task of teaching about the structure of the text or characteristics of the genre, one for the literary critic. The task of the teacher of literature, on the other hand, is to focus on the transaction between the book and the reader, on the literary experience itself, and on ways of extending and deepening it.

Activities such as the above bring pupils and poems together in this kind of 'transaction', to use Louise Rosenblatt's term (Rosenblatt, 1978): literary history, biography and criticism can follow, but this experience of poetry needs to come first. Putting poems into pupils' hands, literally, will mean abandoning the approach which puts poetry on a pedestal as something private, precious and exclusive. Poetry will need to be approached as something much more public and more robust, which if it is well enough made will stand up to a hands-on examination and even a bit of rough handling. Giving poetry 'a special place' in the past has not done it any favours: to treat it in the same way as any other necessary part of the school curriculum will actually do poetry a greater service.

Poetry has an important role to play, not only as an enjoyable and valued part of language development in primary schools, but also as a way of broadening and deepening reading experience in the secondary school. Poetry, after all, *should* appeal to the adolescent reader, the 'reader as thinker' in Appleyard's schema, who looks to literature

> to discover insights into the meaning of life, values and beliefs worthy of commitment, ideal images, and authentic role models for imitation. The *truth* of these ideas and ways of living is a severe criterion for judging them.
>
> (Appleyard, 1990, p. 14)

As a special form of non-fiction, poetry is ideally placed to address the particular demands of these readers for insights, values, 'truths', and to extend their repertoire of roles further, producing what Andrew Goodwyn calls in Chapter 1 a 'sophisticated reader'.

ACKNOWLEDGEMENT

Part of this chapter previously appeared in *Reading* **27** (3), 50–3.

REFERENCES

Ahlberg, A. (1983) *Please Mrs Butler*. Harmondsworth: Kestrel.

Andrews, R. (1991) *The Problem with Poetry*. Buckingham: Open University Press.

Appleyard, J. A. (1990) *Becoming a Reader*. Cambridge: Cambridge University Press.

APU (1981) *Language Performance in Schools: Primary Survey Report No. 1 [1979]*. London: HMSO.

APU (1982) *Secondary Survey Report No. 1 [1979]*. London: HMSO.

APU (1984) *1982 Primary Survey Report*. London: DES.

APU (1988) *Review of APU Language Monitoring 1979–83*. London: HMSO.

Beard, R. (ed.) (1995) *Rhyme, Reading and Writing*. London: Hodder & Stoughton.

Benson, G., Chernaik, J. and Herbert, C. (eds) (1993) *Poems on the Underground*. London: Cassell.

Benton, M. (1992) *Secondary Worlds: Literature Teaching and the Visual Arts*. Buckingham: Open University Press.

Benton, M. and Benton, P. (1990) *Double Vision*. London: Hodder & Stoughton.

Benton, M. and Benton, P. (1995) *Painting with Words*. London: Hodder & Stoughton.

Benton, M. *et al.* (1988) *Young Readers Responding to Poems*. London: Routledge.

Bryant, P. and Bradley, L. (1985) *Children's Reading Problems*. Oxford: Blackwell.

Calouste Gulbenkian Foundation (1982) *The Arts in Schools*. London: Calouste Gulbenkian Foundation.

Carter, D. (1997) *The Power to Overwhelm*. Clwyd: Clwyd Poetry Project.

Cope, W. (1989) *Is that the New Moon?* London: Collins.

Duffy, C. A. (1996) *Stopping for Death*. London: Viking.

Dunmore, H. (1994) *Secrets*. London: Bodley Head.

Goswami, U. and Bryant, P. (1990) *Phonological Skills and Learning to Read*. London: Erlbaum.

Gowar, M. (1986) *So Far So Good*. London: Collins.

Gowar, M. (1992) *Carnival of the Animals*. Harmondsworth: Puffin.

Gross, P. (1995) *Scratch City*. London: Faber.

Harries, S. (1984) *Writers in Schools*. London: Arts Council of Great Britain.

Harrison, T. (1995) *The Shadow of Hiroshima and Other Film/Poems*. London: Faber.

Harvey, A. (1989) *The Language of Love*. London: Blackie.

Hayhoe, M. and Parker, S. (eds) (1990) *Reading and Response*. Buckingham: Open University Press.

HMI (1992) *English: Key Stages 1, 2 and 3: A Report on the Second Year, 1990–91*. London: HMSO.

Johnson, D. M. (1990) *Word Weaving: A Creative Approach to Teaching and Writing Poetry*. Urbana, IL: National Council of Teachers of English.

Lewis, N. (1985) *Messages*. London: Faber.

McGough, R. (1987) *Nailing the Shadow*. London: Viking Kestrel.

Nicholls, J. (1991) *Sing Freedom*. London: Faber.

Patten, B. (1985) *Gargling with Jelly*. London: Viking Kestrel.

Rosenblatt, L. (1978) *The Reader, the Text, the Poem: The Transactional Theory of the Literary Work*. Carbondale, IL: Southern Illinois University Press.

Silver, N. (1994) *The Walkmen Have Landed*. London: Faber.

Thompson, L. (ed.) (1996) *The Teaching of Poetry: European Perspectives*. London: Cassell.

Zephaniah, B. (1994) *Talking Turkeys*. London: Viking.

Chapter 5

Picture Books in Secondary English

Vaughan Prain

In recent years the use of picture books in the classroom has been extended far beyond their traditional role as a stimulating resource for initial literacy learning. Increasingly English teachers are viewing these books as part of the necessary broad range of texts students can study profitably at different levels of secondary school. There are various reasons for this development, including the more sophisticated or 'mature' subject matter in this kind of text, as authors have explored such topics as homelessness, nuclear war and the effects of colonization on indigenous peoples. Teachers have also noted that older students are more interested in, or perhaps dependent on, visually oriented material. In addition, there is a growing recognition in National Curriculum documents of the expanded and diverse nature of literacy learning in the late 1990s. As many commentators have noted, including Green (1997), Lemke (1996) and Hinkson (1991), the ongoing digital–electronic communications revolution is having profound effects on society in general and on the reconceptualization of what literacy for the future might mean. If, as Wexler (1990) claims, we are now living in a 'semiotic society', increasingly shaped by pictorial and multimodal communication, then literacy must necessarily be redefined and extended to include the ability to use and interpret a wide range of mixed visual and print media. Literacy skills can no longer be understood purely in terms of a print-based, page-governed technology, but must now be extended to include the ability to read and use all the current and emerging new forms of literacy. More and more this new literacy includes the intricate blending of linguistic, aural and pictorial meanings.

There is also growing agreement that English in the future will need to concern itself more with what Kress (1995, p. 22) has labelled 'visuality', rather than purely print-based notions of literacy and 'text'. However, the question of which 'texts' might best be studied to develop these new skills, knowledges and values has become increasingly problematic and contested. There has been divided opinion over which current non-print texts, of all the available films, videos and CD-roms, might be appropriate for this work. There is also debate over whether any or most picture books have sufficient 'substance' to count as texts worthy of close study in developing visual literacy skills. Further, there is debate over the question of the year level at which such texts can be studied productively. For example, the decision to include Raymond

Briggs' picture book, *When the Wind Blows* (1982), as a set English text for senior students to study in Victoria, Australia, in 1989, was viewed by some traditionalists as incontrovertible proof of the collapse of literacy standards and goals in that state. By contrast, those who supported the choice of this text argued that it provided a complex ironic mix of visual and verbal meanings that required a considerable degree of student sophistication to interpret its rich play of themes.

The question of which texts should be studied formally in school (and why), as Green (1997) and others have noted, is further complicated by the ways in which media culture has increasingly supplanted schooling as the major site for student social learning, knowledge development and identity formation. In other words, the more influential 'texts' on students' lives are most likely to be experienced outside school. While teachers are expected to encourage student appreciation of 'salient' past cultural texts, such as Shakespeare's plays, they are also expected to develop students' ability to read and contribute to the 'ephemeral' but increasingly supersaturated world of multimedia culture. In such a context of unprecedented technological and cultural change, it is hardly surprising that prescriptions about appropriate texts and strategies to support the development of visual literacy remain, at best, provisional and open-ended. However, in this chapter I would like to review some current claims made for the study of traditional print-based picture books in secondary English, including various educational and cultural justifications for this activity, and to explore the kinds of learning such study might promote.

Educators in the 1990s have made diverse claims for why secondary students should read and analyse picture books. These range from the bluntly pragmatic (this kind of text, like some poetry and short short stories, is well suited to the exigencies of 40- or 50-minute lessons and short attention spans) to claims that pleasurable analysis of picture books can be a productive part of developing students' visual literacy skills and values. For example, educators such as Michaels and Walsh (1990, p. 1) assert that picture books can play an important role in developing student capacities to interpret a 'complex interrelationship between words and pictures'. They argue that picture books are a worthwhile literary 'genre in themselves' (p. 113), and that they can be used, among other things, as an introduction to the conventions of Shakespearean theatre. They also claim that study of these texts can consolidate student knowledge of all the customary concepts of traditional literary studies such as narrative structures and features such as 'interior monologues' and 'gender stereotypes'. These texts, it is also claimed, can provide accessible models for students' own writing, dramatic improvisation and role-play. Picture books, the writers argue, can also enable readers to become 'conscious of their own reading processes' through experiencing a shared meaning-making event in the classroom that is 'just as applicable in the secondary school as in the primary school' (p. 113). Picture books, in that they often take the form of a storyboard, can also be a 'useful tool to explore aspects of the media, particularly film and video' (p. 114), in that they encourage the development of students' technical knowledge about camera shots and angles, and provide models for students' own storyboards. From this viewpoint picture books are one important resource, among many possible options, for the development of visual literacy skills.

For Stephens and Watson (1994) the study of picture books can go far beyond a merely technical view of reading and visual literacy, defined as the ability to 'decode' the linked structures of meaning in a sequence of images and parallel text. These writers assert that picture books can provide pleasurable development of a whole range of skills and values usually associated with critical literacy, or the ability to make analytical judgements about the values, purposes and possible effects of particular texts. They imply that the defining characteristics of the best of these texts, their impressive succinctness and economy of ordering and detail, can offer an exemplary, manageable resource for students to engage with the complexities of recent theories about reading. From their perspective picture books offer focused, powerful texts for developing students' understandings of, and values about, particular ideologies, including feminist, multicultural and post-imperialistic viewpoints. These writers also suggest that recent picture books offer rewarding comparative studies with other media such as movies, video and television programmes in terms of identifying parallel structures, values and intentions.

In this chapter, then, I would like to consider a range of issues relating to picture books, beginning with the relatively new problem of defining this specific genre. This has arisen partly because of the recent effects of technological innovations on what can be created as, or designated, a 'picture book', as well as recent claims about the emergence of new postmodern, as opposed to traditional 'modernist', picture books. I then review in a more extended way some of the current rationales and agendas proposed for using picture books to support literacy development, with a particular focus on the claims made for these texts as exemplary resources for cultural studies and new theories of reading. The final section is oriented more to practical concerns, and considers some general guidelines for classroom use of these texts, as well as some specific questions suitable for different year levels in secondary English. Certainly I agree with those who argue that there are picture books of sufficient complexity to provide a worthwhile resource for the development of students' 'visual literacy' skills and values development, and therefore to justify their study at least up to middle secondary English classes.

DEFINITIONS AND SHIFTING BOUNDARIES

Before considering recent distinctions made between modernist and postmodernist picture books (Bradford, 1993; Lonsdale, 1993; McHale, 1987; Stephens, 1992; Stephens and Watson, 1994), I would like to acknowledge the very strong influence of new electronic technologies on broadening and destabilizing what we now define as a picture book. Whilst this chapter focuses predominantly on print-based picture books, the emergence of new electronic texts needs to be understood as central to any proper coverage of the changing meanings of 'picture book' and 'visual literacy'. Certainly the recent application of information technologies to the basic format of the print-based picture book has had a significant influence on the potential text structures and writer/reader relationships in this kind of text. As Lemke (1996) has noted, the parallel shift in schooling from purely print-based literacy to 'metamedia literacy', 'electronic cognition' and to digital–electronic forms of communication has had profound effects on the technologies of new texts and subsequent new definitions of what might constitute a text and its boundaries.

Clearly these new multimodal texts are altering significantly our ways of understanding reading, writing, illustration, context, authorship and readership, with future effects that are obviously difficult to predict. For example, the emergence of the graphic novel challenges past views on the scope of pictorial illustration in an extended text, just as hypertext encourages much more reader freedom by giving readers a range of options. The hypertext reader is able to browse in a non-linear way before making a more extended commitment to read sections of the text. In this way the reader or viewer will make many more decisions about preferred pathways into and 'through' the possible content of these new texts compared to the page-governed texts of the past. This technology means that different readers can and will construct quite contrasting sequences, emphases and experiences of the text, and hence the question of the boundaries and potential meaning structures of this new kind of reading is far more problematic than in conventional reading. While obviously the broad scope of the content of these new texts is ultimately constrained by the writers' earlier decisions on content, the writer is more like a designer of a golf course on which the reader 'plays' rather than the conventional messenger-sender of earlier models of communication.

Another major consequence of the new technologies, as noted by Kress (1995), Monteith (1993), Tuman (1992), Tweddle *et al.* (1997) and many others, is the shift from single authorship to collaborative composing using multimedia options rather than relying solely on print. Computers can enable much more complex composing processes where writers in different physical settings collaborate in using diverse banks of 'stored' (or newly created) images, speech, text and music to create a multimedia presentation. This technological innovation is no longer simply a matter of futuristic speculation, and is already altering the meaning and experience for students of 'picture books' in schools. The application of multimedia computers, scanners, video cameras and colour printers to student 'writing' has clearly changed the possible structures, expressive options and 'content' of 'new' picture books. For example, middle secondary students in Bendigo, Australia, have produced computer-based personalized interactive picture books for junior primary students (Tweddle *et al.*, 1997). In one particular classroom pairs of older students first talked with the younger child who was the target reader, finding out her or his preferences in story lines, characters and settings. The older students then worked on an interactive picture book which had the following features: hypercard was used to create animated illustrations; characters in the text introduced themselves verbally, spoke to one another and also directly addressed the reader by name; a photograph of the reader was scanned and reproduced in the dedication at the start of the 'book'; and the responses of the reader were sought during the initial development of the storyline.

Another example of a new 'picture book' option currently available to students is use of digitized cameras to record events that then can be viewed on a computer, manipulated in terms of colour, size and image arrangement, and then printed selectively to become part of a factual or fictionalized pictorially illustrated text. Informational technologies can also be used to explore in greater detail the relationship between word and image in a text. For example, in CD-rom interactive books there is scope for the reader to investigate the implications of the narrative by activating various programmed multimedia additions to the text. While such reading practices, like the electronic picture book described above, are still not fully interactive, in that the reader can only react to the options already programmed into the 'text', the possible relationships between text and image are far more complex than in the traditional picture book.

In the face of all these emerging technological applications of multimedia programmes to reading and 'text creation' it might be argued that the traditional picture book represents an obsolete or merely 'historical' technology for literacy development, and is therefore not a preferable starting place for the study of new literacies. This argument might be further elaborated along the lines that the current conventions of print-based technology (such as page turns, sequenced text and a left to right format) represent constraints rather than opportunities for developing student understanding of the expressive possibilities of multimedia. It could be further argued that even those texts, such as Jon Scieszka's *The Stinky Cheeseman* (1992), that attempt to disrupt many of these traditional conventions of print, only succeed in confirming the rule of these 'laws'. For instance, all the disarray of typeface, the disorder of the sequence of content, and the rule-breaking in relation to the boundaries of what the narrator can and does refer to in Scieszka's text, are still ultimately 'framed' by the linear page-turn technology of the traditional book.

However, despite these reasonable concerns I suggest that there are several strong arguments that can form the basis for a rationale for the study of print-based picture books in the secondary classroom. These texts can be read as worthwhile in their own right as a particular genre with a history extending over two hundred years. They are also a valuable resource for developing students' advanced skills in reading, including the development of some aspects of visual literacy. In this regard, the conventions that affect possible meanings in these texts are more clearly understood (because they have been the subject of close study in recent years) than the emerging conventions and possibilities of multimedia texts. Therefore print-based texts offer an accessible, 'stable' starting place for developing student understandings of the potential relationships between print and visual media, as well as a range of other aspects of literacy. At the same time, several possible misreadings of this case need to be clarified. First, these texts should not be viewed as purely simplified precursors to more complex multimedia texts, as though they are only multimedia 'with training wheels'. Print-based picture books, as outlined later in the chapter, offer very effective teaching resources for developing students' understanding of the communicative and expressive possibilities of print-based literacy, which still plays a large part in current understandings and practices of literacy. This is not to argue that these texts cannot be used productively, as well, for comparative purposes with other media, but rather that this should not be viewed as their only or major value.

Nevertheless, despite their current popularity, their place as an important resource for developing students' reading capacities, given the rate of technological change, cannot be guaranteed into a distant future; but this is also obviously true of many other current classroom texts. Also, as this brief coverage of new forms of picture books indicates, the whole future meaning of this category of 'text', like many other kinds of text, is open-ended, with the possibility that particular electronically produced texts will in the future enjoy the cultural status now given to some traditional texts.

MODERNIST AND POSTMODERNIST PICTURE BOOKS

Turning to the question of which kind of print-based picture book should be used in class, Lonsdale (1993, pp. 25–6) makes a useful distinction between the modernist picture book and its postmodernist successor, which she claims emerged in the 1960s. While conceding the dangers of simplification and overlap in attempting to characterize the two types of text, she argues that the modernist text usually has the following features. This type of picture book is generally 'mimetic' in that the author attempts to represent the text's world and characters realistically rather than surreally. In these texts life, despite some surprises and reversals, is viewed as 'ordered and rational', with an authoritative plot resolution enabling the reader to 'close' the story without any troubling loose ends. Such texts usually offer the reader a sense of aesthetic and thematic closure on completion of reading. Pictures and words appear 'naturally' integrated into a harmonious relationship. Lonsdale also claims that this kind of text usually has an 'implicit moral code which values sensible, courageous and unselfish behaviour in individuals, order in society, and innocence in children'. These texts assume that there is one truth rather than 'pluralistic truths', and are likely to offer children a secure world where they do not have to confront 'dissonant or disquieting juxtapositions and ruptures which challenge familiar understandings'. Judging from these attributes it is easy to see how such texts were perceived as suitable for promoting the development of initial literacy in younger readers.

By contrast, the postmodernist picture book inverts all these features. It celebrates diversity and 'relativity of viewpoint', resisting any closure or definitive meanings, with 'uncertainty, ambiguity and paradox . . . privileged over consistency and the unitary viewpoint' (p. 27). Supporting this analysis, Stephens and Watson (1994) and Watson (1996) claim that this kind of text is characterized by the breakdown of boundaries between high and popular culture, and by preferences for non-realistic representations and self-conscious narratives. Such texts often blur the boundaries between genres and worlds, and delight in imitating or 'quoting' past art to create a rich intertextual play of meanings. Following Waugh (1984), Stephens and Watson (1994, p. 53) also claim that these texts are absorbed in their own metafiction, that is, in drawing attention to, and commenting on, how the text has been constructed and the explicit 'nature of its fictiveness'. They see David Macaulay's *Black and White* (1990) as an exemplary instance of this interest, with its four narratives, multiple illustrative styles and teasing 'layering of different but similar fictions' (p. 44) that refuse any final closure. For Lonsdale, Kit Williams' *Ambrose the Beekeeper*, Jon Agee's *The Incredible Painting of Felix Clousseau*, David McKee's *I Hate My Teddy Bear*, and much of the work of Maurice Sendak and Anthony Browne are exemplars of this new kind of text. For instance, she notes that Williams' text is 'full of obscure illusions, weighty complex prose, and striking sensual pictures', where 'both text and illustrations defy rational explanation' (p. 27).

She also points out that all these writers tend to blur deliberately the boundaries 'between ontological worlds' (p. 28), where, for example, Felix Clousseau's painting of a duck, when displayed at the grand contest of Art in Paris, is mocked, until the moment the painting quacks, enabling the author to disrupt playfully notions of the real. She also notes that these texts often borrow eclectically from other cultures, historical periods and past graphic styles to create startlingly new meanings and surprising ideas, but often refusing to provide a closure or a neat coda or key for the text's overall meanings. Of course, this style of assemblage and pastiche is very familiar to most adolescents through their exposure to video clips of popular music and to various 'rule-breaking' humorous television programmes. However, as she notes of McKee's *I Hate My Teddy Bear,* while these texts might be clever, it is sometimes difficult to see any real point to them. Certainly many of these authors refuse to offer their readers, whether young or old, an educative lesson or an instructional moment, preferring to celebrate absurdities or imaginative freedom. Lonsdale recognizes that these authors might 'foreground the surreal and the aesthetic, intellectual conundrums, sociological concerns, pastiche and parody, and the excesses of language and art' (p. 35), but speculates that some of these texts may have lost their capacity to engage young readers in significant ways. She argues reasonably that young readers can still benefit from the vicarious working through of larger philosophical and metaphysical issues to do with life, death, fear, loneliness, love and friendship, the usual domain of the traditional picture book. Clearly a good literature programme would offer students a diversity of reading experiences that included both kinds of texts.

In focusing on the value of postmodern texts for a specifically secondary school readership, Stephens and Watson (1994) argue that the experimentation and rule-breaking of many contemporary postmodern picture books make them especially suitable resources for introducing students to some key concepts central to newer 'critical' literary and cultural theories. However, they also suggest that modernist texts can also be studied in terms of the ways they seek to hide their 'constructedness' and in their espousal of particular values. For instance, they suggest that a text such as David McKee's *Tusk, Tusk* (1978) could be studied to consider the degree to which its apparent theme of the importance of racial tolerance is consistent with a plot line that seems more about 'racial assimilation' (p. 22) than tolerance. In other words, they argue that picture books can be studied in class to explore the question of the potential for unity or indeterminacy and contradictions of meaning in texts that seem, at least on the surface, resolutely decisive or conclusive in their themes. In this way Stephens and Watson assert that picture books offer excellent scope for 'close reading', where students are expected to justify their particular viewpoint on an issue through precise textual or pictorial evidence. They also claim that postmodernist picture books contest the view that the 'true' or 'best' reading experience is one where a universal 'non-gendered' reader discovers unitary and universal meanings and values in any given text.

Stephens and Watson also believe that postmodernist texts 'teach' students about the constructedness of texts, because this element is so often highlighted by the author. They also seek to contest the idea that the 'best' texts are only those in which an author aims to offer a mirror of reality and to disguise the textual conventions by which this effect is achieved. Instead, they argue that factors like gender, social class, age and race inevitably affect how we read and the particular meanings we give texts. They imply that students should be made aware of these varied influences on their judgements, and to become, where appropriate, more tolerant of diversity of responses and values. At the same time, students are expected to recognize where an authorial or reader viewpoint, including their own, might be partial, biased, intolerant and possibly in need of modification.

Clearly this group of claims and agendas is easily recognizable as forming the basis of many recent accounts of 'critical literacy' (Buckingham, 1993; Turnbull, 1993), and evokes all the troubled advocacy and resistances that now seem to accompany any attempt to explain (or justify) English's purpose in these terms. While strongly supporting the value of much of this agenda I believe that this discussion about different types of (and approaches to) picture books should reiterate the point that the reading of texts, of whatever kind, can never be separated from the negotiation and espousal of specific values. These values may include the literary claims made for the text (its merit as 'literature' as part of a tradition, or as innovative), the claimed 'laudable' values of the author evident in the texts, as well as any claims made for the benefit of a particular approach to a text, in terms of the values and attitudes it might engender in all or a particular group of readers. For example, a text might be praised for its positive representation of a particular problem or sub-group. In this sense the development of students' literacy capacities is never merely the acquisition of neutral or functional skills or techniques (or the ability to recognize these skills in the texts of others), but rather the development of particular values about and through literacy practices. With this in mind I would like to turn now to a more extended discussion of a possible rationale to guide the use of picture books in secondary classrooms.

RATIONALES FOR READING PICTURE BOOKS IN SECONDARY ENGLISH

As suggested already, two broad rationales have been proposed recently for the study of picture books in secondary school. These are: first, that the study of this kind of text is justified as a culturally significant practice worthy of attention in its own right (Moss, 1992; Stephens, 1992; Vandergrift, 1990); and second, that the study of picture books can enhance 'reading skills', defined variously as technical or practical capacities in interpreting texts (Michaels and Walsh, 1990; Keck and Phillips, 1996), as part of new visual literacy (Keck and Phillips, 1996), the development of multiliteracies (New London Group, 1996), or as part of 'critical literacy' skills (Meek, 1995; Stephens and Watson, 1994).

Here I would like to consider in more detail the second rationale, but acknowledge that both rationales are often blended, in that knowledge about the traditions, structures and resources for meaning in this genre are inseparable from questions about effective or competent reading. The second rationale relates to claims that these texts are exemplary resources for developing broadly defined 'literacy skills'. 'Skills' in this context includes the acquisition of a set of value-free techniques for extracting apparent meanings from diverse texts, including ones that combine verbal and visual meanings. This view is evident in many national and state English curriculum documents, as, for example, in the expectation students in Victoria, Australia, should 'develop their understanding of the constructed nature of texts' by viewing and reading 'a wide range of novels, plays, films and poetry' (Board of Studies, 1995, p. 59).

However, for the New London Group (1996, p. 78) the notion of one single, standard national literacy should be replaced by the idea of 'multiliteracies'. This concept recognizes that new communication technologies and networks have resulted in a considerable expansion in multimodal forms of 'messaging', where there is 'an increasing complexity and inter-relationship' in the different modes that students are now expected to 'read' today as part of 'visual literacy'. These writers claim that if students are to become literate in a multimedia-saturated world that is no longer 'page-bound' (p. 61) then they will have to learn about and use various interlocking different 'designs' in new kinds of print and electronic texts. The group identifies six major areas of design that are important in these new patterns of meaning as follows: linguistic design, visual design, audio design, gestural design, spatial design and multimodal design (which represents connections between the other modes). While the writers draw heavily on their past use of systemic linguistics as the basis for understanding the patterns and choices in verbal meaning-making, they acknowledge that the means of analysing the other modes are as yet not fully developed. They note that visual meanings relate to the reading of 'images, page layouts and screen formats' (p. 80), and that gestural meaning relates to the interpretation of 'body language and sensuality' (p. 80). However, they admit that the frameworks for analysing the subtleties of each of the five modes and their intricate interconnection remains to be developed. They also argue that students need to develop a critical distance from texts so that they can read the social and cultural context in which designs are produced. In other words, students should learn how to stand back from what they are studying, viewing or producing, and consider critically its effects on themselves and others, to make judgements about the worth of the values texts offer. They admit that all their proposals are 'a tentative starting point' (p. 89) in making literacy education more effective in the future, because these multimodal patterns and links are yet to be identified.

In supporting this call for the development of student critical literacy in relation to multimodal forms of meaning, Stephens and Watson argue that students need to have an appropriate technical vocabulary for discussing the structural features and expressive possibilities of this genre. They need to be able to recognize the structural, formal, pictorial and linguistic options available to authors within this particular technology if they are to understand the innovations writers make and that they themselves can make in constructing their own and others' texts. For example, they suggest that students should understand the role of the 'peritext' (1994, p. 38), those elements of the book other than the story, including covers, endcovers, publishers' blurbs, epigraphs, layout, font type and book format if they are to understand the potential ways in which textual meanings can be confirmed, contested, undermined or consolidated by other elements. For example, in Anthony Browne's *Piggybook* (1986), as in most of his texts, the illustrations establish very precisely the particular social class of the family depicted, while the porcine motif in this book slyly undermines the verbal text. Illustrations can understate, contradict or underline verbal meaning. Students need to know that in Western culture (and traditional aesthetics in general) the left-hand side of the page is the customary starting point for the viewer's gaze, and that this convention may be challenged by the placement of important images in other positions, or by the denial of the viewer's gaze moving in a straightforward way from left to right across a page or double page. Of course, these surprise techniques are used in billboards and other kinds of advertising to grab the viewer's attention. Some texts, such as Maurice Sendak's *We are all in the Dumps with Jack and Guy* (1993), omit the title from the front cover of the book (as in television advertisements that refuse to offer the viewer a verbal or aural clue to their focus) to create a sense of suspense, disorder or abnormality. Students first need to be able to identify these particular features before considering authorial intentions and values in relation to any text.

Needless to say, a knowledge of these structural codes and patterns of texts should not be viewed as an end in itself, but rather related to other issues. If students are to achieve a critical literacy then analysis of further technical issues, such as point of view, reliability of the narrator, angle of vision from which illustrations are represented and style of representation (for example, photorealism or animated cartoon colours), should lead on to the identification of the explicit or implicit values of the text. Students should then consider the extent to which these technical resources are consistent with the espoused themes of the text. Stephens and Watson argue, as do many National Curriculum documents on English, that students should understand the values (and make defensible judgements about the worth of the values) implied in these texts and in their own texts. For example, they suggest that a comparative study of the illustrated representations of Cinderella in a variety of versions of that story, including Perrault and Grimm versions as well as Babette Cole's *Prince Cinders* (1987), can lead students to consider the female behaviour these versions consider to be 'appropriate' or 'natural', and the extent to which the students support or contest these representations.

CLASSROOM PRACTICES

Clearly the 'average' monocultural classroom of highly motivated students of mixed ability has become increasingly a rarity, and texts need to be chosen to match the interests and capacities of particular students in specific contexts. The following proposed texts are suggested only as indicative examples. However, two broad principles are worth noting from the outset.

First, *no text should be studied in isolation.* As with poems and short stories, students are likely to form much sharper impressions of the particular or distinctive features of a text if they can make comparisons with other texts. This is not simply a matter of examining multiple versions of the same story, although such a task is clearly ideally suited to the study of picture books. Comparisons can also effectively range over texts with similar themes, ideologies or perspectives despite quite contrasting illustrative styles, subject matter and diction. For example, students are far more likely to be able to characterize the distinctive features of one pacifist text, such as Roberto Innocenti's *Rose Blanche* (1985) if it is contrasted with, say, Junko Morimoto's *My Hiroshima* (1987). Picture books can also be compared with texts in other genres, such as newspaper reports, as well as television programmes and films in order to establish their particular conventions as well as themes.

Second, *multiple copies of texts should be provided.* As Stephens and Watson (1994, p. 2) comment, detailed group discussion of texts benefits from each group having ready access to a copy of the text. In practice, this means that five or six copies of texts are required, especially if students are expected to substantiate their viewpoints about the texts from specific textual evidence. Stephens and Watson suggest that if budgetary considerations limit the number of multiple copies to only three or four texts, then various texts by Anthony Browne, such as *Hansel and Gretel* (1981), *Piggybook* (1986) and *Changes* (1990), can form a useful basis for teaching junior secondary classes.

ACTIVITIES IN THE CLASSROOM

In order to cover briefly a range of practical classroom options, some focal issues are suggested in relation to three pairs of texts that could be used with students of different ages. These are not intended as exhaustive but rather to indicate some possible lines of approach and types of activities that could develop students' literacy skills. These suggestions could also be modified to suit other pairs of texts. It is assumed that some of the discussion points for younger students would be incorporated into work with older students.

Libby Hathorn, *Way Home* (1994) and
Maurice Sendak, *We are All in the Dumps with Jack and Guy* (1993)

Both texts focus on portraying the experiences and feelings of young homeless people. Hathorn's text is written and illustrated in a realistic style, with the text taking the form of a rap monologue by the main character, a teenager, whereas Sendak's text comprises two traditional rhymes from Mother Goose to represent the emotions and experiences of much younger homeless children. Sendak's text and illustrations are not presented within realistic conventions, but take the form of a disconnected narrative with a strong fantasy element.

With junior secondary students, discussion could focus on students' understanding of the differences and similarities in the texts in their depiction of the theme of homelessness, including a focus on technical or conventional differences in the styles of each book. Before reading either book, students could be asked about their understanding of what being homeless might feel like. Students in pairs, or through group discussion, could jot down a list of relevant words to characterize these feelings.

After reading the two texts the students could share their ideas about what feelings are depicted and the extent to which they match their predictions.

In reading *Way Home* discussion could focus on the following questions:

1 What ideas or feelings are conveyed by the design of the endpapers?
2 How does the visual effect of a ragged break between text and images on each page contribute to the mood or feeling of the story?
3 Why does Shane talk to himself so much? Why does he keep giving the cat different names? Why is the cat so important to him?
4 How do the pictures extend the written text? How do they influence your feelings about and understanding of the story?
5 The pictures show Shane from different angles. He is seen from a low angle, eye level and from above. How does this affect how you respond to his story?
6 Look at the illustrations in Hathorn's book with the words covered and write down your ideas on the story. What are the main visual clues to your interpretation?

In reading *We are All in the Dumps with Jack and Guy* discussion could focus on the following questions:

1   Where does the story take place and how do you know?
2   What are the main problems of the children throughout the story?
3   How do the moon's reactions change during the story? What role does the moon play both in the first half of the story and when it turns into a cat in the second half? How would you explain this?
4   How do the illustrations add to the text?

Comparative questions in relation to both texts could focus on the following issues:

1   What age group do you think each story is written for? How can you tell? If you cannot tell, why not? Do you think Sendak's book would make sense to younger readers? Why/why not?
2   Which text do you think gives you a stronger sense of what it feels like to be homeless? Explain your viewpoint.

With middle secondary students discussion could focus in a more extended way on what has been called 'emotional literacy', or the ability to recognize their own and characters' feelings. Students could be asked to explain in more detail their sense of the characters' feelings in each book and the basis of these feelings.
Further questions on Hathorn's book might include:

1   To what extent do you think this text is a believable account of the feelings and daily survival of a young homeless person? Explain your viewpoint. Do you think there are any gaps in this account? How would you explain these gaps?
2   How would you explain the choice of pictures that Shane has pinned up in his 'home' in the final illustration in the story?
3   Do you think this book has been written for homeless children to read, or to show what homelessness feels like to children who are not homeless? Explain your viewpoint.

Further questions on Sendak's book might include:

1   From whose point of view is the story told? How do you know?
2   What explanations do the pictures offer for the causes of homelessness? How persuasive do you find these explanations? Do you think these explanations would make sense to younger readers? Explain your viewpoint.
3   Sendak has also tried to make his subject strange and dreamlike, to make homelessness seem unfamiliar, as though seen from a new perspective. How has he used images and words to blend the strange and the recognizable aspects of modern city life?

Comparative questions might consider the following:

1   Which book do you think gets its message across more strongly about the suffering of homelessness? Explain.
2   Write a comparative review of each book, explaining the purpose and successes (or failures) of each.

For more able students, discussion could also include analysis of the use of intertextuality in each text; that is, the use of references from other texts and contexts to enrich the meaning of each story.

For example, why has the illustrator chosen to present two very recognizable images from Michelangelo's paintings in the Sistine Chapel as posters early in Hathorn's text, and to repeat one of these images on the final page? What is this reference intended to indicate about Shane's world, feelings and needs?

Why does Sendak 'quote' from some of his past books, such as the drawing on a 'wild thing' on a child's shirt early in the text? What associations from other literature or contexts do the 'house of cards' have in Sendak's text? At the end of this text the moon is represented more naturalistically, and most of the characters are sleeping peacefully. How does the author use associations readers already have about the moon prior to reading the text?

Gary Crew, *First Light* (1993) and *The Watertower* (1994)

Both texts focus mainly on boys' experiences, and are therefore unusual in terms of the general themes of picture books. Both are illustrated in realistic styles, although *The Watertower* is illustrated in a style of heightened realism sometimes associated with science fiction films. It could also be considered a postmodern picture book in that there are many unsolved problems and 'clues' in the illustrations and in that the plot is not resolved at the end of the text. By contrast, *First Light* is about the uneasy relationship between a father and his son.

With junior secondary students discussion could focus on understanding the stylistic similarities and differences in the texts in their depiction of the main characters' feelings.

In reading *First Light* discussion could focus on the following questions:

1 How would you describe Davey's and his father's character at the start of the story?
2 In what ways do the first five illustrations in the text add to our understanding of Davey's feelings about the fishing trip with his father?
3 In what ways have Davey's feelings changed about his father by the end of the story? How would you explain this? How would you describe their relationship at the end of the text? How is this shown by the illustrations?

In reading *The Watertower* discussion could focus on the following questions:

1 Where does this story take place and how do you know?
2 Why do you think the illustrator has included a spiral pattern in the first few pages of the text? What effect is achieved by having the text on each page laid out at right angles to the cover?
3 How does the author build suspense throughout the story? What effect is achieved by the extreme close-up illustration of Spike's face?
4 The story presents many unanswered questions. What happened to Bubba's underpants? What moved on top of the tower? In what ways has Bubba changed? What is the purpose of the watertower?
5 How do the illustrations in the second half of the text add to the sense of mystery?

For older students discussion of *First Light* could focus on the following issues:

1   Some of the illustrations are presented from a viewpoint below water level. How is this relevant to presenting Davey's feelings, his sense of the outer world and his sense of his own feelings 'below the surface'?
2   Each of the illustrations is presented in a 'frame'. What effect does this have on the mood of the story?
3   Do you think the story outcome is believable? Explain your viewpoint.

For older students discussion of *The Watertower* could focus on the following issues:

1   A standard theme of science fiction is the invasion of aliens who recruit locals to their side through devious processes. In what ways does this story suggest it is recycling this theme?
2   This picture book attempts to break some of the usual rules associated with stories and traditional pictorial layout. What examples of rule-breaking can you identify? Do you think this rule-breaking weakens or increases the story's appeal for you? Explain your viewpoint. This text could be compared with David Weisner's *June 29, 1999* (1992).

Comparative questions might include the following:

1   Which of these two stories do you consider more convincing? Which is more enjoyable? Explain your viewpoint.
2   How are the two books similar in their depiction of male qualities? How might the stories be different if the gender of the main characters was changed?
3   Write a picture book for younger readers that breaks as many rules as you can about story expectations and pictorial layout. Are there any rules that cannot be broken and the story still be readable?

Roberto Innoceni, *Rose Blanche (1985)* and Jane Yolen, *Encounter* (1992)
These two texts are concerned with the persecution of racial groups. Yolen wrote her text as a counter-story to the celebration of Christopher Columbus's 'discovery' of the 'New World'. Innocenti's book presents a child's response to the persecution of Jews by the Nazis in the Second World War.

For junior secondary students' discussion of *Rose Blanche* could focus on the following issues:

1   Before reading the book, the class should discuss their knowledge about the persecution of the Jews during the Second World War.
2   In reading the book, consider how the illustrations convey the impression that they are reporting true past events. What mood is created by the illustrations?
3   What impression is created of the mayor?
4   What does *Rose Blanche* achieve? Explain your viewpoint.

In dealing with *Encounter* the following issues could be addressed:

1   Before reading the book, the class should discuss their knowledge of European settlement of the Americas, and consider such points as: Why was the New World settled? What reasons were given for this settlement? Why were the explorers considered to be heroes? What happened to local populations?
2   During the reading the following questions could be discussed:
    a. What does the Indian boy feel about the newcomers?
    b. How do the illustrations make clear his feelings of awe, fear and suspicion? Why are the pictures sometimes presented out of focus?
    c. How do the illustrations try to convince the reader that the story is historically true?
    d. How does the reader view the Europeans after reading the story? How does the writer make us care about the Indian boy's point of view?
    e. What is the main message of the book in terms of how different cultures should be treated?

Questions for older students might be:

1   In what ways are both books similar in terms of the main character's feelings in terms of a sense of displacement or alienation?
2   How do both books try to influence our views of the past? Which do you think is more successful? Explain your viewpoint.
3   Compare the text of *Rose Blanche* with the more detailed version by Ian McEwan (London: Random House, 1985). Which text do you think is more effective in involving the reader in the story?

CONCLUSIONS

In this chapter I have argued that there is a strong case for the study of picture books in secondary English, both as texts in their own right and as resources for the development of visual and critical literacy skills. Many texts in this category are of sufficient complexity to warrant careful student analysis at this level, and, as many teachers have discovered, these texts also have high appeal for students across the ability range. While the proposed focal questions on specific texts in the latter part of this chapter represent only some indicative ways to address visual and critical literacy issues, these questions suggest that picture books have considerable potential in developing students' interpretive skills in mastering the new and emerging forms of literacy.

RECOMMENDED PICTURE BOOKS

Browne, A. (1981) *Hansel and Gretel*. London: Walker Books.
Browne, A. (1986) *Piggybook*. London: Walker Books.
Browne, A. (1990) *Changes*. London: Walker Books.

Browne, A. (1992) *Zoo.* London: Walker Books.

Briggs, R. (1982) *When the Wind Blows.* London: Hamish Hamilton.

Cole, B. (1987) *Prince Cinders.* London: Hamish Hamilton.

Crew, G. (1993) *First Light.* Melbourne: Lothian.

Crew, G. (1994) *The Watertower.* Flinders Park, South Australia: Era Publications.

Fox, M. (1989) *Feathers and Fools.* Adelaide: Ashwood House.

French, F. (1986) *Snow White in New York.* Oxford: Oxford University Press.

Hathorn, L. (1993)*Way Home.* Sydney: Random House.

Innocenti, R. (1985) *Rose Blanche.* Mankato, MN: Creative Education.

Macaulay, D. (1990) *Black and White.* New York: Houghton Mifflin.

McKee, D. (1978) *Tusk, Tusk.* London: Andersen Press.

Morimoto, J. (1987) *My Hiroshima.* Sydney: Angus & Robertson.

Sendak, M. (1993) *We are All in the Dumps with Jack and Guy.* New York: HarperCollins.

Scieszka, J. (1992) *The Stinky Cheeseman and Other Fairly Stupid Tales.* Harmondsworth: Penguin.

Van Allsburg, C. (1995) *Just a Dream.* New York: Houghton Mifflin.

Wagner, J. (1977) *John Brown, Rose and the Midnight Cat.* Harmondsworth: Penguin.

Weisner, D. (1992) *June 29, 1999.* New York: Houghton Mifflin.

Yolen, J. (1992) *Encounter.* New York: Harcourt Brace Jovanovitch.

SECONDARY REFERENCES

Board of Studies (1995) *Curriculum Standards Framework: English.* Carlton, Victoria: Board of Studies.

Bradford, C. (1993) The picture book: some postmodern tensions. *Papers.* Burwood, Victoria: Centre for Research in Cultural Communications, Deakin University.

Buckingham, D. (1993) Going critical: the limits of media literacy. *Australian Journal of Education* **37** (2), 143–52.

Green, B. (1997) Teaching for difference: learning theory and post-critical pedagogy. In D. Buckingham (ed.) *Teaching Popular Culture: Beyond Radical Pedagogy.* London: Taylor & Francis.

Hinkson, J. (1991) *Postmodernity: State and Education.* Geelong, Victoria: Deakin University.

Keck, K. and Phillips, D. (1996) *Picture Books Supporting the Visual Arts and English.* Dromkeen,Victoria: Ashton Scholastic.

Kress, G. (1995) *Writing the Future: English and the Making of a Culture of Innovation.* Sheffield: National Association for the Teaching of English.

Lemke, J. (1996) Media literacy: transforming meanings and media. In D. Reinking *et al.* (eds) *Literacy for the 21st Century: Technological Transformation in a Post-Typographical World.* London: Erlbaum.

Lonsdale, M. (1993) Postmodernism and the picture book. *English in Australia,* No. 103, 25–35.

McHale, B. (1987) *Postmodern Fiction.* Methuen: New York.

Meek, M. (1995) The critical challenge of the world in books for children. *Children's Literature in Education* **26** (1), 15–23.

Michaels, W. and Walsh, M. (1990) *Up and Away: Using Picture Books.* Melbourne: Oxford University Press.

Monteith, M. (ed.) (1993) *Computers and Language.* Oxford: Intellect Books.

Moss, G. (1992) Metafiction, illustration, and the poetics of children's literature. In P. Hunt (ed.) *Literature for Children*. London and New York: Routledge.

New London Group (1996) A pedagogy for mulitliteracies: designing social futures. *Harvard Educational Review* **66** (1), 60–92.

Stephens, J. (1992) *Language and Ideology in Children's Fiction*. Harlow: Longman.

Stephens, J. and Watson, K. (eds) (1994) *From Picture Book to Literary Theory*. Sydney: St Clair Press.

Tuman, M. (1992) *Word Perfect: Literacy in the Computer Age*. London: Falmer Press.

Turnbull, S. (1993) The media: moral lessons and moral careers. *Australian Journal of Education* **3** (72), 153–68.

Tweddle, S. *et al.* (eds) (1997) *English for Tomorrow*. Buckingham: Open University Press.

Vandergrift, K. (1990) *Children's Literature: Theory, Research and Teaching*. Englewood, CO: Libraries Unlimited.

Watson, K. (ed.) (1996) *Word and Image*. Sydney: St Clair Press.

Waugh, P. (1984*) Metafiction: The Theory and Practice of Self-Conscious Fiction*. London and New York: Methuen.

Wexler, P. (1990) Citizenship in the semiotic society. In Bryan S. Turner (ed.), *Theories of Modernity and Postmodernity*. London: Sage.

Chapter 6

Inside the Literature Curriculum

Don Zancanella

The 1980s and 1990s have been a tumultuous period for the school subject of literature. During the past fifteen years almost every facet of literature instruction has been attacked, defended, revised and reconsidered. Among the most intense debates have been those focused on instructional methods (traditional text-centred practices versus reader-oriented practices); on the content of the curriculum (canonical texts versus selections reflecting more diversity of culture and gender); on the control of the curriculum (local control versus control by way of state/national standards and tests); and on the role of literature in the curriculum (the subject of English as literature-centred versus the subject of English as literacy-centred). This reconsideration of literature instruction has been wide ranging and, in some cases, highly public. Literature education has been the subject of best-selling books such as Allan Bloom's *The Closing of the American Mind* (1987) and of editorials and news stories in prominent, widely read newspapers and magazines (the many editorials in British newspapers on the role of Shakespeare in the National Curriculum and the many news magazine reports in the USA about the revision of the Stanford Western Civilization course being two of the more noteworthy cases).

While these debates have been many things – thought-provoking, entertaining, maddening – one thing they have seldom been *is grounded in the day-to-day life of students, teachers and schools*. This shortcoming has meant that discussions of literature education have been pushed in some unproductive directions. Not only have the Western canon and multicultural literature been cast as opposites, but policy-makers and the public have been led to believe that change can be easily imposed on schools and teachers because the day-to-day life of schools is simply not very nuanced or complex. However, as those who have spent time in schools know, complexity and nuance are among the defining characteristics of how literature instruction is shaped at particular school sites. As Freebody *et al.* (1991) put it:

> Untangling the complex patterns of influence on what come to count as literacy and literature in schools is difficult, for unlike the compilation of an authoritative anthology by, for instance, the editorial board of a university press, the selection of school texts and competencies is not a singular decision undertaken by a particular group of teachers,

curriculum consultants, nor by state or provincial governments, schools boards, or publishers. Rather, such decisions are embroidered into the complex politics of curriculum and schooling.

(p. 437)

This chapter attempts to unravel some of the curricular embroidery Freebody and his colleagues refer to by describing in detail the teaching of literature in one school, with particular attention to how some of the recent debates about literature education have played out in this school at this point in history. As such, this study is what Goodson and Ball (1984) call a curricular ethnography – the goal of which, in their words, is to 'provide insights into those factors which mediate between the "espoused" and the "enacted" curriculum as well as emphasizing the realization and experience of the different contents and forms of subject knowledge in the classroom' (p. 91). Based on interviews and observations conducted from 1992 to 1995, this account attempts to map literature as it exists as part of the English curriculum in a single school by drawing on the perspectives of students, teachers, administrators and community members. In what follows, I begin by describing the school, one particular English course in the school, and the context surrounding the course's creation and continuing existence.

CANYON HIGH SCHOOL AND THE 'SOUTHWEST LITERATURE AND CREATIVE WRITING' COURSE

Canyon High School (a fictitious name) is a school of approximately six hundred students in a small town in New Mexico in the southwestern portion of the USA. Located near a larger town and near a large government installation that employs many of the people who live in the town of Canyon, the school serves a population comprised of students from three ethnic/cultural groups – Hispanic students from the town itself, Anglo students who live on the south and west edges of the large town nearby, and Pueblo Indian students who live a few miles to the north. (I should note that the terms I am using to describe ethnicity – *Hispanic* as opposed to *Chicano* for instance – are the terms most frequently used by the participants.) Each of these groups contributes approximately one-third of the school's population. The school stands next to a highway on the outskirts of town and has a rural feeling about it. In fact, people tend to refer to where they live not so much by using the name of the town, but rather by naming the larger area in which the town and school are located, an area they simply refer to as 'the valley'.

Among the courses offered as part of the English curriculum at Canyon High is Southwest Literature and Creative Writing. The specificity of the course title may seem unusual and, indeed, the course is somewhat of an anomaly in the school, but both the course and its title are very clearly a product of the school's recent history. If one were to visit Canyon High School and ask about the origin of this course, the ready response would be that its teacher (I will refer to him as Mr G) invented it. That explanation would have a good deal of truth to it, but the story is considerably more complex. While material describing the course is woven throughout the remainder of this chapter, it may be useful to begin with a brief overview.

THE NATURE OF THE COURSE

Southwest Literature and Creative Writing is a year-long course open to sophomores, juniors or seniors. It fulfils the regular English requirement for whatever year students enrol in it. Mr G, a Hispanic 38-year-old who grew up in a small town in the same part of the state as Canyon, teaches two sections of the course, each of which typically enrols between 20 and 25 students. The content of the course consists of reading, discussing and writing about literature from the Southwest, mostly by Hispanic and Native American authors such as Rudolpho Anaya, Jimmy Santiago Baca, Denise Chavez and Leslie Silko, and a large amount of writing which tends to take the form of personal narratives, poetry, and, occasionally, fiction. The readings come from a variety of sources – mass market paperbacks, small press paperbacks, and selections gleaned from more traditional school textbook anthologies.

Mr G's customary way of working is to ask students to read a story, poem or memoir, engage students in small group discussion about the piece, and then encourage students to write pieces similar to the ones they have read. The small group discussions are typically guided by lists of discussion questions that invite students to make connections between the literature and their own experience. For example, one day, while students were in the midst of reading Anaya's *Bless Me Ultima* (a coming-of-age novel set in northern New Mexico) Mr G distributed one copy of the following set of questions to each of five groups:

> Older people, figures who represent wisdom and knowledge, play an important role in Anaya's novels. Anaya says in the Hispanic culture a great deal of respect is given to older people. Do you agree or disagree with this statement? Is it important and of value to listen to the old ones, the more experienced? Why or why not? Do all cultures place emphasis on the importance of the elders or is it your experience that some cultures do more than others? Discuss a learning experience you've had with an older person.

Later on during the study of the same novel, Mr G read an excerpt from an interview with Anaya in which the author discusses the autobiographical roots of his book. When he had finished reading he said, 'Over the next few days, we're going to be looking back into our own childhoods and seeing what stories we might write from those experiences, just as Anaya does in his work.' On another occasion, Mr G used an autobiographical essay by Gary Soto about an after-school job to prompt student writing about their own work experiences.

When asked about this pattern of teaching, Mr G was quite explicit about its purpose:

> I want them to see that they have things to write about. Most of the authors we read have backgrounds very similar to theirs and that's evident in the literature itself. So it shows the students that they have something to say.

On another occasion he said:

I want them to have some sense that the world of books and of people in books has something to do with them. I don't think a lot of kids really feel that very clearly or deeply.

Both my interviews with Mr G and my observations of the class showed that the course had two relatively consistent emphases. The first was reading texts that matched the cultural background of the students in school more closely than the traditional canonical works taught in other English classes in the school and other schools in the region. The second was writing in forms similar to those found in the readings – poetry, personal essays, short fiction – rather than in more traditional school forms such as the literary essay.

Given the tradition of autonomy in the English curriculum, it may be tempting at this point to simply view Mr G's course and its particular emphases as idiosyncratic. However, one of the most striking shortcomings in educational curriculum and policy studies is the failure to link local particulars with broader trends and issues. In some sense *all* classrooms are idiosyncratic in that they are the product of the vision of a particular teacher working with particular students in a particular situation. What needs further exploration is how the local, the personal and the specific are linked to the wider social and political environment. In the next sections, the Southwest Literature and Creative Writing course is viewed from a variety of perspectives, each of which provides a partial explanation of why the class exists and what it means in this school context.

The internal history of the class

The Southwest Literature and Creative Writing course has been in existence for three years. However, it originally carried the title 'Hispanic-American Literature and Creative Writing.' In the first two years of the class, Mr G included only Hispanic-American authors (his term) and there was some emphasis on work in Spanish. For example, on one day I visited during those first two years, students were listening to *corridos* (ballads) from some old 45 r.p.m. records Mr G had found in his mother's garage, as well as reading a *corrido* ('The Ballad of Gregorio Cortez'), all in Spanish. Spanish ability in the class ranged from two or three students who were fluent to two or three who understood no Spanish (for whom translations were provided), with the majority falling in between. After listening to the songs and reading 'The Ballad of Gregorio Cortez', Mr G led a discussion of the characteristics of *corridos*, asking students what they noticed about the poetic form and what sort of events appeared to be typically chosen as subject matter for these songs. Students then wrote their own *corridos*, some choosing to write in Spanish and some in English. By the end of the class period, students had begun writing songs about contemporary figures such as HIV-positive basketball player Magic Johnson and Rodney King (whose beating triggered the 1992 Los Angeles riots), having learned that *corridos* typically focus on larger-than-life figures and tend towards the tragic. The following day they returned to class with their completed songs and read them aloud to one another, with a few students improvising melodies to accompany their words.

Later, when I spoke to Mr G about the *corrido* lesson, I was surprised to find him dissatisfied. This was because he had noticed that the Hispanic students (approximately one-third of the class) had responded to the lesson with more enthusiasm and thoroughness than the Pueblo and Anglo students had.

'I've been thinking about this all year', he said. 'It really doesn't make sense to have a class on just Hispanic literature when you look at our school. It leaves too many people out.'

I returned the following autumn to find he had changed the course to Southwest Literature and Creative Writing. To his reading list he had added Native American authors such as Silko and Momaday, and Anglo authors of the Southwest such as Edward Abbey and John Nichols, a change he was pleased with partly because he had had some difficulty finding a sufficient number of works by Hispanic authors of the American Southwest published in editions that were available, affordable and accessible to his students. Along with the change in readings came a gradual shift away from work in Spanish, although he continued to include some, such as his *corrido* lesson.

The course had originated in Mr G's own growing dissatisfaction with what he perceived as the ethnic and cultural narrowness of the English curriculum at his school. His first effort, Hispanic-American Literature and Creative Writing, had been a straightforward attempt to draw on aspects of himself – his own ethnic heritage and his passion for writing – as a means of combating that narrowness. The revision, after two years, occurred because he believed he hadn't adequately taken into account the characteristics of the students he was teaching.

The history of the course within the school

Mr G was allowed to create this course because of two events in recent school history. First, the English department was in the process of shifting to an 'elective' system (defined at Canyon High as a curriculum in which students can choose from a menu of one-semester English courses rather than requiring all students to take particular courses such as 'English 11' at particular grades) because members of the department felt that no one was teaching enough writing but that they *would* teach writing if only they could teach it in conjunction with content they personally enjoyed and valued. Thus, one teacher created a mythology course and another a short story course, and so on. Second, and shortly after that, the school became a 'Re:Learning' school – that is, a member of the Coalition of Essential Schools movement (Sizer, 1984), a high-profile school reform effort that was being strongly supported by the state department of education in New Mexico. Becoming part of the Re:Learning Network was interpreted by the principal not as reform towards any specific end, but more as simply a mandate for change. Consequently, when Mr G asked if he could create his course, the English department chair and the other teachers in the department were supportive because his idea fitted into the new elective system and the principal was supportive because he had adopted a general stance of encouraging innovation.

Thus Mr G's personal reform agenda (diversify the literature curriculum) converged with the reform agenda of the English department (teach more writing), which in turn converged with the school and state department of education reform agendas (encourage school-based, teacher-driven innovation). While this conjunction of agendas might seem serendipitous for Mr G, as the following section shows, other forces in the school were less supportive of his course.

The course and English department politics

The shift in the English department's curricular structure and in the school's attitude towards innovation created an opening that allowed Mr G to go around some obstacles he probably would not have been able to go over or through – namely, the majority of the department, including the chair, who remained, for the most part, committed to an English curriculum that focused on canonical works of literature and traditional modes of discourse. For example, the chair of the department teaches a course titled simply 'American Literature' which is essentially her old eleventh-grade English class retitled for the elective system. Students read works by authors such as Thoreau, Hawthorne, Twain and Fitzgerald, and write in-class essays. They also spend a good deal of time on preparation for college admissions tests. When asked about the relationship between student needs and the curriculum, the department chair said, 'I look at their needs almost entirely in terms of what can better prepare them for after they get out of school. What can they use in their life. Especially, what can they use in post-secondary education.' On another occasion, in describing her approach to teaching writing, she said:

> Knowing that most students are going to have to have some kind of post-secondary instruction, whatever they decide to do – they're going to have to be able to do at least short research papers – so they're going to have to be able to do that correctly. They should be able to write an opinion paper. And they need a sound vocabulary. In fact, they need a good vocabulary to do well at all on SATs or ACTs. Those are some of our department's aims.

(It is important to note that I am using the chair as a representative for views that were held throughout most of the department. This was not a case of two individuals having differing opinions but rather of one teacher having different views from the majority of the department in which he taught.)

Where does Mr G fit into this? While one reason given for the institution of the elective system was to promote the teaching of writing, another reason, according to several teachers in the department, was to defuse disagreements about the kinds of literature that ought to be taught, how language skills should be taught, and which discourse forms should be emphasized. Mr G and the department chair (who is also Hispanic) represent the poles of this discussion. The department chair favoured teaching canonical works of literature, the writing of traditional literary essays, and a drill-and-practice approach to the teaching of language, while Mr G favoured the teaching of non-canonical works, writing in personal and literary forms, and teaching language as part of the process of reading and writing. They also had different feelings about the role students' languages and cultures should play in the curriculum. When I asked the chair about the use of Spanish in English classes she said:

> We need to emphasize English, not bilingualism. I suppose I bring my culture to class with me to any class I teach, whether it's a literature class or composition class, because I am Hispanic and that's my point of reference. But I see a great need, especially among minorities, to really work on English skills.

Mr G's course, on the other hand, was the only course to emerge from the new elective structure that explicitly (or even implicitly) attempted to respond to the cultural and linguistic diversity of the school and community. While the climate of change certainly helped him find support for the course he wanted to create with the administration, it may be that the support of the rest of the English department was similar to the process of 'mentioning' Tyson-Bernstein (1988) describes in her analysis of American textbooks. That is, new, potentially controversial issues and information are 'mentioned' – included in the curriculum in limited, compartmentalized ways and not developed in depth. Thus schools (or, in this case, the department) can argue that the diverse needs of students are being met despite the fact that the curriculum change is highly circumscribed.

The role of textbooks in the curriculum

A fourth perspective relates to the role of textbooks and other materials in shaping the course. In the first year of the course, Mr G discovered that many of the authors he wished to have students read were not on the state-approved book list and, consequently, were not available through the standard textbook distribution system. Furthermore, while some of the other newly created electives matched up nicely with anthologies and publisher packages on the market (mythology is an example), he would have to buy multiple volumes, many of which were published by rather obscure small presses. (When I would visit Mr G's classroom in my capacity as a researcher, he never failed to have some question related to a book's availability. For example, one day he said he had heard that Sandra Cisneross *The House on Mango Street* was being republished by a major publishing house and asked me if I knew who that publisher was). As the class evolved, he was able to collect a few copies of this title and a few of that title. But then, after the first year of the course, he discovered a new anthology, published by Houghton Mifflin, titled simply *Mexican American Literature*. He ordered a class set, but, as he later reported, the single, concentrated focus of the anthology actually contributed to his interest in broadening the course to 'Southwest Literature'. He said:

> Having this big fat anthology reminded me, in a way that the little paperbacks didn't, that there ought to be literature by lots of different groups. And it could still speak to our kids about who they are and where they live.

Yet another twist in the text problem occurred with the change to Southwest Literature because the school did have a class set of John Nichols' novel, *The Milagro Bean Field War*. He used it, but later had second thoughts because it's such a long novel that it tended to dominate a good part of the semester in which students read it. He was concerned that, after his careful shaping of the class to include Hispanic and Native American volces, an author who is neither had become the centrepiece.

In this era of large chain bookstores, huge multinational publishing conglomerates and electronic media that can allow people on opposite sides of the globe to communicate instantaneously, it is easy to think that problems related to the accessibility of texts must be a thing of the past. Surely a motivated teacher must be able to get copies of any book under the sun for his or her students to read? In Mr G's case, however, limited access to the texts he wished to use was a significant obstacle. The problem was threefold: obtaining the books he wanted through the existing school bureaucracy; knowing what books existed that might fit his curricular framework (he was an eager reader but many small presses of the kind that typically publish Hispanic or Native American authors do not have the resources to advertise or distribute their books widely or to get them reviewed); and the simple shortage of appropriate titles. A common tradition in the teaching of literature is using an existing body of literature as the starting point for creating a course. To some extent, his vision of what he wanted to teach ran ahead of the literature available to help him realize that vision.

A biographical perspective

Another useful way to view the creation of the course is through the lens of Mr G's and the department chair's personal and professional biographies. Mr G grew up in northern New Mexico and had aspirations to be a journalist. After two years at a small college not far from his home town, he went away to a large state university. There he spent a single semester feeling so isolated and out of place that he decided to return to the small college and become a teacher so that he could live and work in the region he knew best. He views the time he spent at the large university as a watershed experience and describes it this way:

> The university was so huge. It was the first time in my life I got depressed. I was a kid from a small town and I was lonely. I remember working at night for campus security and getting home at midnight. There were masses of people, but it was just a sea of faces.

What this has to do with the Southwest Literature and Creative Writing course is that a very strong strand in it – almost its central goal – is to help students appreciate and understand their home communities and develop self-esteem and confidence about themselves as readers and writers, but not for the purpose of preparing students to leave for the big world beyond the valley. This contrasts dramatically with the department chair. Like Mr G, she grew up in northern New Mexico. However, she went away to college, married, and then spent a number of years teaching in Los Angeles. One of her primary goals is, as has already been demonstrated, preparing students for post-secondary education. In one of our interviews she said:

> The valley is a very traditional Hispanic community – there are Indian influences, but mostly Catholic/Hispanic. They [the students] see the valley as their home and it will always be their home, but that's naive because the jobs aren't here and the valley is changing and they need to be prepared for more than just what's here.

The life experiences of Mr G and the department chair have led them toward substantially different views about the purpose of high school English. Mr G believes that, while some students will leave the valley, part of his job is to prepare them to stay. However, he also believes that what he is teaching provides a broad foundation that will serve those students who go on to higher education as well. During one interview, he told about meeting a former student at an ice cream stand and being pleased when the student told him she was doing well in freshman English at college, success which she attributed to what she learned in his class. About the encounter, he said, 'I think I'm teaching them to be readers and writers and I think that's what they really need. The finer points, maybe they'll need them if they want to be English majors, but there aren't many of those.' When I asked him what he meant by 'the finer points', he spoke of 'writing an essay about Hamlet or something like that'.

THE STUDENTS' PERSPECTIVE

Since the move to the elective system, the students can choose the English courses they want to take and they approve of that. Many choices are made on the basis of what classes friends are taking and on the basis of personal feelings about teachers. However, the department chair reported that 'college-bound kids tend to congregate in certain courses – they more or less track themselves'. That appears to be true. For example, comparing the American Literature course taught by the chair to the Southwest Literature course, the students in the former course are more likely to be enrolled in advanced maths and science courses than those in the Southwest Literature and Creative Writing course. A majority of the Anglo students, many of whom come from upper-middle-class families in the large town nearby, have a strong tendency to choose the American Literature course. It is difficult to tell the extent to which this tracking was anticipated as part of the institution of the new elective curriculum.

Interestingly, this appears to be an instance where the usual research findings about tracking – that classes filled with college-bound students tend to be challenging and engaging while classes for the non-college-bound tend to be mind-numbing and repetitious – is contradicted. The perception in this particular school is that college-bound students need to write in particular forms (the 'five-paragraph essay' being the most common) and, as the chair's remarks in the earlier sections suggested, do a good deal of test preparation, most of which should focus on improving students' vocabularies. In fact, preparation for college admissions exams occupies a significant amount of time in the department chair's American Literature course – on average, about one day a week – with most of this instruction taking the form of worksheets and drill-and-practice activities. Thus Mr G's Southwest Literature and Creative Writing course, populated primarily by students who do not intend to go on to college, tends to include more various and extensive writing experiences and more engaged discussion of texts than the department chair's American Literature offering.

From the perspective of students (and their parents) it's not surprising that a class called 'American Literature', whether it is part of the old 'four-years-of-required-English' structure or part of the new elective structure, would look more respectable, serious and essential than a course called 'Southwest Literature and Creative Writing'. Mr G's title, on the other hand, tells students that his course is about their home region and that they should expect to write in wide-ranging and self-expressive forms – both, perhaps, invitations to students who have felt themselves to be ill-fitted to the expectations and teaching methods found in more traditional English courses. Thus, even by themselves, the titles of these offerings carry clear messages about how they are positioned in relation to student needs, the perception of teachers, parents and community members beyond the English department, and the traditions of the English curriculum.

CONCLUSIONS

From the outside, the creation and evolution of the Southwest Literature and Creative Writing course may seem like one more example of the debate about which texts to teach – the so-called 'canon debate'. However, perhaps the most interesting thing about it is that several other issues operating below the surface are the real engines of controversy and change, so much so that it might be said that the canon debate is merely a sideshow.

One important thread that runs through Mr G's remarks as well as remarks made by the department chair is the role of the English class in preparing students for life beyond secondary school. Mr G believes it is possible to build literacy that will be useful in the adult world by matching reading and writing experiences to student life experiences. Other members of his department, however, typically attempt to match the reading and writing experiences they offer to what they perceive to be the literacy tasks required by the next level of the educational system. In the case of literature, this means that those teachers teaching canonical works appear to be doing so largely because they believe reading Hawthorne will better prepare students for college than will reading Anaya.

One way to view this difference of approach is through the lens constructed by Appleyard (1990), in his book about the development of readers of literature. Appleyard posits five stages through which he believes readers pass as they mature (p. 122). Stage Four, 'The Reader as Interpreter', is 'the reader who studies literature systematically, typically the college English major or graduate student or teacher', while Stage Five, 'The Pragmatic Reader', is 'the adult reader' who 'consciously and pragmatically' chooses from among all the ways of reading available (for escape, for wisdom about life, for analysis, etc.). The department chair, it appears, wishes to move students directly into Stage Four while Mr G, assuming that few students will become English majors or English teachers, is attempting to move students to Stage Five, helping them to use reading in more diverse ways. For Appleyard, this is a 'split' in the developmental path of readers (p. 122) and in this school we have Mr G taking one fork of the path and other teachers taking the other.

It would be difficult to overstate the importance teachers other than Mr G placed on the expectations they believed to be held by college English programmes. Throughout my interviews, I got the strong feeling that most of the teachers would abandon Hawthorne for Anaya if a large university or two would assure them that to do so was an acceptable course of action. In my entire three years of visits, I heard no talk about the importance of the great books as civilizing or humanizing influences, about 'cultural literacy' or about the importance of tradition. It may be that teachers are simply used to responding to parents and other outsiders in utilitarian terms and therefore they gave me more of the same, but if so, it was a continuous and uniform façade. On the other hand, it may also be that the canon debate is a convenient stand-in for more fundamental disagreements about what students need to know and be able to do. Mr G tended to focus on those students who were likely to stay in the local area and thought they would need to be broadly and flexibly literate to succeed in the job market or perhaps community college. Most other teachers tended to focus on students leaving for higher education and thought they would need knowledge of the authors and texts and interpretative approaches they remembered as important in their own college course work.

A second important thread is the way in which literature instruction is intertwined with writing instruction. Indeed the impetus for the change to the elective programme, which from the outside looks literature-driven, was in fact driven by writing instruction. For Mr G, this shift involved moving writing more to the foreground, as suggested by the title of his course, as well as emphasizing different kinds of writing – primarily personal essays, poetry and fiction – than the kinds he'd emphasized in the past. For most other teachers, however, more writing meant more writing about literature. Interestingly, Mr G's experimentation with the writing curriculum made other teachers more uncomfortable than his reading selections. In interviews, teachers were more likely to make negative remarks about 'Creative Writing' and its validity than they were about 'Southwest Literature'. And while most department members could provide only a vague defence for the literature they taught, their defence of the kinds of writing they asked students to do was clear and unequivocal. Success in college required the ability to write formal essays and so that was where the emphasis in the high school curriculum should clearly lie.

What lessons can we take from the story of Mr G and the Southwest Literature and Creative Writing course? At first glance, it may appear that most of what can be learned should be directed towards policy-makers. For example, this case suggests that curriculum standardization of the kind currently in place in the UK and being widely promoted in the USA (see Hirsch, 1996 for one example) will endanger locally invented curricula of the kind found in Mr G's room. This is not a new finding but it is one that deserves repeated restating because those with the most power to influence curricula – the state, test makers, textbook publishers – seem most sanguine about the positive benefits resulting from standardization. However, this case also has implications for individual teachers and schools. Perhaps the most compelling is Mr G's crafting of a curriculum whose primary focus is not on college entrance exams but instead focuses on leading students towards the kinds of rich, constructive literacy currently being called for in such documents as the *Standards for the English Language Arts* (1996) created by the National Council of Teachers of English and the International Reading Association. It would be interesting to see a school in which local literature formed at least one part of English for all students, perhaps as a stage in a curriculum that moved from local literature to national literatures to world literatures (or vice versa).

A second lesson from Mr G's course is that culture matters in English class and that an open, enquiring multiculturalism need not lead to the 'tribalism' many conservative critics warn against. One of the striking things about the evolution of the Southwest Literature and Creative Writing course was the way in which Mr G was constantly reshaping it, adding texts, revising assignments, changing the focus, all in the interest of making the work more inclusive and more connected to students' lives. One example of this is a unit he added during its third year focusing on 'work and jobs' because so many students had after-school jobs.

Ultimately, however, Mr G's course is most interesting not as an example of how literature and English ought to be taught but as an example of the kind of curriculum that can be built by a sensitive teacher being responsive to students and where they come from. That is, rather than argue that we should all construct courses that look like Mr G's, I would argue that we should resist the standardization of the curriculum and work to give one another the kind of support and curricular space necessary for the construction of our own locally valid versions of English. And this support can only come from an increased understanding of the process of curriculum creation, which is a challenging task when the subject in question – literature – is so dynamic, so value-laden, and so connected to the personal passions and beliefs of teachers.

REFERENCES

Appleyard, J. A. (1990) *Becoming a Reader: The Experience of Fiction from Childhood to Adulthood*. Cambridge: Cambridge University Press.

Bloom, A. (1987) *The Closing of the American Mind: How Higher Education has Failed Democracy and Impoverished the Souls of Today's Students*. New York: Simon & Schuster.

Freebody, P., Luke, A. and Gilbert, P. (1991) Reading positions and practices in the classroom. *Curriculum Inquiry* **21** (4), 435–61.

Hirsch, E. D. (1996) *The Schools We Need: And Why We Don't Have Them*. New York: Doubleday.

Goodson, I. and Ball, S. J. (1984) *Defining the Curriculum: Histories and Ethnographies*. London: Falmer Press.

National Council of Teachers of English and International Reading Association (1996) *Standards for the English Language Arts*. Urbana, IL: NCTE.

Sizer, T. (1984) *Horace's Compromise: The Dilemma of the American High School*. Boston: Houghton Mifflin.

Tyson-Bernstein, H. (1988) *A Conspiracy of Good Intentions: America's Textbook Fiasco*. Washington, DC: Council for Basic Education.

Chapter 7

Adolescent Girls' Responses to Female Literary Characters: Two Case Studies

Holly A. Johnson and Dana L. Fox

We all need a mythology to live by. Cultures use stories, myths, heroes, and heroines to create role models. Stories transmit moral values, tell us ideally how we should live, help us distinguish correct behavior from incorrect, and identify those traits considered desirable by a group or society . . . cultural values and norms circumscribe women's lives so strongly.

(Rebolledo and Rivero, 1993, p. 189)

To read resistantly is to read with a critical eye toward assumptions or 'norms' that are often so firmly ingrained in each of us that they have become all but invisible and thus taken for granted. Reading resistantly involves, among other things, asking questions in alternative ways and maintaining a skeptical outlook on the messages authors convey, as well as the interpretations others draw from those messages.

(Alvermann, 1997, p. 182)

Recent research conducted by Lyn Mikel Brown and Carol Gilligan (1992), Myra and David Sadker (1994), Maureen Barbieri (1995) and the American Association of University Women (AAUW, 1992) points to the complex problems which young females face daily in classrooms around the world. Most recently, clinical psychologist Mary Pipher (1994) has written poignantly about her work with adolescent girls, asserting that 'particularly junior high seem[s] like a crucible' where '[M]any confident, well-adjusted girls [are] transformed into sad and angry failures' (p. 10). Questioning the 'more dangerous, sexualized, and media-saturated culture' (p. 12), she writes:

As I looked at the culture that girls enter as they come of age, I was struck by what a girl-poisoning culture it was. The more I looked around, the more I listened to today's music, watched television and movies, and looked at sexist advertising, the more convinced I became that we were on the wrong path for our daughters. America today limits girls' development, truncates their wholeness and leaves many of them traumatized.

(p. 12)

With a culture pressuring girls to become *less* than they are, Pipher asserts there are four general ways in which girls can react: they can conform, withdraw, be depressed or get angry. Often those who become angry are considered delinquent or equally misconstructed or unrecognized by society. Most girls, like Shakespeare's Ophelia, submerge themselves and lose relationship with themselves, and many also enter into false relationship with others (Brown and Gilligan, 1992).

We believe that one very important aspect of the socialization of young girls centres on their transactions with literary texts (Cherland, 1994; Christian-Smith, 1990; Davies, 1989; Trousdale, 1995). Louise Rosenblatt (1938/1995) suggests that literature is an enculturating agent. Few would argue with this statement, yet what should be acknowledged, especially related to girls and women, is the *type of influence* literary texts may have over readers. Pipher (1994) describes the content of adolescent girls' reading as the 'big lie' that girls may not see. This lie is about deficiency, about superficial beauty and behaviour, and about the critical reading and sophisticated thought that are required of girls in a technological age that can change images and representations with a few punches on a keyboard. Through this 'lie', girls become lost or submerge their own need for relationship with the self for the sake of relationships in the world, which often places them as less than total and equal participants (Brown and Gilligan, 1992; Christian-Smith, 1990; Roman *et al.*, 1988).

Even though we continue to value our relationships with the young male students in our classrooms and even though we know that gender is a complex, socially constructed category of experience, we worry about the difficulties and dilemmas faced by adolescent females in our schools. How do educators help young female students 'resist' the messages sent to them through texts? How do we help adolescent girls become more critical, sophisticated readers? The purpose of our work reported in this chapter was to focus closely on the voices, perspectives and experiences of female readers. From a feminist perspective (Maynard and Purvis, 1994), we wanted to learn more about their text choices, the literary characters they notice and admire, and their overall impression of literature written specifically for adolescents. Through in-depth interviews and observations, we sought to learn more about the role that literature plays in the lives of 13- and 14-year-old girls. We attempted to utilize what Taylor *et al.* (1996) call 'a voice-centered method' of enquiry, which 'means that we build theory from listening – in this case, listening to girls' (p. 14). We were aware that the questions we were asking could provide an opportunity for these girls to become more conscious of the norms related to female identity and womanhood that are so ingrained in texts and readers alike. Throughout the project, we also found ourselves interrogating our own positions as female readers and teachers.

In this chapter, we begin by discussing our professional relationship, our research process, and the school and community contexts for our work. We then present narrative portraits of two adolescent female readers and discuss a number of important themes which emerged from our research. Finally, we suggest several implications and ideas for positive action for teachers, parents, authors and others who are involved in the lives of female adolescents.

As we briefly summarize and compare the case studies (Merriam, 1988) that follow, our purpose is not to generalize about all adolescent females, nor is it to pronounce judgement on these two individuals, their schools or communities. 'Generalizations from story are at best precarious', writes Kathy Carter (1993). 'It is important to remember that stories, because of their multiplicity of meaning and resistance to interpretation, teach in ambiguous ways' (p. 10). Nevertheless, as Carter suggests, stories may provide us with patterns, themes or 'explanatory propositions with which we can make sense of the dilemmas and problematics of teaching [and learning]' (p. 10). The stories of Angie and Gillian[1] provide us with important insights concerning the experiences of adolescent female readers, allowing us to become more thoughtful and critical about our own roles as readers and educators.

THE CONTEXT AND METHODS OF THE STUDY

Background for the project

Both of us have spent a number of years teaching adolescents and working closely with other English-language arts teachers. The two of us first met in the autumn of 1994, when our enquiry began in Dana's graduate seminar on gender and literacy at the University of Arizona where Holly was a doctoral student. Our work together continued when Holly enrolled in two additional seminars which Dana facilitated the following spring, one focused on reader response theories and the other on teacher research. Our interactions around the issues of gender equity, reader response and teacher enquiry in these courses enabled us to begin a productive collaborative partnership. Since that time, we have co-taught a graduate course on qualitative research, co-edited a special themed journal on gender issues in teaching English language arts (Fox and Johnson, 1997), and are currently co-authoring a book on educators' beliefs and knowledge about the complex relationship between gender and literacy (Fox *et al.*, forthcoming).

Through our conversations both inside and outside the university, we found that we were both intensely interested in female readers' perspectives. Our qualitative research with females in Holly's eighth-grade classroom is an outgrowth of our initial work together at the University of Arizona. Working with Cathie Fallona, a fifth-grade classroom teacher who was also a student in the three doctoral seminars, we initiated a formal study and wrote a grant to support our enquiry (Fox with Johnson and Fallona, 1995). Even though data from Cathie Fallona's classroom are not reported in this chapter, we collaborated with Cathie throughout the process of data collection and analysis and are indebted to her for her help in generating many of the ideas we discuss in this chapter.

Data collection and analysis

The primary goal of our project was to investigate eighth-grade girls' transactions with literature. Drawing upon interview and observational data that Holly collected in her own eighth-grade classroom, we wanted to learn more about adolescent girls' responses to female protagonists in adolescent literature. We were particularly interested in hearing girls' analysis and critique of the books they chose to read on their own, which included books from the two popular Goosebumps and Fear Street horror series by R. L. Stine as well as a number of selections identified as either contemporary realism, humour, adventure or fantasy novels written for young adult audiences.

Unlike some studies which seem to focus on the perspectives of 'young women of privilege' within the culture of a private school (Barbieri, 1995), the female participants in our study represent a range of socio-economic levels and attend a public school situated in a small town of the desert Southwest in the USA. By listening closely to the perspectives of these young female readers, we sought to answer various questions: How do adolescent girls choose texts? What do they notice about the characters in the books and stories they read? What types of protagonists are they attracted to? What similarities or differences do they observe in male and female protagonists, and in male and female authors of young adult literature? As our study progressed, we became especially interested in their perceptions of characters (particularly male and female protagonists), their text choices, and their analysis and critique of books written by both male and female authors of literature for adolescents.

Working with Cathie Fallona, the two of us collaborated over the course of a year in all aspects of the study, from the conception of the project to data analysis and writing. Multiple data-gathering methods for the study included (a) *in-depth, phenomenological interviews* (Seidman, 1991) with a total of 17 students; (b) *participant observation*; and (c) the *collection of written artefacts* (such as students' written responses to literary texts, journal writings, class work and so on). Interviews were audio-taped and transcribed verbatim. Data were analysed by means of analytic induction (LeCompte and Preissle, 1993) and constant comparison (Glaser and Strauss, 1967), and categories were derived from the data. In order to enhance the trustworthiness and reliability of our study, we first read and colour-coded the data independently; then, we met together as a team on several occasions for collaborative conversation and analysis (Wasser and Bresler, 1996). For the purposes of this chapter, we focus most closely on the data collected in Holly's eighth-grade classroom and draw heavily from our interviews with and informal observations of two eighth-grade female adolescents: Angie and Gillian.

School and community contexts for the study

Holly's eighth-grade classroom is located several miles south and southwest of Tucson, Arizona, in a small town amidst the great expanse of the Sonoran Desert. Desert Middle School is situated among several mountain ranges and within a forest of cholla cacti in the recently incorporated town of Desert View. The town itself consists of a post office, a one-stop market, a bar and grill, and a pecan factory. Most residents either work at the pecan factory, in the nearby pecan groves, or commute to work in the larger city to the north. Near an interstate highway, the school is located two miles from the pecan groves and serves students from a variety of communities – from the San Xavier Indian Reservation to the north, Vail to the east, Arivaca to the west and Tubac to the south. Desert View School District is the largest school district in the state, yet it still has the neighbourliness of a small town.

Desert Middle School, a circular structure with open hallways, trees and a grassy lawn, supplies the education for over 450 students. These students are socially and culturally diverse, coming from the artist colonies of Arivaca and Tubac, trailer parts in the pecan fields and along the reservation, 'ranches' next to the mountains and old mines, and up-scale subdivisions surrounding a nearby retirement community. About 58 per cent of the school population is Anglo, while the other 42 per cent is Mexican or Mexican-American – all three terms used by the students to describe themselves. In Holly's class, twelve of the 26 students are Mexican-American and fourteen are Anglo. Of these students, sixteen are girls and ten are boys, and they range from 13 to 14 years of age.

SUMMARIES OF THE TWO CASE STUDIES

Even though we had the opportunity to work closely with a number of girls during this investigation, two individuals stood out because they were representative of and respected by their female peers. Angie and Gillian emerged as interesting case studies partly because they represented attributes that we had not possessed as young women – a sense of passion and a sense of their own value. They were not afraid to speak their minds or question their roles as young women in what seems to be a male-dominated world. They were articulate and giving, rebellious and caring, and patient and exasperated at any given encounter. They defied stereotypes, yet were typical of the young women within Holly's classroom. They were female leaders whose voices resonated with the truth of their classmates, yet they maintained their individuality.

A profile of Angie

[What bothers me the most about female characters is] they're so sensitive, and 'ohhh,' you know? If something bad happens to them, they just start crying and give up. I mean, golly, take a chance or something! I just feel like yelling at the author and saying, 'Why don't you make this girl more . . . stronger?!' I mean, usually the girls are so wimpy . . . And that's when I close the book.

Angie, dishwater blonde hair either flowing down her back or sailing behind her as she runs, is the undisputed class leader. An eighth-grader in Holly's classroom, Angie is respected by both male and female classmates, yet knows she reacts too quickly to the boys' teasing comments of 'woman's place' and male superiority. The boys know she will rise to their bait, and thus have a good time at her expense. A basketball *aficionada*, Angie plays ball with the boys whenever there's a break, while the rest of the girls choose to play basketball or talk among themselves. She holds her own on the court, so she is not hassled about her athletic ability. Basketball is her first love, though she has recently taken up playing softball. Angie would not be insulted if you called her the quintessential tomboy.

Angie has never been seen wearing a dress, since she feels more free in shorts or pants. She wears her shorts to her knees, as is the style, with T-shirts and hightop Nikes. She wears glasses that accent her blue eyes, and she is quick to smile or joke about most things. Intelligent and not afraid to share her views either in her writing or in classroom discussions, Angie is 13 years old. She has an older sister and brother, and lives with her family in the larger city next to the school district. Both her parents work for the local high school. Given the opportunity to transfer to the city school nearer her home, Angie refused. She was afraid she wouldn't be on the first string basketball team at the larger school.

Besides schoolwork and sports, Angie also is involved with questioning current politics and wonders about the state of her country, although she would say she is not too political. She thinks students should have a say in what happens in the classroom, and she wishes that teachers and students could talk to each other more than they currently do. She is actively looking for a role model and is not afraid to state it.

'I like reading', Angie reports, 'but I don't like reading boring books.' Her favourite genres are 'horror and funny books'. When asked what she notices about characters in the books she reads, Angie says she likes to connect with characters, and she focuses first on their personalities: 'I notice usually their personality, what they're like, and I can say to myself, "Oh man, I don't like her!" or "I don't like him!"' Angie is quick to point out that she enjoys 'smart' characters, and she often encounters intelligence in 'really mean characters': 'You love the bad guy, but you hate the bad guy, too. And that's what I like mostly 'cause the bad guy is like, so smart.' Angie contrasts this smart antagonist to other 'stupid' characters who seem plentiful in all kinds of texts she reads or views:

> [I dislike] stupidity. You know how those movies, like, the scary movies where you know the killer is in that room, and they're all stupid enough to go in? It's the same about the book. You know that house is abandoned, you don't want to go into this abandoned house, but you do anyway . . . I really don't like that, and people think it makes the book more interesting, but I think, 'Ah, it's just stupid.' And it makes the book more predictable.

In her discussion of these 'stupid' characters, Angie says that more often than not, the 'stupid' characters are female: 'R. L. Stine is a guy, [and] he makes the girl stupid. Like in *Hitchhiker* [Stine, 1993], not the killer, but the friend of the killer, she was really stupid.' Angie goes on to say that when this female character was trying to identify the killer, she jumped to conclusions quickly and 'never thought of the other possibilities'.

As a reader, Angie notices that authors often patronize females, denying them intellect, courage or self-reliance:

> I haven't read one of R. L. Stine's books where he makes the girl the hero, except for in *The Babysitter* [Stine, 1989] . . . [Male authors portray girls] as wimps, sometimes. Like, they don't know how to take care of themselves, 'cause they always have, in all R. L. Stine books, they always have a guy by their side to help them. Always the guy is coming to help.

Angie says that she does like intelligent female characters and has encountered a few female protagonists who are smart ''cause they usually know what to do in bad situations and stuff . . . [m]ost of the time these girls are like, "Oh let's leave" or something. I mean, that's good if you're in this house with like ghosts and stuff.' However, Angie has difficulty recalling very many intelligent female characters: 'I mean, I don't know, I don't think there's very many books that I've read that have a girl actually like that, you know?'

Male characters, Angie believes, 'always seem to be coming out as the brave, brave ones': 'They don't take anything from anybody, you know? And if they do, it's always, "Well, I've got to punch this guy out now" . . . [The guy's personality, I notice], he's usually got a big ego . . . gotta prove something all the time.' Angie perceives that authors 'make [male] characters out to be this strong, brave person that's not afraid of anything – "I'm Superman, I'm Mr Man", all that.' Like female characters, male characters are often portrayed as unintelligent: 'The guys are, like I said, have the ego, and they're just stupid and punch out anybody that's in their way.'

Interestingly, Angie believes that both male and female characters she has encountered in books are highly stereotypical and generally unbelievable:

> Usually, it's sensitivity in girls, and like, big, buff dudes, and stuff like that. I guess that's okay, 'cause that's how books have always been, and I guess that's how they're always going to be. [It] don't bother me, it's just a stereotype, no more than that. I know it's just fiction, and it's not going to happen . . . I know it's just fiction.

Males, says Angie, are stereotyped as active, macho, 'tough', and physically violent; females are stereotyped as overly sensitive, inactive, 'wimpy', and dependent. On the one hand, Angie says these sweeping stereotypes 'don't bother me'; on the other, she reveals that she becomes impatient with these stereotypical characters and longs to meet more complex female and male characters. Different comments she makes about both male and female characters disclose her wishes:

> I know guys aren't that brave, no guy is. Some guy has to be afraid of something. I just know it's not true, and I know it can't, I mean, I know some guys are [not afraid of anything], but every guy is afraid of something . . .
>
> In action books usually you don't see a girl being like Arnold Schwarzenegger built and saving all these people. But it would be nice to see that one day . . . I just want to see, just one time, where this girl can take care of herself, just kicks the girl's or guy's butt that's trying to attack her. And that's all I really want to see, you know? I don't want to see some guy coming to the rescue.

Overall, Angie believes that 'the truth' is missing from the fiction she reads, and she has a strong message for authors of adolescent literature. She reflects, 'I mean, sure, a lot of girls are always going, "Ah-h-h, oh no, get that spider away from me!" Even I'm like that, I don't like spiders.' However, she continues, 'But every girl, like every guy, has a weak point, but every girl has a strong point. And I think that's what they should put more in books.'

A profile of Gillian

> [What bothers me about female characters is] when they're sort of like, 'Okay, sure' [in a high-pitched tone], you know, whatever, because I don't think that's how most females are. So well, most of my friends are [laughs]. But most girls aren't really like that, I don't think . . . [They really aren't] like blondes! You know, 'Okay, sure, whatever you say [in a high-pitched voice], oh mighty male.' That's not really what girls are like, that's just how they are portrayed.

Gillian, dyed red hair and masses of freckles, also reads, but would much rather question the *status quo* and defend her rights at school. Of all of Holly's students, Gillian has spent most of her time in either the principal's office or in-school suspension. And while she caused no trouble in language arts class, except to question the boys' logic on truth and justice, she was regularly referred to the office for either her choice of clothing (mid-drifts and overalls, boxer shorts exposed under her pants, Green Day T-shirts with 'dookie' on the back) or her decisions to spend time in the desert instead of school. She was silent many days in class so as not to start problems, but when she spoke, she had the girls' attention and the boys' frustration or anger. Slim, pleasant and controversial, she questioned Christianity and thought she might believe in reincarnation, and thus was called 'Buddha' by both insensitive teachers and students. Gillian is of Anglo descent, yet her real name (not used in this chapter) is a Spanish word which means a type of desert flower. Her parents are divorced, and she lives with her mother, who reads philosophy and shares her views with her daughter.

The year before, Gillian added to the controversy that surrounds her by piercing her nose, and she remains the only girl in school to do so. And while Gillian has many friends at the middle school, most of them are older and that is where she gets her self-esteem. She readily admits that she is racist, but also readily admits she is working hard to alleviate these racist tendencies from her life. Honest and reflective, she laughs easily, rolls her eyes regularly, and shrugs her shoulders when asked about her constant discipline problems. For 14-year-old Gillian, school is something she must do on her way to doing what she wants to do (which is to grow up); thus, while she has been known to cry because the principal would not listen to her side of the story, most of the things that happen in eighth grade will be forgotten or chalked up as just a bad year.

Gillian is not afraid to state she is a feminist, as opposed to Angie who grudgingly admits she is 'kinda a feminist', yet in the living out of their feminism, both girls are equally strong. Angie is much more action-oriented and louder in her views, yet it is Gillian and her voice of exasperated reason that infuriates the boys and wins the respect of the girls in Holly's classroom.

As a reader, Gillian, like Angie, notices characters' personalities and 'how they like, fit into my life. [I look for] a character who's sort of like me. I like books I can sort of identify with ... [And] if I'm trying to identify with the character, if it's a girl, it sort of matters because, you know, she's a girl and I'm a girl.' When female protagonists are absent, however, Gillian says that with 'male characters, well, I enjoy like, how I would like to be [like that] as a woman, you know?' Revealing something about her own identity, Gillian says she looks for characters who share her own perspectives or who can model alternative perspectives and lead the reader to think:

> I like characters who sort of take everything in hand, and know what they're doing ...
> and who aren't shy. And I like characters who are, like, my own age. I like characters who
> are my age because I can sort of think like, 'Well, that's a different way of thinking it' or
> 'I think that way, too'. And characters who are in control and stuff just because ... I don't
> know ... I think I can see how other people might handle other situations and stuff.

A reader of adventure and fantasy stories, Gillian appreciates female characters who are believable: '[Y]ou want to think that maybe that's what they are really thinking, even if it's just a made-up character.' Gillian reports that most of the fantasies she has read contain female characters.

Unlike the 'wimpy', stereotypical female characters in the R. L. Stine series which Angie reads, some of the characters in the fantasies read by Gillian are 'the take control ones': 'It sort of takes place in, you know, knight days or whatever. I don't think that seems logical that the females would be, you know, they are the ones who are like men and travel and stuff.' Specific female characters in fantasy novels remain memorable to Gillian because these characters defy strict gender roles and even serve as models or guides:

> I forget the name of the book, but it was this elf-human thing that was, her name was Wren, and she was like . . . perfect! She wasn't, she fought and everything, but she was like, not completely masculine and not completely feminine. I guess, like in the book, she had been raised with a guy who was deaf, and she understood a lot of different things. And it's just like the way I want to be . . . to understand, and not be so prejudiced.

Like Angie, Gillian believes that both male and female characters she has encountered in books are stereotypical, lacking in complexity and authenticity. 'I think that males in most books, a lot of times they're the tough ones, or the "save-the-day" ones, most of the time', Gillian reflects. In discussing her perceptions of female authors writing about boys, she continues, 'I really think that we don't understand [males] as much as we think we do. I think we think, "Okay, so, like they're totally masculine, and they want to fight, and everything." But I don't think that's how guys really are . . . So I think [stereotyping] is true a lot.'

Reflecting on the ways in which female characters are stereotyped, Gillian says, 'I think a lot of times books portray girls as one extreme or the other.' She explains, 'Like either really tough and really like, "I'm not going to take anything" or either like "I'll take anything" [high-pitched voice]. You know, I mean a lot of girls aren't one or the other.' Often, says Gillian, male writers portray female characters as one-dimensional, supporting a culture that seems to reward stereotypical behaviour:

> I think they make girls sound like dumb blondes, which is sort of a bad way to put it, 'cause I have tons of blonde friends and none of them are dumb. They just like to act that way because it gets them attention. And you know, if you're going to act like a smart girl who won't take it from people, then you're not going to get the attention they think that they want!

Like Angie, Gillian desires to meet more complex, female characters who are strong and assertive and who can help guide her into becoming the type of woman she wants to become. She seeks female characters who 'take control':

> And I think that people don't usually realize that part of women . . . besides that they take control of children. But I mean other things in life. People say, 'Yeah, they know how to control children, but they couldn't handle death or whatever.' And I think women characters can do that . . . That's the kind of personality I would like to have when I get older, or, not that I want to copy their personality at all, but something like I could sort of look up to.

Even though Gillian clearly describes the kind of female literary character she is searching for, she reports that she rarely finds such characters in the books she reads. 'I think overall, female characters I don't really relate to', Gillian declares, 'because, you know, they're like . . . prissy, and I don't like that.' Again, Gillian searches for a character who can provide her with an alternative to the *status quo*: 'I'm trying not to be like what everyone expects girls to be . . . prissy and stay home.' Even though she says she finds few such characters, Gillian remains hopeful: 'I think it's changing now, though. I don't have to [be like what everyone expects girls to be].'

WHAT WE LEARNED FROM LISTENING TO GIRLS: IMPLICATIONS FOR TEACHERS, PARENTS, AUTHORS AND TEACHER EDUCATORS

From our close attention to Angie's and Gillian's responses to literature, we have come to understand more about adolescent girls' text choices, the literary characters they notice and admire, what they appreciate and prefer in literature, and what they feel is missing in their literature. Even though this chapter focuses on only two girls' perspectives, we believe that Gillian and Angie represent the perspectives of many of the other adolescents with whom we have worked, both male and female.[2] Given what we have learned from Angie and Gillian, we are even more convinced of the power and potential influence of literature on adolescent girls' developing sense of self. The following observations may help teachers, parents and others as they struggle to provide both theoretical and practical alternatives to conventional educational practices, especially as those practices relate to adolescent female readers.

The power and potential of literature

The role of literature in the negotiation of identity
Both Angie and Gillian longed for female characters who were more realistically like *them*. They wished to see themselves mirrored in the literature they read: '[I look for] a character who's sort of like me. I like books I can sort of identify with.' Both Gillian and Angie also sought strong female characters who could serve as role models for them: 'not that I want to copy their personality at all, but something like I could sort of look up to.' However, since they were quick to recognize predictable, stereotypical characters, neither Angie nor Gillian found female characters who met their needs directly: 'I think a lot of times books portray girls as one extreme or the other . . . You know, I mean a lot of girls aren't one or the other.' Even though they noted both male and female stereotypes, we think that it is especially significant that they disdained one-dimensional female characters, describing them as lacking in self-confidence, whining and even 'stupid'.

In a study of girls' attitudes towards contradictory sex-role ideologies, Anyon (1984) suggests that the girls she studied both *resisted* and *accommodated* the cultural ideology of femininity they encountered. Anyon believes that this 'dialectic of accommodation and resistance' is a natural response to contradiction and oppression. As Cherland and Edelsky (1993) point out:

Critical educational theorists have frequently used the word 'resistance' to mean the action of individuals or groups by which they assert their own desires and experience and contest the ideological and material forces that are imposed upon them by their culture (Weiler, 1988). People exercise agency to resist the imposition of forces that work to construct their places within the society. McRobbie (1989) has suggested that 'negotiation' may be a better term for the processes by which individuals come to terms with these forces.

(p. 30)

While we see Angie and Gillian's awareness of stereotypes and their negotiation of meaning and gender ideologies in their reading as positive, we realize that adolescent girls may not often be encouraged to explore seriously the female norms they see represented in magazines, movies and books. We believe that educators should work to enable both female and male adolescents to become more conscious of the power such images embody as enculturating agents. Perhaps literature does not impose meaning on readers, but it constructs readers' identities in complex ways. Teachers need to support students as they critically negotiate their relationships with the characters they meet in texts.

Genre and female representation in young adult fiction

As we consider the power and potential of literature in adolescents' lives, we need to look carefully at the relationship between genre and female representation in young adult literature. The girls in our study were highly interested in genres which are not often the focus of study in English-language arts classrooms: fantasy, horror, humour, and adventure. According to Angie, females were often victimized in horror books she read, especially those books authored by R. L. Stine. 'I haven't read one of R. L. Stine's books where he makes the girl the hero', reflected Angie. '[Girls in these books] don't know how to take care of themselves, 'cause . . . they always have a guy by their side to help them.' In adventure novels, Gillian and Angie found both male and female characters to be stereotypical. They identified the males in these books as macho, 'tough', and physically violent, while they described the females as overly sensitive, 'wimpy', and dependent. In contrast, Gillian found some of the female characters in fantasy novels to be strong and independent. Even though Gillian desired strong female characters, she was a bit confused by the 'take control' female characters in fantasy novels: 'I don't think it seems logical that the females would be . . . like men.' Interestingly, the most memorable female character she encountered, the 'elf-human' Wren, wasn't even fully human.

Reading and studying fiction, adolescent females have the opportunity to experience and confront a culture of femininity and to construct meaning for themselves in their present and future lives. Cherland and Edelsky (1993) argue that, generally speaking, texts provide girls with patterns of culture and womanhood with which they are not entirely satisfied. In this situation, girls need to be supported in their struggles to critically analyse female representations in adolescent fiction. Looking across multiple genres, students need to read characters critically, trying them on and analysing their behaviours. As Christian-Smith (1993) suggests, teachers of literature are involved in a political practice:

[i]t is important that educators help students to locate the contradictions between popular fiction's version of social relations and their own lives as well as to help them to develop the critical tools necessary to make deconstructive readings that unearth the political interests that shape the form and content of popular fiction.

(p. 63)

The need for more complex characters in adolescent literature

Our study reveals adolescent girls' strong desires for more complex female and male characters. This may seem quite obvious to some readers, but we think Angie's and Gillian's comments are important because they help us see that adolescent girls do have insights into the socially constructed nature of gender. Both girls pointed out characters who defied strict gender roles and, significantly, these were the characters they sought as models for their own lives. Looking for more complexity in characters, Angie reflected that '[e]very girl, like every guy, has a weak point, but every girl has a strong point. And I think that's what they should put more in books'. Describing the elf-human character in the fantasy novel she read, Gillian called her 'perfect!', 'not completely masculine and not completely feminine . . . just like the way I want to be'.

Citing the work of Cixous (1986), Moi (1987) and Wilshire (1989), Bronwyn Davies (1993) suggests that metaphors and storylines of binary thought and the male/female dualism permeate our lives. Davies maintains that it is possible to create texts and readings of texts which move us beyond dichotomous thinking towards multiple ways of knowing and being. Gillian and Angie seem to recognize the inadequacy of this male/female dichotomy and long for characters who demonstrate multiple aspects of the self. Davies argues that teachers need to help readers like Angie and Gillian develop skills to engage in critical readings of all kinds of texts, both those that sustain and create male/female dualisms and those that attempt to move readers beyond dualisms. This is a complicated matter in both instances, as Trousdale (1995) and Davies (1989, 1993) have shown in their research with young readers. Davies (1993) illustrates:

> The multiple readings that can be made of any one story that attempts to achieve a feminist storyline compound the complexity of the task of creating new narrative forms. In *Frogs and Snails and Feminist Tales* (1989), I showed how a story like *The Paperbag Princess* (Munsch and Marchenko, 1980) with a female hero who ultimately rejects the romantic myth and dances off alone into the sunset without the prince, can be read as a traditional story about a heroic prince who is better off without a princess who didn't know how to be a princess.
>
> (p. 150)

In her discussion of classroom pedagogy, Davies suggests that students should be taught 'conceptual strategies' in order to engage in multiple interpretations of texts and to examine how those interpretations occur. 'They need to be able to crack the code of dominant gender ideologies for themselves', she writes, 'to understand how they are constituted through discourse, how they might invent, invert, rethink, rewrite a new world' (p. 159).

Fostering a culture of critique in the classroom

How do teachers help both female and male students negotiate meanings in reading? What specific practices might enable students to 'crack the code' of gender ideologies represented in discourse and texts? How do we support students in their becoming more sophisticated, critical readers? In the final section of this chapter, we offer an overview of how to develop what we call the 'culture of critique' in literature classrooms, drawing from theoretical models of reading and suggesting multiple ideas and strategies for positive action.

Towards a social-cultural model of reading
Recent publications on the teaching of literature have noted promise in the confluence of reader response theories and cultural studies, because such a union moves both in a new direction (Sims Bishop, 1997; Rogers and Soter, 1997). Kathleen McCormick (1994) argues that educators should consider supporting students by inviting them to move beyond either cognitive or expressivist models of reading literature. She advocates instead a social-cultural model of reading, which encompasses Giroux's (1983) idea of critical literacy. McCormick explains:

> Critical literacy consists not only of being able to comprehend texts one reads or to link them with one's own personal worlds. Rather, to be a critically literate reader is to have the knowledge and ability to perceive the interconnectedness of social conditions and the reading and writing practices of a culture, to be able to analyse those conditions and practices, and to possess the critical and political awareness to take action within and against them.
>
> (p. 49)

McCormick's model of reading follows a cultural studies framework as developed by Stuart Hall. Combining the ideas of cultural studies and transactional, reader response theories, McCormick views readers as balanced between autonomy and social determinism. This balance places readers within a discursive practice that regards them as 'active producers of meaning within specific cultural constraints' (p. 53). Reading pedagogy, then,

> should enable students to articulate their own readings of cultural objects [in our case, female characters in young adult fiction] and introduce them to discourses that can help them explore ways in which cultural objects are historically and socially produced . . . [a]nd if students are to become "active makers of meaning" of texts, they must also be given access to discourses that can help them historicize their own reading position.
>
> (pp. 53–4)

Within reading pedagogy, readers need to be encouraged to interrogate their own relationship to the text. In essence, they should begin to think about and articulate their transactions with a particular text and the tensions and connections made within those transactions. In doing so, they become more sophisticated readers.

Rogers and Soter (1997) suggest that 'it is the power of literature as artistic as well as cultural texts that persuades us and our students to be moved enough to look deeply at both the aesthetic and cultural contributions they make and to look outward from the works to their social meanings' (p. 2). Within any reading event, we find multiple cultural texts. The reader's culture, the author's culture, and the cultural text produced within a particular time and place are areas worthy of exploration. The context of the reading event itself and the social and cultural frameworks within which that reading event occurs are also areas for enquiry. There are issues of resistance and acquiescence within the reader as well as issues of race, class and gender that need to be addressed within the transactions of any reading event. Especially important in questioning and challenging dominant versions of femininity encountered in texts is Gilbert and Taylor's (1991) notion of reading 'against the grain':

> Learning to read and write against the grain . . . is therefore about learning to read and write against conventions that construct women in ways that are demeaning and restricting. It is . . . about learning to read and write in ways that offer constructions of female subjectivity that are not fixed and static, but are dynamic and shifting. It is about learning to understand the discursive construction of subjectivity and the potential spaces for resistance and rewriting.
>
> (p. 150)

As we encourage students to 'read and write against the grain' in order to disrupt conventions, we believe that teachers should also take care to reflect regularly on their own positions and roles in raising students' consciousness (Johnson, 1997a). As teachers, we should ask the following questions: Whose position is being privileged in this classroom? Which stances gain the most attention? What do we believe students should become more conscious of, and why?

Pushing students beyond both basic comprehension and expressivist, reader response orientations to their becoming more critically literate would well serve young readers. Becoming sophisticated, critically literate readers would allow adolescents to be more conscious of themselves as cultural subjects within a social, cultural and historical context. An understanding and appreciation of readers' positions would well serve our society and schools and may allow for the acknowledgement and validation of difference. Through a critical and feminist pedagogy, reading could encourage an understanding of multiple cultures and multiple realities.

Fostering critical reading and critical literacy in the classroom
Several classroom practices can facilitate the development of critical literacy among adolescent readers. Discussion and dialogue are paramount in the promotion of critical reading in the classroom (Barnes, 1992; Pierce and Gilles, 1993). Indeed, as Judith Langer (1995) suggests, 'Literature instruction is an essentially social activity' (p. 79). We believe that teachers should work with students in order to create a classroom atmosphere that promotes talk and interaction among all participants. Langer (1995) describes the nature of such an environment:

> In literary communities . . . students learn to develop their own capabilities as thinkers and participants in the complex social relations of the class and the broader community. As they learn to listen to and confront one another, students enter into dialogue in the sense that Bakhtin (1981) describes. Such dialogue permits participants to consider

other ways of interpreting and to view the individual selves within the class community as interwoven; the participants, and thus the community itself, are open to difference, empathy, awareness, and change.

(pp. 53–4)

In developing such a classroom atmosphere, Langer suggests that teachers use particular strategies conducive to critical reading. She recommends that teachers

1   invite students into the literary experience by easing access to the literary work;
2   invite students' initial understandings of the work;
3   support students in developing their interpretations of the work;
4   encourage students to take a critical stance towards the work;
5   engage in stocktaking (rather than closure or consensus) by summarizing key issues, acknowledging agreements and disagreements, and pointing out concerns not adequately addressed (pp. 88–92).

We also believe that educators need to teach students how to dialogue with one another and to become more aware of the gendered nature of their readings and talk (Cherland, 1992).

Creating such a lively literary community in the classroom is not without contention or conflict. In her book, *Teaching to Transgress* (1994), bell hooks suggests, 'Making the classroom a democratic setting where everyone feels a responsibility to contribute is a central goal of transformative pedagogy' (p. 39). However, we have learned that the process of creating a classroom community does not necessarily create 'cozy, good feelings' for everyone involved; it may be joyful and pleasurable at times, but we've also found the process to be difficult, troubling, and even painful (Taylor and Fox, 1996). Few concrete examples exist in our professional literature which demonstrate how teachers and students can work together to transgress usual boundaries and map out 'terrains of commonality and connection' in the classroom community (hooks, 1994, p. 130).

We suggest that conflict and dissonance are inevitable (and essential) in any learning community, and are especially important as students engage in questioning their own and others' stances, cultural models (Beach, 1995) or cultural maps (Enciso, 1997). Because students are 'discursively located readers' (Alvermann, 1997), their interpretations of literary texts are greatly influenced by their 'values, beliefs, race, class, and gender (as well as any number of other historically situated sociocultural practices)' (p. 182). Their socially constructed positions and ways of knowing and viewing the world affect their stances towards literary characters and others within the classroom community. Even as students are invited to engage in response-based activities *in addition to discussion*, such as freewriting, sketch-to-stretch drawings (Short and Harste with Burke, 1995), role-playing, or writing their own parallel texts, we believe educators should be aware of the nature of dissonance and the potential promise of conflict in their classroom communities. We believe that literature classrooms can become *both* the 'contact zones' *and* the 'safe houses' that Mary Louise Pratt (1991) describes. Although battling in 'contact zones' to explore differences across textual locations and cultures is essential, students also need the space for tentative reflection and development of ideas, the 'temporary protection from the legacies of oppression' that 'safe houses' provide

(p. 40). Creating such a classroom community takes time, however, and involves everyone's commitment and participation. Multi-age classrooms, where students work together with the same teacher over several years, provide one alternative arrangement where long-term commitment may occur.

We also propose that teachers (re)consider and rethink their own roles in the teaching and learning of literature. Teachers need to be fully vested participants in literature discussions, offering their own responses to texts and their critiques of characters' motives and authors' storylines. Choosing texts for classroom study is an especially important aspect of the teacher's role. Even though student choice is important, Johnson (1997a) suggests that teachers themselves need to make informed choices and should select read-alouds and other texts for whole-class discussion that expose students to a variety of cultures and stories students may not have chosen to read on their own. For instance, popular media texts such as movies, magazines or advertising should be included to generate a critical discussion of female representation in texts. In choosing titles that provide examples of strong female protagonists in young adult literature, we have found a number of sources to be helpful (Barbieri, 1995; Barbieri and Rief, 1996; Johnson, 1997b; Shay, 1997; WEEA Equity Resource Center, 1997; Whaley and Dodge, 1993; WILLA, n.d.). Barbieri (1996) warns us, however, to take care as we select texts for adolescent girls: 'We must be aware of the trap of urging books on them because the female characters are aggressive, feisty, physically undaunted . . . The solution to our girls' dilemma is not to have them turn into boys' (p. 39). We agree with Barbieri that female representation in texts is a highly complex issue, and we also want girls 'to recognize and cherish qualities such as compassion and empathy without giving them signals that such qualities constitute the entire script for their lives' (p. 39).

Finally, we believe that teachers need to be careful listeners and active 'kidwatchers' (Goodman, 1985). In Barbieri's (1996) terms, we need to listen especially closely to adolescent girls' 'words under the words' as they struggle to make sense of the world (p. 37). More than listeners or observers, however, we believe teachers need to take thoughtful action to help students question their unreflective stances and become more critical, sophisticated readers. In doing so, we must create opportunities for meaningful engagement with literature that might help students consider alternative responses, interpretations and texts:

> We can help our girls ask questions of their books, reading against the text when necessary, and in the process provide opportunities for rich classroom discussions of what it means to be human in the world we all share. We can pursue the quietest girls, those most willing to be passive, by valuing their ambivalence and tentative thinking. We can eschew consensus and welcome conflicting points of view, urging girls to develop the habit of asking tough questions: From whose perspective is this story being told? What other perspective might there be? How are the female characters presented? What does it mean to be a woman? What are the responsibilities, challenges, opportunities women have today? What trade-offs do decisions involve? And what does this text have to say about these?
>
> (Barbieri, 1996, p. 40)

NOTES

1   Pseudonyms are used throughout this chapter to protect the anonymity of students. Pseudonyms are also used for names of the school and school district.

2   It is important to note that not all of the girls in our study sought 'strong' female characters. Unlike Gillian and Angie, a few of the Mexican-American girls and one of the white girls in our study saw the female characters they encountered in young adult literature as 'good enough'. See Johnson (1997a) for a more detailed discussion of the intersections of race, class and gender as they relate to adolescent girls' responses to female protagonists in young adult literature.

REFERENCES

American Association of University Women (AAUW) Educational Foundation (1992) *How Schools Shortchange Girls*. New York: Marlowe.

Alvermann, D. E. (1997) Commentary. In S. McMahon and T. Raphael (eds) *The Book Club Connection: Literacy Learning and Classroom Talk*. New York: Teachers College Press.

Anyon, J. M. (1984) Intersections of gender and class: accommodation and resistance by working-class and affluent females to contradictory sex role ideologies. *Journal of Education* **166** (1), 25–47.

Bakhtin, M. (1981) *The Dialogic Imagination* (trans. C. Emerson and M. Helquist). Austin, TX: University of Texas Press.

Barbieri, M. (1995) *Sounds from the Heart: Learning to Listen to Girls*. Portsmouth, NH: Heinemann.

Barbieri, M. (1996) Words under the words: learning to listen to girls. *Voices from the Middle* **3** (1), 33–40.

Barbieri, M. and Rief, L. (eds) (1996) *Voices from the Middle* **3** (1). Special themed issue: 'Girls'.

Barnes, D. (1992) *From Communication to Curriculum*. Portsmouth, NH: Heinemann.

Beach, R. (1995) Constructing cultural models through response to literature. *English Journal* **84** (6), 87–94.

Brown, L. M. and Gilligan, C. (1992) *Meeting at the Crossroads: Women's Psychology and Girls' Development*. New York: Ballantine.

Carter, K. (1993) The place of story in the study of teaching and teacher education. *Educational Researcher* **22** (1), 5–12, 18.

Cherland, M. (1992) Gendered readings: cultural restraints upon response to literature. *The New Advocate* **5** (3), 187–98.

Cherland, M. (1994) *Private Practices: Girls Reading Fiction and Constructing Identity*. Bristol, PA: Taylor & Francis.

Cherland, M. and Edelsky, C. (1993) Girls and reading: the desire for agency and the horror of helplessness in fictional encounters. In L. K. Christian-Smith (ed.) *Texts of Desire: Essays on Fiction, Femininity and Schooling*. London: Falmer Press.

Christian-Smith, L. (1990) *Becoming a Woman Through Romance*. New York: Routledge.

Christian-Smith, L. (1993) Sweet dreams: gender and desire in teen romance novels. In L. K. Christian-Smith (ed.) *Texts of Desire: Essays on Fiction, Femininity and Schooling*. London: Falmer Press.

Cixous, H. (1986) Sorties: out and out: attacks/ways out/forays. In H. Cixous and C. Clement (eds) *The Newly Born Woman*. Manchester: Manchester University Press.

Davies, B. (1989) *Frogs and Snails and Feminist Tales: Preschool Children and Gender*. Sydney: Allen and Unwin.

Davies, B. (1993) Beyond dualism and towards multiple subjectivities. In L. K. Christian-Smith (ed.) *Texts of Desire: Essays on Fiction, Femininity, and Schooling*. London: Falmer Press.

Enciso, P. (1997) Negotiating the meaning of difference: talking back to multicultural literature. In T. Rogers and A. O. Soter (eds) *Reading Across Cultures: Teaching Literature in a Diverse Society*. New York: Teachers College Press.

Fox, D. L. and Johnson, H. A. (eds) (1997) *Arizona English Bulletin* **39** (2). Special themed issue: 'Gender Issues in Teaching English Language Arts'.

Fox, D. L., Johnson, H. A., Anders, P. L. *et al.* (co-ordinating eds) (forthcoming) *Gender and Literacy: A Self-Study of Educators' Beliefs and Knowledge*. Mahwah, NJ: Erlbaum.

Fox, D. L. with Johnson, H. A. and Fallona, C. (1995) Girls, texts, and their 'poems': transacting and interacting with literary characters in fifth and eighth grades. College of Education Summer Research Support Grant, University of Arizona, Tucson, Arizona.

Gilbert, P. and Taylor, S. (1991) *Fashioning the Feminine: Girls, Popular Culture and Schooling*. Sydney: Allen & Unwin.

Giroux, H. (1983) *Schooling and the Struggle for Public Life*. Minneapolis: University of Minnesota Press.

Glaser, B. G. and Strauss, A. S. (1967) *The Discovery of Grounded Theory: Strategies for Qualitative Research*. New York: Aldine De Gruyter.

Goodman, Y. (1985) Kidwatching: observing young children in the classroom. In A. Jagger and T. Smith-Burke (eds) *Observing the Language Learner*. Newark, DE: International Reading Association.

hooks, b. (1994) *Teaching to Transgress: Education as the Practice of Freedom*. New York: Routledge.

Johnson, H. A. (1997a) Reading the personal and the political: exploring female representation in realistic fiction with adolescent girls. Unpublished doctoral dissertation, University of Arizona, Tucson, Arizona.

Johnson, H. A. (1997b) Strong female protagonists in adolescent literature. *Arizona English Bulletin* **39** (2), 59–62.

Langer, J. (1995) *Envisioning Literature: Literary Understanding and Literature Instruction*. New York: Teachers College Press.

LeCompte, M. D. and Preissle, J. (1993) *Ethnography and Qualitative Design in Educational Research* (2nd edn). San Diego: Academic Press.

McCormick, K. (1994) *The Culture of Reading and the Teaching of English*. Manchester: Manchester University Press.

McRobbie, A. (ed.) (1989) *Zootsuits and Second-Hand Dresses: An Anthology of Fashion and Music*. New York: Unwin Hyman.

Maynard, M. and Purvis, J. (eds) (1994) *Researching Women's Lives from a Feminist Perspective*. London: Taylor & Francis.

Merriam, S. B. (1988) *Case Study Research in Education: A Qualitative Approach*. San Francisco: Jossey-Bass.

Moi, T. (1987) *Sexual Textual Politics: Feminist Literary Theory*. London: Methuen.

Munsch, R. and Marchenko, M. (1980) *The Paper Bag Princess*. Toronto: Annick Press.

Pierce, K. M. and Gilles, C. J. (1993) *Cycles of Meaning: Exploring the Potential of Talk in Learning Communities.* Portsmouth, NH: Heinemann.

Pipher, M. (1994) *Reviving Ophelia: Saving the Selves of Adolescent Girls.* New York: Ballantine.

Pratt, M. L. (1991) Arts of the contact zone. *Profession 91*, Modern Language Association, 33–40.

Rebolledo, T. D. and Rivero, E. S. (1993) *Infinite Divisions: An Anthology of Chicana Literature.* Tucson, AZ: University of Arizona Press.

Rogers, T. and Soter, A. O. (1997) *Reading Across Cultures: Teaching Literature in a Diverse Society.* New York: Teachers College Press.

Roman, L., Christian-Smith, L. and Ellsworth, E. (1988) *Becoming Feminine: The Politics of Popular Culture.* London: Falmer Press.

Rosenblatt, L. (1938/1995) *Literature as Exploration* (5th edn). New York: Modern Language Association.

Sadker, M. and Sadker, D. (1994) *Failing at Fairness: How America's Schools Cheat Girls.* New York: Charles Scribner's Sons.

Seidman, I. E. (1991) *Interviewing as Qualitative Research: A Guide for Researchers in Education and the Social Sciences.* New York: Teachers College Press.

Shay, J. (1997) *Just Girls: Books that Celebrate Girls.* Catalogue published five times a year, aimed at families with girls ages 4 to 14. For more information, write: Just Girls, PO Box 34487, Bethesda, MD 20827, USA.

Short, K. G. and Harste, J. with Burke, C. (1995) *Creating Classrooms for Authors and Inquirers.* Portsmouth, NH: Heinemann.

Sims Bishop, R. (1997) Foreword. In T. Rogers and A. O. Soter (eds) *Reading Across Cultures: Teaching Literature in a Diverse Society.* New York: Teachers College Press.

Stine, R. L. (1989) *The Babysitter.* New York: Scholastic.

Stine, R. L. (1993) *Hitchhiker.* New York: Scholastic.

Taylor, J. M., Gilligan, C. and Sullivan, A. M. (1996) *Between Voice and Silence: Women and Girls, Race and Relationship.* Cambridge, MA: Harvard University Press.

Taylor, M. and Fox, D. L. (1996) Valuing cultural diversity. *English Journal* **85** (8), 87–90.

Trousdale, A. (1995) 'I'd rather be normal': a young girl's response to 'feminist' fairy tales. *The New Advocate* **8** (3), 183–96.

Wasser, J. D. and Bresler, L. (1996) Working in the interpretive zone: conceptualizing collaboration in qualitative research teams. *Educational Researcher* **25** (5), 5–15.

WEEA (Women's Educational Equity Act) Equity Resource Center (1997) *Resources for Educational Excellence: 1997 Catalog.* Washington, DC: US Department of Education. For more information: Web site: <http://www.edc.org/CEEC/WEEA>. E-mail: <WEEApub@edc.org.>

Weiler, K. (1988) *Women Teaching for Change: Gender, Class, and Power.* South Hadley, MA: Bergin & Garvey.

Whaley, L. and Dodge, L. (1993) *Weaving in the Women: Transforming the High School English Curriculum.* Portsmouth, NH: Boynton/Cook.

WILLA (Women in Literature and Life Assembly) (n.d.) *Guidelines for a Gender-Balanced Curriculum in English Language Arts.* Urbana, IL: National Council of Teachers of English.

Wilshire, D. (1989) The uses of myth, image, and the female body in re-visioning knowledge. In A. M. Jagger and S. R. Borno (eds) *Gender/ Body/ Knowledge: Feminist Reconstructions of Being and Knowing.* New Brunswick, NJ: Rutgers University Press.

Chapter 8

Adapting to the Textual Landscape: Bringing Print and Visual Texts Together in the Classroom

Andrew Goodwyn

In this final chapter, I shall examine some key ideas about reading in relation to that most problematic of areas, the media. In the first instance I shall cover certain issues about the reading environment in which we all live and discuss what I call the 'textual habitat'. This evolving habitat has profound implications for all teachers in terms of how texts are changing, and, therefore, for the specific texts that they select for students' attention. We have lived through almost the whole of the second half of the twentieth century, a postwar, postmodern era, in which the humanist concept of the unique self is constantly challenged, yet one in which we continually strive to make sense of our lives as individuals. This enduring paradox is central to young people who are surrounded by the all-encompassing, universal media, yet struggle to create a particular identity within their social and cultural context. Reader response theory has provided an account of reading which confronts this tension by stressing the value of the personal as a means of understanding ourselves and the broader social and cultural determinants which shape our lives. However, my own research evidence, as well as that of others (Masterman, 1985; Davies, 1996; Goodwyn *et al.*, 1997; Goodwyn, 1992a, 1992b; Hart and Benson, 1992, 1993), suggests that literature teachers and teachers generally are still ambivalent and deeply unsure about work related to media texts.

In this chapter, I shall develop an argument which provides a rationale for extending the parameters of what we habitually regard as textual study. This argument will range extensively over a number of key topics that tend to restrict the way literature teachers approach media texts. I shall focus then on an area which is particularly germane to the literature teacher – the adaptation – and treat it, not just as a mechanism for moving a text between media, but as a concept which in itself is evolving and becoming revitalized. The latter part of the chapter will present some ideas for classroom work that offer literature teachers some ways forward in this especially complex but potentially rich area.

SIGNS FOR THE TIMES

To begin with the personal, a police officer once remarked to me, with some irritation and justification, 'Can't you read!' In a moment of geographic, traffic-induced uncertainty, I had just tried to drive the wrong way down a one-way street. I might have pointed out to him that he should have said:

> Did you neglect to observe the large symbolic icons on both sides of the street, both of which provide striking visual clues, using red for danger and a broad bar across a white field suggesting no entry – these icons now being in common use throughout Europe and, indeed, much of the world?

Fortunately for me, and the traffic building up around me, I decided to say nothing and simply to turn round and drive on in as humble a manner as possible.

The police officer expected me, an adult in a country with universal education, to be able 'to read'. That was a reasonable assumption although it is still very possible to be functionally illiterate in such a country but, even if I were, the visual representation of such, a clear sign as 'No Entry' might have prevented my mistake; that I am sure the policeman meant 'read' as in recognizing the sign, not particularly the words. What I had done, in a stressful situation, was to fail to read that vital sign, one amongst thousands, in a complicated city-scape. This event happened to take place in London, in Trafalgar Square, a historic site that also contains, in its symbolic centre, Nelson's column, a vast nationalistic icon and, along one side, the National Gallery, a huge collection of symbolic representations. I did not think about these cultural and historic riches at the time; in fact I was barely aware of them, except as familiar markers on a recently altered route. One's attention is always, necessarily and crucially, selective, and this is a key point in thinking about how to broaden the reading scope of adolescents in schools. We recognize that we have only so much time and attention in school in which to help our students prepare for an extraordinarily demanding reading environment; it is a radically different environment to that of even a decade ago and we must teach accordingly.

However, despite the police officer's doubts, I can read; so can you. I can also make another, reasonable assumption: that you are concerned about reading in some professional way – such readers being the implied audience of this text. I can also make the assumption that you, as a highly skilled reader of print, especially this kind of more academic text, know that I, the author, am up to something with this anecdote. You are waiting for my point. If this were a novel or a film, I might keep you guessing for some time and you would probably tolerate this uncertainty as part of the learned pleasure of such delay. Here, however, you are reading mainly, in Rosenblatt's sense, efferently (Rosenblatt, 1978); you want to take something useful and usable from this text.

My first point is that your skills as a reader are multifarious, hence you have different expectations of this text from a novel or a narrative film: so far, so obvious. We, sophisticated readers (a term I have defined quite specifically in Chapter 1) and people interested in the process of reading, must give young people as much opportunity as possible to have the same multifarious skills. However, as people professionally and personally interested in reading, we must respond to significant changes in what I am going to call the textual habitat, that is the textual environment which affects us and which we affect. Trafalgar Square (or Washington Square in New York or any similar, historically determined urban arrangement) is part of such an environment, so is any library full of books, so are people's homes, so is the classroom. The textual habitat has changed in the twentieth century and will continue to evolve rapidly in the next century, where our students will spend their adult lives. One major change to this habitat will be that the importance of print will continue to be great but its temporary domination (perhaps a few hundred years) is coming to an end. Sophisticated readers like us have a tremendous appreciation of and loyalty to print, and we tend to be very defensive about its supreme importance. However, we already know how much we gain from, and enjoy a vast repertoire of other texts, mostly visual. Sophisticated readers, then, can recognize how much is gained from a sophisticated reading of almost any text. It is also important to state that the ending of print's domination will not make it less important; it will become even more important but in a rather different way as it becomes more obviously simply one, very particular, form of communication.

This chapter tries to explore the implications of this very obviously changing textual habitat for young people learning to read it and to read in it. So my second point is that those teachers in school who claim the main responsibility for improving students' reading can surely recognize how multifaceted reading now is and will continue to be. For example, the screen, whatever its shape and size, is a primary site for reading and this includes reading in the most iconic way to the most literary. I write this 'on' a screen which offers me various writerly icons and which recognizes my pen and paper upbringing. An easily recognizable image of scissors tells me that I can 'cut and paste' a text that has no solid, physical existence – this is a reassuring symbol for me but it hides how utterly different the textual habitat is now to the one in which I learned to write. Literary teachers, i.e. teachers of the letter (Latin *litera* 'letter'), are becoming aware of the enormous implications of such changes to the process of textual composition but are often unsure how to view these changes or make use of them as teachers (Goodwyn, 1997). I should like to stress here that we are all in the same state of uncertainty and that this inevitably produces collective anxiety and, often, a somewhat reactionary desire to hold on to what we felt 'worked for us', i.e. reading print (Lanham, 1993; Goodwyn *et al.*, 1997). Teachers, whose responsibility is for the future as well as the past, need to help each other to have courage to look forward as well as to the past; what we cannot afford to be is backward.

My third point is that we know a great deal about reading and that the literary understanding of texts is of immense value and, in my view, is not made redundant by either technological change or the undeniable fact that *the majority of adults choose to watch texts*. As I stressed above, the apparent (it was never real), absolute dominance of print is ending and we need to adapt our knowledge to a new environment. To broaden reading for our adolescent students means making them engage *consciously* with a wider range of texts from a wide range of media. Defined like this it does not mean less reading, as so many teachers fear; it means both more reading and more intelligent reading of texts *in relation to each other*. For this reason I plan to explore the area of adaptations in some detail later on.

Finally, I shall be drawing on a range of sources to build my argument and to provide some practical examples of its implementation in teaching. I shall look at some issues about visual and literary reading; explore the applicability of aspects of reader response theory to visual as well as printed texts; focus on theories of reading development, using Appleyard's schema (Appleyard, 1990) reviewed in Chapter 1, in detail; and consider how we may need some different concepts to help us make our teaching coherent both for ourselves and for our students.

LITERATURE TEACHERS AND THE REAL HEATHCLIFFE

As I have mentioned above, the processes of change generate much anxiety and all readers, who, like me, come from a particular species that might be designated 'the print species', often find some of the claims made for the digital future (Negroponte, 1995) more alarming than invigorating. However, as I shall continue to argue, we must all recognize that the print species (a fairly intelligent life form) must evolve. In reviewing my own history as a dedicated consumer of texts and someone who is conscious of being changed, I am reminded of when I was studying for a Masters in Victorian Literature. Coming close to the end of that arduous course, I was walking home, passed a girls' secondary school, and noticed, over the hedge, a group of girls, probably 11 and 12 years old, engaged in an intense game. Several of the girls were racing around, arms outstretched, calling out to each other; I could just make out one repeated word, 'Heathcliffe!' I smiled, amused by their intensity and touched by their naivety but also bemused, pondering on that extraordinarily dark book, *Wuthering Heights*, and its contrast to a hot, bright afternoon. I had not enjoyed the book very much myself but recognized its strange, almost crude power. I remember thinking that these girls must have really visualized those bleak moors in order to create a play world of their own. Heathcliffe has always seemed to me to be a kind of fantasy figure in the modern sense of someone (or rather something) that excites fantasies. Of course, the girls were young and relatively inexperienced readers; perhaps that meant that Heathcliffe could, paradoxically, be very real?

Or were they viewers? It had not occurred to me, not once in twenty years, until writing this chapter, that they might have seen, for example, the 1939 film (much shown in British secondary schools) in which Laurence Olivier plays Heathcliffe. At that stage in my life, all those years ago, I was very definitely dominated by print, quite prejudiced against popular visual media and still struggle with that legacy today. I hope this reassessment of my understanding serves as an example of how the limits of one's literariness can be exposed. I was making assumptions and thinking narrowly about texts, two decades later, in the age of the screen; both I, and all of us, need to think more broadly.

I shall never know where that powerful image of Heathcliffe came from for that group of girls. However, I know that experienced readers currently often express their dissatisfaction with a particular film 'version' of a book they have read because the visual text does not match the one stored in their memories. As Harriet Hawkins observes (Hawkins, 1993, p. 124) in discussing *Gone with the Wind*, 'if a film adaptation fails to satisfy readers who "couldn't put the book down", "didn't want it to end" and thought it would make a *great* film, it will inevitably fail'. She quotes *Time* critic Richard Corliss who states, 'Novel readers are a possessive lot – they have already made their own imaginary film version of the book – cast it, dressed the sets, directed the camera.' His focus is the failure, in his view, of the film of Tom Wolfe's novel, *Bonfire of the Vanities*. Actors and actresses in particular frequently fail to embody the imagined Heathcliffe or Emma. One might interpret this readerly phenomenon, disappointment at a film 'version', in various ways.

For example, advocates of reading as the 'real thing' may wish to argue that written texts are the definitive and truly demanding experience because each reader imagines their own. John O. Thompson reviews some of these issues commenting that 'the adaptation phenomenon has always made people uneasy' (J. O. Thompson, 1996, p. 11). He argues:

> there is a tangle of grounds for unease – I am thinking of considerations of 'authenticity' (the original is authentic, the adaptation is a simulacrum), of 'fidelity' (the adaptation is a deformation or dilution of the original), of art-form 'specificity' (the literary original, if it is valuable must unfold its material in terms of distinctive literariness, and this must be lost in a filmed version, while the film version itself represents a lost opportunity to develop material of a specifically filmic sort) and of 'massification' (the original must be harder, more cognitively demanding, than the adaptation, or the latter would not be the more popular form for a mass audience; but then the easy access to the material must involve deskilling the reader/viewer).

For me this is an excellent summary of the unease felt by members, like myself, of the print species. For the print species the film of *Wuthering Heights* or *Emma* is therefore almost inevitably second-best and disappointing.

Other readers/viewers, in absolute contrast, may wish to criticize these narrow 'readers', pointing out that this is not so much a version but really a different text based on one narrative; it should be different and an intelligent viewer will enjoy the new text alongside the old, having been enriched by the intertextual experience. Some might even go a step further and argue that the new text will add to our understanding of the 'old' one; any 'new' interpretation raises challenges for our responses and our understandings, therefore the more adaptations the better.

Where should teachers of literature place themselves on this spectrum of opinion? Should they be 'purists', devoted to the authenticity of the total reading experience of a demanding novel, with Heathcliffe only truly living on the page? Should they be intertextualists, excited by the opportunities opened up by a new and powerful interpretation, one very likely to hold their students' full attention? Should they even embrace postmodernism and seek for as many textual variants as they can track down, destabilizing the archaic notion of the singular text once and for all? Well, frankly, that depends, and it depends on a number of contextual elements which will be explored as the chapter progresses, but I would argue from the outset that our 'real' Heathcliffe, whether in the novel or in a stage, film or television adaptation, is a set of codes that we read and so imbue with textual life. Such a statement is, of course, the bold, confident assertion of a sophisticated reader. Adolescents are much more concerned about 'fidelity', 'authenticity' and whether fiction in whatever form is 'realistic'. Characters are real to them. So real, in fact, that it may be true to say that reading matters far more to them than to mature readers – reading can really affect their lives.

For example, the adolescents whom I have taught were far and away the strictest critics of adaptations; on the grounds of authenticity and fidelity in particular they would ridicule, as only insecure teenagers can, the whole artistic enterprise of a particular film or television version. This is their response to the 'unease' defined above, and something we all share. But surely it is a relatively naive position? Are we not, as teachers of texts, trying to ease our students towards more thoughtful and considered personal and critical positions? Heathcliffe has never had an existence, yet he exists in a multitude of minds. Olivier, on screen, is not Heathcliffe but for some viewers he may be the 'definitive' Heathcliffe. Once one can hold this paradox in mind, without unease, then one recognizes the power of the mind to respond to these codes, to 'know' they are codes and yet to enjoy their reality; they do affect our reality.

Literature teachers, especially those who specifically define themselves as 'Literature teachers', are much preoccupied with adulthood. Many of the claims made about adolescents studying literature, especially 'Serious Literature', are that such study will benefit them as adults, and in fact that it will make them mature (this is discussed more fully in Chapter 1) and responsible adults. (Good examples in the UK context can be found in the Kingman and Cox reports (DES, 1988, 1989), which form the basis for the National Curriculum for English.) There is a kind of mythology that adults who read 'serious' fiction are more civilized and cultured than those who do not. Whether such reading actually does have this effect will always be almost impossible to prove but I, for one, believe it has some truth. However, I think a more practicable, honest and realistic benefit of textual study is that adolescents can be helped to be more sophisticated adults and *potentially* morally superior ones. They can be made better readers of all texts including that multiplicity of texts we loosely call reality. Our students will engage as adults, and eventually as parents, with a vast number of challenging texts; most of them, of course, will be visual texts. They will choose, as do professional educators (Goodwyn, 1997), all kinds of texts from the most complex to the most banal, according to their needs at the time. Our emphasis as teachers needs to be less on making adolescents 'discriminate and resist' (Leavis and Thompson, 1933) and more on being understanding, i.e. knowledgeable, self-conscious readers and, therefore, selective. There is a great deal of more recent research evidence to suggest that adolescents are already quite independent and resistant to all kinds of texts (Benton, 1996; Buckingham, 1993a, 1993b; Goodwyn, 1992a; Sarland, 1991; Moss, 1989).

I am not suggesting, however, that adolescent readers need some kind of *amoral* training in decoding. The aim is not to distance them from texts but to make them knowledgeable about how texts become intimately involved in our thoughts and feelings. Indeed, almost all texts, visual or printed, obviously deal with value systems, and adolescents are helped by exploring value systems in texts; it is one of the very few ways that adolescents can get to grips with value systems at all since they can be so much more 'visible' in texts than in our daily narratives. Appleyard (see Chapter 1) characterizes the adolescent as 'The Reader as Thinker'. 'The adolescent reader looks to stories to discover insights into the meaning of life, values and beliefs worthy of commitment, ideal images, and authentic role models for imitation' (Appleyard, 1990, p. 14). In other words, adolescents bring powerful value judgements into all their textual experiences; if anything they need help to see the limitations that those values often produce. It is an illusion, of course, that these value systems are made static in texts. However, it can be a helpful illusion to students and teachers: just like the illusion of moving pictures that are made up of static images, we are able to feel as if we can see the whole thing at once.

As Louise Rosenblatt has so expertly demonstrated, the crucial point is that we are enabled to make some satisfying interpretation of the particular text at the time and so we are able to turn our attention to other texts (Rosenblatt, 1938). That interpretation is then, in a sense, stored in our textual archive at the conscious and subconscious levels. We consciously recall a text when a mental event, usually engaging with another text, calls for comparison. Most of the time each text is subsumed in a general pool of textual knowledge.

For me this is why the fate of Heathcliffe is very indicative. As part of a Masters course I ask adults, who are also teachers, to read *Wuthering Heights*. For most of the group, certainly 90 per cent, this means re-reading the book. Each time I have done this, half the class have been thrilled by their re-reading, the other half deeply disappointed. The first group are happy because the second reading has retained the remembered excitement of the first; for the second group the remembered excitement has unfortunately been replaced by boredom, they can no longer see what all the fuss is about. Heathcliffe in particular, as one teacher put it, 'acts like such an idiot all the time'. However, both groups tend to agree that this text, based on their memories of their own adolescent encounter with it, must be essentially a good read for adolescents.

This retrospective readerly phenomenon is well known, and reader response theory (Rosenblatt, 1938, 1978) has given it a sound, psychological underpinning. The original, textual interpretation has been relatively static but these readers have changed enormously. They respond differently now, not essentially because they are teachers (note that the group, who are all teachers, have markedly different responses) but because they are adult readers. All these adults have continued to mature and to read; there is clearly some connection but one does not simply explain the other – the act of reading is clearly not in itself the *cause* of maturity. However, these readers, re-reading *Wuthering Heights*, have also absorbed countless visual texts in the intervening years. What difference has that made to their textual knowledge? Has not some of their sophistication and understanding, whether they enjoyed or disliked their mature encounter with Heathcliffe, come from their reading of, for example, television and film texts? Ultimately then, we need to help adolescents draw on all their textual knowledge in order to assist them towards sophisticated understandings of the new texts they will encounter, both with and without us.

ADAPTING TO THE TEXTUAL LANDSCAPE

English teachers, it has been claimed, are the heirs of Leavis either consciously or unconsciously (Eagleton, 1983; Davies, 1996). That is to argue that they promote reading as a highly serious, usually moral engagement with a text; close reading, in Leavis' sense, suggests an almost spiritual as well as physical intimacy with a book. Leavis was interested in the media, yet he despised it as the enemy of close, serious reading, seeing it symptomatic of a culture in decline. He made it clear that his approach was not designed to help the majority but a minority of highly specialized discriminating readers, the preachers of culture in a debased environment. His implicit message was that one should not adapt to such an environment.

Literature teachers today have lived through rapid technological change and inhabit a very different textual landscape. They ought to have far more awareness of and engagement with this change to the textual habitat than their adolescent charges for whom the present is everything. Yet old habits die hard and many literature teachers have difficulty accommodating these changes in relation to schooling and/or have seen them as evidence of decline, a decline in the predominance of print, which is their favourite medium. However, if we genuinely want our teenage students to be good readers and to become sophisticated adult readers, it is time for change. We need to broaden our definitions of textual study and to escape some of the narrow boundaries and strict limitations of traditional literature study in the secondary school, especially when current curriculum pressures in many English-speaking countries are very conservative (Jones, 1992; Myers, 1996; Green, 1993). We need to engage with a whole spectrum of texts in a way which is meaningful to our students, acknowledging that the landscape they inhabit is dominated by visual texts and it is time for literature teachers to redefine themselves in essence, if not in name, as textual teachers. The textual landscape is evolving and is now more crowded, probably more stimulating, than ever before. We need new teaching approaches to help our students to cope with the new landscape; some older approaches need to be either adapted or abandoned. I am aware that many literature teachers are already and frequently making use of media texts; my argument is that they now normalize this element of their teaching.

One reason why it is important to normalize this approach is so that teacher and students can normalize their relationship. During the period of about 400 years between the invention of the printing press and the invention of the camera, textual teachers were dealing with printed texts; as I argued in Chapter 1, being educated was really synonymous, almost exclusively, with being able to read print. The whole discourse of education and, to a large extent, society, centred around print. Since the arrival of 'universal' television about forty years ago, a confusion has arisen about the discourse of education. The old definition of being educated has been overtaken by technology and has not been lost but subsumed. Our educations come from many sources (as indeed they always did, we have always learned most from people) and we now have more choice about where to focus our attention to learn about the world. Back in 1975, a study (Murdock and Phelps, 1975) found that teachers were mostly removed from 'ordinary' culture and were perceived by students as trespassing in that territory if they brought it into their teaching. My argument is that teachers now live much more in both territories, the 'old' education discourse and the new media culture, also inhabited by their students.

It is useful here to turn for some help to linguistics, a subject which is increasingly turning its attention from the micro (the word, the sentence) to the macro level, often using the term 'discourse' as the chief category. James Gee, among many others, is a linguist deeply interested in literacy. He defines literacy not as a limited outcome of education but as a 'social practice', arguing that:

> *Types* of texts and the various *ways of reading* them do not flow full-blown out of the individual soul, (or biology); they are the social and historical inventions of various groups of people. One always and only learns to interpret texts of a certain type in certain ways through having access to, and ample experience in, social settings where texts of that type are read in those ways.
>
> (Gee, 1994, p. 44)

I would argue that bringing in media texts alongside print texts allows us to help students to understand the social contextuality of all texts, both contemporary and historical.

Gee goes further and examines the notion of discourse and, most importantly, of primary and secondary discourse. To sum up his complex argument for my purposes, he suggests that 'schooling' has a well-established discourse that relates to the privileged elements of society. Many students' primary discourse does not relate to this discourse; the discourse of schooling is secondary for them.

I agree with this argument but I want to use the concept to provide us with a helpful way of thinking about our teaching of texts, particularly adaptations. I would argue that society's dominant conversational discourse relates to the increasingly visual world; students are then very knowledgeable about television, for example, but since it is a primary discourse, they are not especially aware of it. Literature teachers, when teaching, adopt a print discourse and so feel much less comfortable in the visual discourse, which is secondary for them. What we need is for teachers to recognize the limitations that this print discourse places on them so that they can enter more fully into understanding the mainstream discourse where their students live. The irony is that my research (Goodwyn, 1997; Goodwyn *et al.,* 1997) suggests that educators generally are quite at ease with media culture in their own lives; when they enter the school they become guilty and confused about the relationship between their own valuing of, and enjoyment in, media and their 'professional role' as a representative of high culture. In other words they feel the tensions between the discourses and need to accept this and to acknowledge its power. I think it is very similar to the idea of the 'unease' surrounding adaptation. However, it also means recognizing that the students will be working from their primary discourse into the secondary one; they too feel this tension. As Gee points out, the more a teacher can use the primary discourse the more chance of bringing students into an understanding of discourses more generally, their own and that of others. If the aim is to create a sophisticated understanding of print, of literature in particular, then students are more likely to gain this through the way teachers relate texts to each other instead of, in a sense, outlawing some from the classroom.

Good literature teachers already recognize that a film text based on a novel is a valuable resource. Yet to fail to treat the film text as a text in its own right is to remain within the boundaries of the existing discourse. One approach is to 'start where the kids are'. In other words, let's grab their attention and then slip in the serious stuff, i.e. the literature, before they know it. Conversely, there are many literature teachers for whom the video version of a printed text is still a kind of carrot to entice the donkeys; the students have to be dragged through the written text in order to enjoy the carrot of the 'film' at the end of their study time. I am well aware why the carrot model happens and I know that 'it works', having used that approach a number of times myself. What that model suggests is that visual texts are motivating and that printed texts appear to demotivate students. However, this superficial truth also perpetuates the problem. Students understand this somewhat behaviourist model, 'If we are good we will get our reward, the soft option of enjoying the movie.' In this way the message to everyone is, 'Print texts are a problem, visual texts are unproblematic.' We should recognize that the carrot model institutionalizes and almost ritualizes all the participants into negative positions; worst of all it places the literature teacher in the ironic position of appearing to accept that students only really enjoy the movie version.

My argument begins with the point that the carrot model developed from a time when print texts were still the basis of schooling. First television and then video came along, and literature teachers added these technologies into their print-dominated approach. This was perfectly successful in its own terms; but now the terms are different, the textual landscape has changed them. We now have access in school to the wide range of textual resources available outside school and this has a simple but profound implication for a literature teacher: we must abandon the carrot model. It will be appropriate to work sometimes on a print text exclusively and sometimes with several 'mixed' print and visual texts; however, it will surely be worth working at times on a visual text exclusively. This should change the message to all the participants and recognize that the textual habitat has changed and is rapidly changing, and that we are all experiencing the challenge of uncertainty and change.

READERS' RESPONSES TO PRINT AND VISUAL TEXTS

Reader response theory has developed a position which recognizes that readers need a personal engagement with a text in order to have a response to it (Rosenblatt, 1938, 1978). By 'personal' response some, the heirs of the New Critics, might still negatively interpret a merely emotional and also narrowly subjective response; however, there is no such thing as a purely objective response to a novel – if any human produced such a response then they must have misunderstood what a novel is and must also be a very strange human being. A response, especially an initial one, is likely to be a tentative and interpretative one, seeking to clarify meaning and to create a sense of satisfactory understanding in the reader. Reaching a satisfactory and temporarily stable view of a text involves an integrated relationship of the cognitive and the affective, with an implication also of the objective and the subjective. This will be my definition of response throughout the chapter. We have a very every-day and entirely phenomen-ologically accurate phrase for this: our interpretation has to 'feel right'.

Drawing on reader response in relation to all texts brings in the potentially problematic use of the term 'reading' for some non-print texts. Many teachers, as well as many non-teaching but highly educated adults, will immediately be uneasy with the term 'reading' if applied to a 'purely' visual text. I will need to examine this territory to some extent but only in relation to teaching. A more useful starting point than the genuine and important differences between, say, print and visual media texts is the simple but absolutely crucial unifier, that these are all texts. When adolescents come to the classroom they are, almost all of them, highly experienced with texts of all kinds. They have a great repository of textual knowledge to draw upon; much of it, usually the vast majority, will be visual text. The point for the literature teacher is that this textual knowledge provides a very valuable base for work with all kinds of texts but also specifically for literary texts. All readers use their life knowledge and their textual knowledge to interpret texts; that is what makes texts meaningful for them, hence textual knowledge of all kinds can be used by adolescents to make sense of all kinds of texts.

We feel that we, i.e. literature teachers, know far more about the nature of print reading than we do about the processes by which readers absorb visual texts, and yet we still know relatively little about print reading. What is known most about is the period of the very early years where literacy is (or is not) acquired. As readers become more experienced the research evidence gets slimmer and the attention of research seems to turn away from models of adult reading altogether. Ironically, the great mass of 'teachers' in university literature departments treat readers as unproblematic in the sense that their main work is concerned with theories of literature as opposed to theories of reading (Evans, 1993). I. A. Richards' experiments with students as actual readers, reported in *Practical Criticism* (Richards, 1929), has eventually had a great effect but not, arguably, in literature departments. In other words, although students and teachers in such departments spend all their time talking about texts and about issues of critical theory and ideology, the term 'reading' is still treated as relatively neutral and clear. Most literature teachers spent several years in literature departments discussing texts and learning to leave out much of their textual and life knowledge from such discussion (Evans, 1993).

Of course, literature students themselves are constantly assessed on their response to print texts. However, as Colin Harrison points out about a person's response to reading:

> Can we see it? Can we measure it? Can we store it and replay it? Can we make it available in any direct way for further examination, moderation, discussion? . . . Reading involves the construction of meaning and in this sense is an active process, but most of the activity is private.
>
> (Harrison, 1995, p. 68)

We can only ever gain a secondary view of the reading process; the reader can only give us some form of account of his or her reading experience and the same is true of reading visual texts. In that sense then print and visual text reading are very similar and offer the same opportunities and problems to the teacher who is concerned with encouraging and developing response.

Claims are frequently made that viewing, unlike book reading, is usually a very social act (as in the home) or even a public activity (as in the cinema) but this contextual and potentially affective difference should not delude us. We respond as we do to a book, in an interior way. As Colin Harrison affirms, our response to the text must be articulated in some way – exteriorized – for others to have access to it, for whatever purpose. What we might find valuable as teachers is to look at how our contemporary style of adult book reading dramatizes the privacy of the act. Most people apparently read at home, on their own, and seem to prefer to read in relative quiet. I would argue that this is our stereotypical image of readers and it is a very dated one. Reading tends to be portrayed as not just an interior activity but an isolated one.

However, many people read in crowded, noisy environments, e.g. restaurants or in transit by whatever form. Even in libraries, where the tradition is of a quiet atmosphere, the individual is surrounded by others. It is an important difference that print readers in public spaces are usually reading different texts whereas, for example, cinema audiences are consciously enjoying the same film. However, it was not so long ago that people used to scream and faint at Dickens' public readings and a few, 'literary' people, some of them teachers, still go to public readings. Our most intimate form of reading is probably exemplified by the parent–child or older–younger sibling partnership but this is both very private and very public, a public performance in a private space. An obvious, but somewhat overlooked, key point is that, for teachers, the majority of their reading and that of their students is extremely public and very often, literally, out loud and everyone is (or is supposed to be) looking at the same text at the same time. The text in the classroom, whether film or novel, is studied socially with response being developed simultaneously by all students. Overall then, print reading is a far more public and visible act than the stereotypical image suggests.

It may be worth reflecting on the apparent difference in control in reading and viewing situations. Viewers in the cinema, as in the theatre, give themselves up to a temporal, finite experience and often choose, quite consciously, to go with others to share in this discrete experience. Readers of, say, novels expect to take some time over their reading and to tolerate frequent, even lengthy interruptions to their narrative. These differences are real and socially and culturally powerful; we may be defining ourselves publicly by choosing to be a member of a certain type of film audience, the Woody Allen rather than the Arnold Schwarzenegger. This experiential difference should be explored in school, and adolescents' understanding of texts can be substantially deepened by exploring the concept of audience. Very strikingly, a consideration of audience has long been a feature of film and media studies and only relatively recently an issue in the literature classroom, a topic I shall return to later. However, there is a basic commonality, in that the book we hold up on the plane or train defines us just as much as our visit to the movies and, even if read in private space, still has to be bought or borrowed. We are engaging in a social act of definition through our choice of reading.

The final and especially crucial point for teachers is that video initially confused and now, I believe, has clarified the commonalities between reading print and visual texts. With video the reader is given back textual control, the ability to pause, to re-view and to reflect and, most simply, to enjoy the text again. Teachers were in a sense conceptually confused initially by video because they felt it gave them this 'new' opportunity to stop and examine texts, i.e. to interrupt them. Students still very often complain at this disruption, 'Can't we see it to the end?' Literature teachers might very well read a complete poem, possibly even a short story without interruption, but an entire novel or a whole play? Literature teachers interrupt texts all the time and go back and forth over them; they consider this technique to be close, textual analysis and therefore 'a good thing'. In other words re-reading and re-viewing, or putting in a reflective pause, have exact parallels and are about the same idea, that of textual knowledge and reader response.

Another distinction still made about video is the obvious fact that books are still far more portable and independent; however, this is simply a matter of technology. As Peter Reynolds succinctly expresses it:

> even the so-called enlightened student of literary texts sometimes inadvertently confuses the material solidity of printed books with the true nature of what they contain ... What the symbolic language of the printed word is constructed by its reader to mean is, of course, the result of a dialectical process in which the reader continually makes and re-makes the text according to his or her cultural, social and historical circumstances.
>
> (Reynolds, 1993, p. 3)

Books may feel solid and permanent but their meanings are not. However, there is an important difference in that video is *dependent* on technology as well as the reader for it to 'work' and the same is true of, for example, audio-books and CD-roms. The print reader feels in control of the physically independent text, especially a solid, three-dimensional book. Ultimately this is a technological advantage that will ensure the survival of the book. However, it does mask the fact that this is just as artificial a text as a video or film, and that it is a mass-produced object. Emily Brontë did not produce my copy of *Wuthering Heights*. Literature teachers feel that a book is authentic in a way that a video is not. This is a misconception.

To take this point further, we are not bothered by print page numbers on the page although, in a typical adult novel, they bear no relation to an author's original manuscript, i.e. they are accidental in relation to the book's form. In an illustrated text or a children's book an author may have designed a text in pages. In a film the narrative is usually realized in scenes and the script will number and paginate these scenes; what we watch simply leaves these out. When we see *Romeo and Juliet* at the theatre, divisions between acts and scenes are marked for the audience but not by someone holding up a print sign. In books we expect page numbers because that is the reading script. We pay more attention to chapters and sections. Victorian novelists especially liked to stop the text and give us a little lecture before 'carrying on', but is voice-over very different? People comment on the three-dimensionality of books, their physical shape, their smell and even their sensual appeal. These are real attributes and pleasures but they are relatively minor side-effects of a production process. Almost paradoxically videos on shelves look very much like books, have covers and blurbs, and presumably their own smell. Literature teachers might usefully reflect on the point that when they sometimes say that it is the text that really counts, i.e. the meta-text not the particular book, at other times they expend much emotional energy on books as objects (I have done it myself many times and still do); the message to many students is that literature teachers see books as, literally, precious, even sacred, objects. They were not dubbed 'The Preachers of Culture' (Mathieson, 1975) for nothing. We must recognize that this is a learned, culturally inflected disposition; it has nothing to do with, say, the intrinsic value of a text. Overall then there are interesting differences to explore about print and visual texts but there are at least as many commonalities; many of the practices of literature teachers do not identify actual differences, they artificially produce them.

DEVELOPING AND EXTENDING READERS' RESPONSES THROUGH WHAT WE KNOW

I am adopting the unoriginal point of view that we should use what we feel we 'know' about reading to develop our understanding of the way that humans generally, but young people in particular, make sense of all texts. That is, we should make the most of our textual knowledge of printed texts and see it as complementary to our broad textual knowledge. It is time, however, to recognize the limitations of our knowledge. Literature teachers have been shown to be, unsurprisingly, relatively inexpert with some kinds of media texts (Buckingham, 1992; Masterman, 1985; Hart and Benson, 1992, 1993) because they tend to apply literary techniques to non-literary media texts.

This narrow approach is simply a result of literary training and needs to be recognized as such. As I am arguing, there are commonalities and differences between print and media texts, and both elements are interesting; literature teachers are bound to need help to expand their understandings and their teaching repertoire.

Equally we should unashamedly draw on our literariness whilst recognizing that literary reading is peculiar in the strict sense of the term. Our students will go on as 'ordinary' adults to consume thousands of texts, mostly just for enjoyment and relaxation, some for information, and a few texts will affect students deeply. How can we help them to read all these texts and to make the most of them in their daily lives?

First, we need to think more about reading and less about Literature with a capital L, and to consider how to place reading in relation to the normal dominant activity of viewing. There is a special place for watching 'versions' of novels in the literature classroom. There is also a special place for examining the genres of reading that cross all textual boundaries, such as romance, horror and crime. These genres are in the true sense phenomenally popular and can be studied as phenomena. The reader as thinker and interpreter can find much to say about texts here; the individual texts act principally as exemplar, rather than as particular icons. Such genres also have quite visible histories. This contrasts with the rather isolating reading of 'sacred' texts whose study is frequently validated by the adjectives 'timeless' or 'universal'. It is equally interesting to involve teenagers in the study of ephemera since it is the main diet of all of us whilst the epithet 'universal' perhaps applies very powerfully to a media genre such as soap opera.

To take Appleyard's schema here (see Chapter 1), the adults are the pragmatic readers, and they are the ones in their many millions choosing to engage with, for example, soap operas. The adolescents are still in the thinking and interpreting stage, open to exploring and considering the whole range of texts. It is not that the literature teacher can somehow inoculate future generations so that they can withstand some corrupting textual virus; the great majority of students will continue to enjoy soap operas, in one form or another, probably until they die, and they will not die because of over exposure to television. What textual teachers can do is to explore our reading of soap operas, investigate them as phenomena, and interpret and question their status in the world.

TEXTS AND THEIR MUTATIONS (ADAPTATION, EVOLUTION, CHANGE)

I have argued elsewhere for the subject of English to embrace media texts in a positive and catalytic way, so that the subject itself will be changed in the process (Goodwyn, 1992a). However, in this section I am going to concentrate on that nexus where literature and media teaching both meet and collide: the adaptation. Before discussing some examples and practical approaches to classroom work I need to extend my earlier metaphor about habitat and to speculate about how texts, rather like species, are changing and being changed. I think it is helpful to look at texts as dynamic entities, under pressure to change in a number of ways, and I shall explore this concept through the metaphors from biology of adapting and mutating.

Mutant is variously defined in dictionaries but its modern use shares the idea that an organism has undergone usually sudden and rapid change. Its older usage was far more neutral, its earliest definitions being to do with musical change (for example, a mutation stop on an organ or changes to syllables in Germanic languages). I suspect that the term for present-day readers of this chapter conjures up images from a range of visual texts in which monstrous creatures have been produced through pollution or radiation; this equates mutants with unnatural and catastrophic changes and with our collective guilt about the way we may be abusing our planet. An adaptation is very different. To adapt is to change in harmony with the environment – to fit in, in a positive sense.

An adaptation in the textual sense is something created by a human agent or agents, transferring a text from one medium to another. Such agency gives the impression that individual human artists remain at the centre of this adaptive process. Mutation, however, carries the connotation that powerful, usually inhuman, forces have caused change; what might it mean in the textual environment?

It might be worth thinking about what is happening to texts as a combination of mutation and adaptation. For example, at the time of writing, Jane Austen's work has been very prominently adapted in the English-speaking world. Each text has been adapted by someone; an example is Emma Thompson who not only adapted but also starred in *Sense and Sensibility*. What makes her text unusual is that many readers of the film actually might know she adapted it but only because she is also a 'star' in the traditional, Hollywood, sense of the term. Most audiences watching *Sense and Sensibility* would consider it to be by Jane Austen; the adapter would be even less known than the director.

First then, literature teachers could usefully extend their repertoire by beginning to engage with the whole concept of adapters and adaptation. That involves not just using the film of the book but actually exploring adaptation as a *phenomenon in itself*. There is, for example, human agency involved and so the use of a screenplay in the classroom can be extremely educative for all concerned. However, screenplays have to be 'realized'; they are not at all easy to read whereas novels are (usually) readerly. Teaching the concept of adaptation means that students will need to know about the novel, how it has been adapted, and the nature of the adaptive process. This means exploring more than just the human and aesthetic dimensions and bringing in the larger, relatively impersonal forces that affect texts.

It is in this sense that adaptations may also be treated as mutant texts. In a sense the 'original' literary text is itself the first adaptation. The vision of the world offered by any artist is a representation of reality, not reality itself, and is necessarily moulded by the social and cultural context of its production. Writers may adapt to this context in a confirmatory or innovatory way, but they are essentially situated within an evolutionary stage in terms of language and consciousness, and work within the parameters of these constraints. For example, Dickens' novels may be seen as a powerful critique of Victorian life but they are essentially part of that life. Subsequent re-adaptations produced in a different historical and social context, for a new audience, work with different conceptions of social experience. Thus the text will undergo changes due to a translation from a purely verbal to a visual/filmic/ televisual/dramatic medium; it will also be altered by the external, even impersonal forces which exert their power on the text. Patsy Stoneman's book, *Brontë Transformations: The Culural Dissemination of 'Jane Eyre' and 'Wuthering Heights'*

(1996), provides an extraordinary account of the literally hundreds of adaptations that have been made of these two famous texts. She argues that not only do 'people transform texts . . . and texts transform people' but 'texts transform themselves' (p. 1). She analyses how these texts have gone through infinite re-inventions. In particular *Wuthering Heights* has been subjected to very different emphases in order to reflect the extent to which the love between Heathcliffe and Cathy could be considered conventionally romantic or sexually subversive.

When Thackeray's *Vanity Fair* was serialized by the BBC as one of its 'Classic Serials' in the autumn of 1987, it was chosen partly because it seemed to offer some critique of modern, Thatcherite Britain (Giddings *et al.,* 1990), yet at the same time it had to be a costume, and therefore authentic, period drama reflecting the manners of the original era. It also had to be reproduced so as to be exportable around the world to a family audience. Thackeray himself had to write in such a way as to conform to Victorian readerly expectations but the directors of the serial had to acknowledge changes in viewer expectations and yet conform just as much to the definition of 'family viewing' in the late 1980s. The case study of *Vanity Fair* in *Screening the Novel* (Giddings *et al.,* 1990), provides a rich picture of the myriad of forces playing on this adaptation. Simply placing it within the classic serial slot meant that very particular commercial forces were at play; such classic serials have been defined as

> The production of a mythologised British 'history' and 'tradition' . . . in strictly domestic economic terms [they] are expensive but become 'a good investment' when guaranteed foreign sales are involved. The marketing of British culture as a televisual commodity has become almost a corollary of the British tourist industry, and fulfils a similar role in international terms.
>
> (Gardner and Wyver quoted in Kerr, 1982, p. 9)

It would be very valuable for students to explore such issues around television adaptations; not just that they have a very different timescale to films, i.e. many episodes that are usually of exactly the same length, but that they are designed to 'fit' particular slots whose conventions they must address. These conventions may well include being marketable as a cultural export.

Thus I would argue that Emma Thompson's *Sense and Sensibility* is both a re-adaptation and a mutant text. It is not just different to the original novel text but also to various other visualizations and dramatizations produced in the twentieth century. Thompson's *'Sense and Sensibility': The Diaries* (E. Thompson, 1996) reveals the actress/director dealing with a whole range of processes in order to create a film which is good as a film, as an adaptation and for the studio, especially as the film was financed with American money. Austen's *Pride and Prejudice*, which is considered to be her most popular novel, has existed in even more mutations. The main point is that external, even impersonal forces have exerted their power on these texts. Literature teachers, unless still under the spell of the ahistorical New Critics, would almost certainly want to look at the social and historical context in which *Pride and Prejudice* or *Great Expectations* was produced. With adaptations there is more complexity to address. As well as the original author, there is the adapter or, very often, the adapters. Again Emma Thompson's diaries show just how dynamic and changing is the process of creating a film over three months, influenced by factors as varied as the whole production team simultaneously suggesting how to get the best from a particular scene on film to dealing with the difficulties of British weather and farting horses.

It seems more and more evident that authors are being recycled by generations who find something powerful in their works. For example, the 1980s was the era of E. M. Forster (there were film versions of *Howards End, A Room with a View, Maurice* and *A Passage to India*). All we can do is explain it by theorizing about Forster's adaptability, the interest of his subject matter for the audiences of the time, and the relatively new phenomenon of which Jane Austen is clearly a part of the using up of textual species. That is, if one text successfully adapts then the others may be similarly treated; this phenomenon becomes a part of the shaping habitat for the text, one of the forces of mutation. The lifeblood of the textual habitat is, obviously, texts; there must be more texts, they have to come from somewhere.

This concept can be translated into classroom practice in a number of ways. It is already reasonably common practice, when working on a single, printed text (usually a novel), for a class to be asked to consider how 'adaptable' a text is. Questions about genre, setting and suitable players for the various characters make useful starting points. However, as with the use of *Heart of Darkness* for *Apocalypse Now*, students might be asked to consider how to use a basic narrative to reach an audience in a particular way. Equally, the way *Clueless* is wittily based on *Emma,* provides an excellent model for considering where an adaptation should have a 'close fit' and where real changes might be made. These general questions can lead students into writing sections of script, and visualizing and trying out scenes.

Students can also be grouped around competing adaptations of a text, having to 'sell' their version to a group of students role-playing financiers and producers. In this kind of activity they can begin to explore this idea of mutation. What forces make a particular text become relevant to a new time-frame? In the same way, students can consider the endless recycling of texts such as *Dracula* and *Frankenstein.* These texts are re-imagined by, it seems, each generation and each version is inflected by that generation's angst. Students might be usefully engaged in speculating about what the next version will be like, what forces will influence the text, and what issues may be appropriately explored within its particular tradition. With younger students there is plenty of opportunity to look at how television for children adapts and recycles key heroes such a Superman, Batman and Spiderman. This is even more interesting now since Hollywood has begun to make blockbuster versions of these essentially cartoon figures.

This approach leads on, very appropriately, to an examination of the original literary text and to a consideration of why it was produced at a specific historical moment. Contrasts between Laurence Olivier's 1940s *Henry V*, made as part of the war effort in the Second World War, and Kenneth Branagh's 1990s version, made after the Falklands War, provide an excellent example, not least because Branagh is clearly making a kind of auteur statement in response to Olivier. One world-famous actor-manager consciously follows another, not simply taking the same, 'original' text, a text with very particular national resonance at a time of nationalistic anxiety, but also making a claim for the predecessor's pre-eminent status (as Shakespeare's Henry V does to his own father, Henry IV). Branagh has also directed a Frankenstein text and claimed to have gone back to the original giving the film the title of *Mary Shelley's Frankenstein.* Just this simple act of 'reclaiming' provides an excellent focus for a class looking at the concept of adaptation and originality. It also provides an excellent means of students reflecting on the fascination of certain modern myths, e.g. the created but destructive monster and their varying representations through print, stage and screen.

Students can develop this work by searching for texts themselves that will make a good adaptation and presenting them to classmates, having researched who owns the text, bringing in an understanding that stories can 'belong' to individuals and companies. This idea can be further developed by working on the idea of sequels, which are not owned in quite the same way. If *Rocky* can have four 'sequels', what about a sequel to *To Kill a Mockingbird* or *Of Mice and Men*? Students can be asked to look in the library or even the English department's shelves and to select a novel to 'sequelize'. They can work in groups, acting like film producers, looking for the right sequel, taking into account its appropriate market, and considering what kind of audience it might appeal to and how much knowledge of the original such an audience might have.

The concept of audience, as mentioned above, is still relatively rare in the English classroom despite the very positive changes that have taken place in the teaching of writing in particular over the last twenty years, where students have been asked to write for real audiences. At any time in the future it is highly likely that whenever a class might be working on the concept of adaptation, there will be several current adaptations in the cinema, on video or on television or radio. Linked to these adaptations will be numerous artefacts; for example, if it is Disney these artefacts will run into thousands of objects and advertising franchises, if it is a classic text then there may be only some literal promotional material and a new edition of the 'original'. Whichever end of the promotional scale a text may occupy it will have an audience and the scale will be very real evidence of the economic impact that the text is expected to make. The way texts are placed at the centre of huge marketing campaigns illustrates perfectly this idea of the textual landscape, but it also emphasizes how adaptations occupy a special and significant place within that landscape. Emma Thompson touches on this briefly in her diaries, 'We discussed the "novelization" question. This is where the studio pays someone to novelize my script and sell it as "Sense and Sensibility". I've said if this happens I will hang myself. Revolting notion. Beyond revolting' (E. Thompson, 1996, p. 16). She published her diaries, however, and students might find it useful to consider the inter-relationship between Emma Thompson's use of American money to finance her film and the studio's expectations of making a profit.

Adaptations also dramatize landscape in a very literal sense. The television adaptation of *Middlemarch* was filmed in a small English town called Stamford and not in its 'real' setting of Coventry. Since the filming the number of visitors to the town has increased dramatically and these visitors have come to 'see' Middlemarch (see Rice and Saunders, 1996). When *Brideshead Revisited* was shown on American television it generated a huge interest in the landscape and settings of the series, leading to the reproduction of the leading character's, Sebastian Flyte's bear, Aloysius, by a leading American designer (Golub, 1993). These two details, one a setting, the other a key artefact, open up rich possibilities to students for reflection on ideas about culture and heritage and identity. For example, students might investigate how an idea of period is evident in films of Dickens or Austen or, equally, of *The Color Purple* or *To Kill a Mockingbird*. They might look precisely for key artefacts, those that are redolent with meaning for modern audiences. Students can also be asked to think about texts that might be set in *their* location. If a certain text was going to be filmed in their area or neighbourhood, what degree of artifice would be needed to make the setting convincing in terms of the necessary atmosphere? Or, how would the text have to change to fit the landscape? These activities draw very precisely on students' textual knowledge, both print and visual, asking them to inter-relate the areas and to 'materialize' their ideas.

There is also interesting work to be done around the commercialization of certain literary habitats. England is full of marketed landscapes such as Hardy country, Shakespeare's country and countless others. Stoneman's book on the Brontës provides a fascinating account of how the Bradford-based British Wool Marketing Board, when planning to advertise its products in Japan, was asked to base their presentations on *Wuthering Heights*. The result was that musuem staff from the Brontë Museum worked with the Board to produce *The Romance of Wool*, a musical spectacle based on Heathcliffe and Cathy (Stoneman, 1996, p. 217). Students might be asked to research the commercial potential of authors with local connections and to develop some innovative 'uses' for these connections.

CONCLUSIONS

This chapter has tried to cover a great deal of ground in order to develop a comprehensive argument for including media texts within a literature-dominated curriculum. I have tried to demonstrate that print is, in a sense, being realigned alongside other kinds of text. However, this realignment is not reducing the status of literature texts although changing it. I have concentrated on adaptations to show how powerful and dynamic are the relationships between texts from different media. The proliferation of adaptations is not accidental; as I have tried to suggest, texts are being changed both by direct human agency and through the influence of much larger and longer-term societal pressures. The one constant element is our insatiable desire for texts. I have concluded with practical suggestions that I hope literature teachers may find attractive and manageable.

My final, crucial point has been touched on above and needs spelling out at this point. Literature teachers have always been, in a sense, evangelical, seeing themselves as missionaries, determined to help their students appreciate the special qualities to be found in the best literature (see my extended discussion in Chapter 1). However noble in intention, this approach tends to put off many students and also to imply that there are two types of reader: those who have been 'saved' and the rest who choose to read from that great mass of unworthy texts which proliferate in the world. I suggest that this division was always false but is now made untenable in our new textual landscape. In that landscape, teachers and students alike are enjoying a whole range of texts from the simplest to the most complex; their interests are, arguably, converging. We can all enjoy being knowledgeable about texts and bringing that knowledge into the classroom to consider together. Adaptations dramatize that convergence, offering wonderful opportunities for the teachers' literary and historical knowledge to be employed in enhancing the developing textual understanding of students, whether they would ever choose 'classic' texts for themselves or not.

Adapting remains the key concept. Texts, so apparently object-like and static, are evolving and adapting even as we pick them up and turn a page or turn them on. Literature teachers need to adapt and, as I have said, being an intelligent species, can recognize where change is inevitable and inescapable and where it is more of a potential, something we can have power over and can influence for the good of all of us. I might sum this up by suggesting that the proliferation of adaptations helps students to see the remarkable energy and staying power of texts and their extraordinary longevity; like certain other species, they survive and they show no signs of imminent extinction. To make one further use of the textual habitat metaphor: why not come down off the high moral plateau, where life can be dry and cold, and join life in the valley where the terrain is fertile and where everything is growing and changing? No doubt a new Heathcliffe is springing up somewhere.

REFERENCES

Appleyard, J. A. (1990) *Becoming a Reader: The Experience of Fiction from Childhood to Adulthood.* Cambridge: Cambridge University Press.

Benton, P. (1996) Children's reading and viewing in the nineties. In C. Davies *What is English Teaching?* Buckingham: Open University Press.

Buckingham, D. (1992) English and media studies: making the difference. In M. Alvorado, and O. Boyd-Barrett (eds) *Media Education: An Introduction.* London: British Film Institute and Open University Press.

Buckingham, D. (1993a) *Children Talking Television: The Making of Television Literacy.* London: Falmer Press.

Buckingham, D. (ed.) (1993b) *Reading Audiences: Young People and the Media.* Manchester: Manchester University Press.

Davies, C. (1996) *What is English Teaching?* Buckingham: Open University Press.

DES (1988) *Report of the Committee of Inquiry into the Teaching of English Language* (The Kingman Report). London: HMSO.

DES (1989) *English for Ages 5 to 16* (The Cox report). London: HMSO.

Eagleton, T. (1983) *An Introduction to Literary Theory.* Oxford: Basil Blackwell.

Evans, C. (1993) *English People: The Experience of Teaching and Learning English in British Universities.* Buckingham: Open University Press.

Gee, J. (1994) *Social Linguistics and Literacies: Ideology in Discourses.* 2nd edn. London: Falmer Press.

Giddings, R., Selby, K. and Wensley, C. (1990) *Screening the Novel: The Theory and Practice of Literary Dramatization.* London: Macmillan.

Golub, S. (1993) Spies in the house of quality: the American reception of *Brideshead Revisited.* In P. Reynolds (ed.) *Novel Images: Literature in Performance.* London: Routledge.

Goodwyn, A. (1992a) *English Teaching and Media Education.* Buckingham: Open University Press.

Goodwyn, A. (1992b) Theoretical models of English teaching. *English in Education* **26** (3), 4–11.

Goodwyn, A. (1997) The secondary school and the media: how are schools preparing for the global mass media environment of the 21st century? Paper delivered at The European Conference of Educational Research, Seville.

Goodwyn, A., Adams, A. and Clarke, S. (1997) The great god of the future: English teachers and information technology. *English in Education* **30** (2), 54–63.

Green, B. (ed.) (1993) *The Insistence of the Letter: Literacy Studies and Curriculum Theorizing.* London: Falmer Press.

Harrison, C. (1995) The assessment of response to reading: a postmodern perspective. In A. Goodwyn (ed.) *English and Ability.* London: David Fulton.

Hart, A. and Benson, T. (1992) *Models of Media Education: A Study of Secondary English Teachers Teaching Media, Part 1, Overview.* Occasional Papers, 11. Southampton: Centre for Language in Education, University of Southampton.

Hart, A. and Benson, T. (1993) *Models of Media Education: A Study of Secondary English Teachers Teaching Media, Part 2, Profiles and Lessons.* Occasional Papers, 12. Southampton: Centre for Language in Education, University of Southampton.

Hawkins, H. (1993) Shared dreams: reproducing *Gone with the Wind.* In P. Reynolds (ed.) *Novel Images: Literature in Performance.* London: Routledge.

Jones, K. (ed.) (1992) *English and The National Curriculum: Cox's Revolution?* London: Kogan Page.

Kerr, P. (1982) Classic Serials: To Be Continued. In *Screen* **23** (1), 6–19.

Lanham, R. (1993) *The Electronic Word: Democracy, Technology and the Arts.* Chicago: University of Chicago Press.

Leavis, F. R. and Thompson, D. (1933) *Culture and Environment.* London: Chatto & Windus.

Masterman, L. (1985) *Teaching the Media.* London: Comedia.

Mathieson, M. (1975) *The Preachers of Culture.* London: Allen & Unwin.

Moss, G. (1989) *Unpopular Fictions.* London: Virago.

Murdock, G. and Phelps, G. (1973) *The Mass Media and the Secondary School.* London: Macmillan.

Myers, M. (1996) *Changing Our Minds: Negotiating English and Literacy.* Urbana, IL.: National Council of Teachers of English.

Negroponte, N. (1995) *Being Digital.* London: Hodder & Stoughton.

Reynolds, P. (ed.) (1993) *Novel Images: Literature in Performance.* London: Routledge.

Richards, I. A. (1929) *Practical Criticism: A Study of Literary Judgement.* London: Routledge & Kegan Paul.

Rice, J. and Saunders, C. (1996) Consuming *Middlemarch*: the construction and consumption of nostalgia in Stamford. In D. Cartmell *et al.* (eds) *Pulping Fictions: Consuming Culture across the Literature/Media Divide.* London: Pluto Press.

Rosenblatt, L. (1938) *Literature as Exploration.* New York: Appleton-Century.

Rosenblatt, L. (1978) *The Reader, the Text, the Poem: The Transactional Theory of the Literary Work.* Carbondale, IL: Southern Illinois University Press.

Sarland, C. (1991) *Young People Reading: Culture and Response.* Buckingham: Open University Press.

Stoneman, P. (1996) *Brontë Transformations: The Cultural Dissemination of 'Jane Eyre' and 'Wuthering Heights'.* Hemel Hempstead: Prentice Hall/Harvester Wheatsheaf.

Thompson, E. (1996) *'Sense and Sensibility': The Diaries.* London: Bloomsbury.

Thompson, J. O. (1996) Vanishing worlds: film adaptation and the mystery of the original. In D. Cartmell *et al.* (eds) *Pulping Fictions: Consuming Culture across the Literature/Media Divide.* London: Pluto Press.

Index

adaptations of texts 21,
132–48
Agee, J. 86
Ahlberg, A. 72
Alvermann, D. E. 110, 124
American Association of
University Women
(AAUW) 110
Anaya, R. 100
Andrews, R. 69–70, 77, 78
Anyon, J. M. 119
Appleyard, J. 1, 8, 77, 107,
132, 134, 142
Arvon Foundation 76
Assessment of Performance
Unit (APU) 62–4, 69–71,
73, 75
Auden, W. H. 72
auracy 5
Austen, J. 28, 32
Emma 32
Pride and Prejudice 144
Sense and Sensibility 143

Barbieri, M. 113, 125
Barnes, D. 123
Barrie, J. M.
Peter Pan 44
Barthes, R. 27, 34
Beach, R. 124
Beard, P. 64
Benson, G. 76
Benton, M. 27–8, 65, 76, 78
Benton, P. 3–4, 134

Bloom, A. 98
Board of Studies (Victoria,
Australia) 88
Bond, C. 58
Book Marketing Report 3
Booth, D. 52–3
Boulton, M. 50
Bradford, C. 83
Branagh, K. 45
Briggs, R. 81–2
Britton, J. 13
Brontë, C. 31, 37
Brontë, E.
Wuthering Heights 132, 141
Brown, L. M. 110, 111
Browne, A. 86, 89, 90
Bryant, P. 64
Buckingham, D. 6, 88, 134, 141
Byron, K. 64
Byron, Lord 36

Carter, D. 65
Carter, K. 112
Cherland, M. 111, 119, 124
Children's Literature
Research Centre 4
Chopin, K. 31–41
Christian-Smith, L. 111,
120–1
Cisneross, S. 104
Cixous, H. 121
Cole, B. 90
computers and reading 5, 6,
81, 83

Corcoran, B. 15
Corliss, R. 132
Cox, B. 24
Cox Report 134
Crew, G. 93–4
critical literacy 7, 36, 88–9,
122–5
cultural literacy 2, 98

Dahl, R. 67
Davies, C. 6, 129, 135
Davis, B. 111, 121
deconstruction 27
Department for Education 44
Dickens, C. 34, 39, 143
All the Year Round 36
Great Expectations 34, 36,
40, 144

Eagleton, T. 27, 36, 135
Eaton, A. 29
Eliot, T. S. 26
Elliott, A. 25
Enciso, P. 124
English, models of 13, 24, 27,
30
Evans, C. 139

Fallona, C. 112, 113
Film Education 57
Fish, S. 50
Forster, E. M. 145
Fox, D. 112
Foucault, M. 34

Freebody, P. 98–9
Freire, P. 7

Gee, J. 136–7
Gee, P. 5, 13
gender and reading 110–12,
   114–22
Gibson, R. 38
Giddings, R. 144
Gilbert, P. 123
Glaser, B.G. 113
Gleitzman, M.
   Two Weeks with the Queen
   51
Golub, S. 146
Goodman, Y. 125
Goodson, I. 99
Goodwyn, A. 3, 6, 10, 12, 24,
   30, 53, 79, 129, 131, 134,
   137, 142
Goody, J. 5
Goswami, U. 64
Gowar, M. 76
Graff, H. 14
Green, B. 81, 82, 136
Greig, N. 46, 57
Gulbenkian Foundation 76

Hall, C. 4
Hall, L. 75
Hall, S. 122
Harding, D. W. 13
Hardy, T. 32, 40
Harries, S. 76
Harrison, C. 139
Harrison, T. 76
Hart, A. 129, 141
Hartley, L. P. 23
Hathorn, L. 91–3
Hawkins, H. 132
Hayhoe, M. 79
Her Majesty's Inspectors
   64–5
Hinkson, J. 81
Hirsch, E. D. 2, 108
hooks, b. 124
Hornbrook, D. 45
horror fiction 17, 32, 40,
   112–13, 115, 118, 120
Howard, J. E. 48

Ingarden, R. 47
Innocenti, R. 90, 94

James, H.
   Turn of the Screw 40
Janssen, T. 10
Jensen, T. B. 74, 78
Johnson, D. M. 77
Johnson, H. A. 123, 125
Johnston, B. 17–18
Joyce, J. 26

Keck, K. 88
Kelsall, M. 45, 48, 50
Kempe, A. 45, 46, 48, 52, 53,
   77
   Gregory's Girl 52
Kerr, P. 144
King, S. 40
Kingman Report 134
Kress, G. 4, 81, 84

Langer, J. 123–4
Lanham, R. 131
Leach, S. 29–30, 57
Lear, E. 67
Leavis, F. R. 16, 25, 134–5
LeCompte, M. D. 113
Lemke, J. 81, 83
literacy 4–7, 14, 16–17, 19, 81,
   107
literary heritage 24–7
literary theory 27, 39
Lonsdale, M. 83, 86, 87

Macaulay, D. 86
McCormick, K. 122
McHale, B. 83
McKee, D. 86, 87
McRobbie, A. 120
Masterman, L. 129, 141
Mathieson, M. 141
Mattenklott, G. 74
Maynard, M. 110
media education 3, 6, 28–30,
   81, 83, 129, 132–48
Meek, M. 88
Merriam, S. B. 111
Michaels, W. 48, 82, 88
Milligan, S. 63
Moi, T. 121

Moon, B. 35
Morgan, C. 76
Morimoto, J. 90
Morris, M.
   Two Weeks with the Queen
   51, 54–5
Moss, G. 88, 134
multi-cultural literature 98,
   108
Murdock, G. 136
Myers, M. 136

Nash, O. 72
National Curriculum (UK) 1,
   6, 23, 26, 59, 75, 81, 90, 98,
   134
Negroponte, N. 132
New Critics 16, 25, 138, 144
New London Group 88–9
Nichols, J. 104
Nichols, P.
   *A Day in the Death of Joe
   Egg* 43–4, 47, 57
Nicholson, H. 53

Olivier, L. 132, 134, 145
O'Neill, C. 47
oracy 4

Patten, B. 67, 73
Piaget, J. 8
Pierce, K. M. 123
Pipher, M. 110–111
Planche, J. P. 58
Plato 10
Poe, E. A. 40
postmodernism 24–5, 41, 83,
   86–8
Pratt, M. L. 124
Priestley, J. B.
   An Inspector Calls 52, 57
Pullman, P.
   *Sherlock Holmes and the
   Limehouse Horror*
   49–51, 52

Rebolledo, T. D. 110
Reynolds, P. 140
Rice, J. 146
Richards, I. A. 139
Robinson, K. 47

Rogers, T. 122
Roman, L. 111
romantic fiction 32
Rosenblatt, R. 79, 111, 130, 135, 138
Russell, W.
  Our Day Out 52

Sadker, M. 110
Sand, G.
  Lelia 37
Sarland, C. 134
Scieszka, J. 85
Sefton-Green, J. 6
Seidman, I. E. 113
Sendak, M. 86, 89, 91
Shakespeare, William 1, 28, 46, 50, 51, 52, 53, 56, 57, 82, 98
Shay, J. 123
Shelley, M.
  Frankenstein 36, 40
Shelley, P. B. 36
Short, K. 124
Showalter, E. 37
Sims Bishop, R. 122
Sizer, T. 107
spectator role 13–14

Squire, J. 79
Stephens, J. 82, 83, 86, 87, 88, 89, 90
Stine, R. L. 113, 115, 118
Stoker, B.
  Dracula 40
Stoppard, T.
  Rosencrantz and Guildenstern are Dead 47
Storeman, P. 143–4, 147
Street, B. 5, 14
Styan, J. L. 44, 47, 48

Taylor, J. M. 110
Taylor, M. 124
Thackeray, W.
  Vanity Fair 144
Thomas, D.
  Under Milk Wood 55–6
Thompson, E. 143–6
Thompson, J. O. 133
Thompson, L. 74
Tolstoy, L.
  Anna Karenina 37
Trousdale, A. 111, 121
Tuman, M. 84
Turnbull, S. 88

Tweddle, S. 84
Tyson-Bernstein, H. 104

Vandergrift, K. 88
Vygotsky, L. 12–13

Walker, S. 4
Walsh, M. 88
Wasser, J. D. 113
Watson, K. 86
Waugh, P. 86
Weiler, K. 120
West, A. 26, 36
Wexler, P. 81
Whaley, L. 125
Whitehead, F. 3
Wilkinson, A. 4
Williams, K. 86
Williams, R. 26
Willis, P. 3, 17
Wilshire, D. 121
Wolfe, T.
  Bonfire of the Vanities 133

Yolen, J. 94–5

Zeffirelli, F. 46